Stone to Silicon

A History of Technology and Computing

Roger Whatley, Ph.D.
and
Bill Inmon

Technics Publications
SEDONA, ARIZONA

TECHNICS PUBLICATIONS

115 Linda Vista, Sedona, AZ 86336 USA
https://www.TechnicsPub.com

Edited by Steve Hoberman
Cover design by Lorena Molinari

All images whose sources are not cited are created by Roger Whatley.

First Printing 2025

ISBN, print ed.   9798898160166 (hardcover)
ISBN, print ed.   9798898160340 (paperback)
ISBN, Kindle ed.   9798898160173
ISBN, PDF ed.   9798898160180

Library of Congress Control Number: 2025946777

To all the unsung heroes of the digital revolution: the eccentric inventors, the tireless programmers, the frustrated debuggers, and the perpetually bewildered users who, through their triumphs and failures, have shaped the wonderfully chaotic world of technology. May your stories, both grand and absurd, continue to inspire and entertain. This one's for the ones who wrestled with punch cards, cursed at cryptic error messages, and accidentally deleted entire hard drives (we've all been there). And a special nod to the ghosts in the machine: those enigmatic glitches and unexpected behaviors that remind us that even the most sophisticated technology has a quirky, sometimes humorous, side.

Contents

Acknowledgments _____ 1

Preface _____ 3

Introduction _____ 5

Chapter 1: The Dawn of Computation: From Abacus to Babbage _____ 7
 Ancient Calculating Devices and Their Limitations_____ 7
 The Analytical Engine: A Vision Ahead of Its Time _____ 11
 Early Punched Cards and the Birth of Programmable Machines _____ 15
 The Human Element: The Unsung Heroes of Early Computation _____ 18
 The Role of Women in Early Computing _____ 19
 Anecdotes, Musings, and Recollections_____ 22

Chapter 2: The Transition to Electronic Computing: The First Steps_____ 25
 Mainframes: The Dawn of Large-Scale Computing _____ 25
 The Early Pioneers: The ABC (Atanasoff-Berry) to the Cray _____ 26
 The Rise of Versatile Computing _____ 33
 Anecdotes, Musings, and Recollections_____ 36

Chapter 3: The Rise of Programming Languages: From Assembly to Abstraction _____ 43
 The Early Days of Assembly Language: A Low-Level Approach _____ 43
 The Invention of High-Level Languages: Making Programming More Accessible _____ 46
 The Evolution of Programming Paradigms: Different Approaches to Problem Solving _____ 50
 The Impact of Programming Languages on Software Development Efficiency and Innovation_____ 54
 The Ongoing Evolution of Programming Languages: Meeting the Demands of Modern Computing_____ 55
 Anecdotes, Musings, and Recollections_____ 58

Chapter 4: Data Storage and Management: From Punch Cards to the Cloud _____ 65
 Early Data Storage Methods, Limitations, and Innovations _____ 65
 The Rise of Databases: Organizing and Managing Information Efficiently _____ 71
 Data Warehousing Building Centralized Repositories of Information_____ 74
 Cloud Computing and Data Storage: The Modern Approach_____ 76
 The Future of Data Storage: Emerging Technologies and Trends_____ 79

Chapter 5: Problem Solving Techniques in Computing: Algorithms and Beyond _____ 83
 The Fundamentals of Algorithmic Thinking: Breaking Down Complex Problems _____ 83
 Data Structures: Efficiently Organizing and Accessing Information _____ 86
 Data Architecture: Designing the Blueprint for Information Flow _____ 89
 Algorithm Analysis: Measuring Efficiency and Performance _____ 90
 Software Engineering Principles: Building Reliable and Maintainable Systems_____ 91
 Advanced Problem-Solving Techniques, Artificial Intelligence, and Machine Learning _____ 94
 Anecdotes, Musings, and Recollections_____ 96

Chapter 6: The Personal Computer Revolution: From Hobbyists to Households _____ 97
 The Early Days of Personal Computing: The Rise of Hobbyist Culture _____ 97
 The Birth of the Microprocessor: The Heart of the Personal Computer _____ 101
 The Software Revolution: Operating Systems and Applications _____ 103
 The Rise of Personal Computer Manufacturers: Competition and Innovation _____ 106
 The Societal Impact of Personal Computers: Changing the Way We Live and Work _____ 110
 Anecdotes, Musings, and Recollections_____ 113

Chapter 7: The Internet and the World Wide Web: Connecting the World _____ 115
 Early Networking Technologies: ARPANET and the Precursors to the Internet _____ 115
 The Invention of the World Wide Web: Making the Internet Accessible_____ 118
 The Rise of E-commerce and Online Services: Transforming Industries_____ 122

The Social Impact of the Internet: Connecting People Globally _____ 125
The Future of the Internet: Emerging Technologies and Trends _____ 128
Anecdotes, Musings, and Recollections _____ 131

Chapter 8: The Smartphone Revolution: Mobile Computing Takes Center Stage _____ **133**
Early Mobile Phones: From Analog to Digital (From Bricks to Clicks) _____ 133
The Rise of Smartphones: Convergence of Computing and Communication _____ 136
Mobile Operating Systems: iOS vs Android _____ 139
Mobile Apps and the App Economy: Transforming How We Interact with Technology _____ 144
The Societal Impact of Smartphones: Connectivity, Convenience, and Concerns _____ 147
Alone Togetherness: The Art of Being Socially Antisocial _____ 150
Anecdotes, Musings, and Recollections _____ 154

Chapter 9: Artificial Intelligence: From Science Fiction to Reality _____ **155**
From Fiction to Function: Sci-Fi's Blueprint for Innovation _____ 155
Early AI Concepts and Research: The Foundations of the Field _____ 156
The Rise of Machine Learning: Algorithms That Learn from Data _____ 160
Deep Learning, Neural Networks, and Their Applications _____ 164
AI in Everyday Life: Applications and Impacts _____ 168

Chapter 10: The Semiconductor Revolution: Tiny Chips, Giant Impact _____ **173**
The Invention of the Transistor: A Fundamental Breakthrough _____ 173
The Development of Integrated Circuits, Miniaturization, and Efficiency _____ 177
Moore's Law and the Exponential Growth of Computing Power _____ 180
The Manufacturing of Semiconductors: A Complex and Precise Process _____ 184
The Future of Semiconductor Technology: Beyond Moore's Law _____ 187

Chapter 11: Cybersecurity: Protecting the Digital World _____ **189**
Early Cybersecurity Challenges: Protecting Mainframes and Networks _____ 189
The Rise of Malware and Cybercrime: Evolving Threats _____ 192
Cybersecurity Technologies: Protecting Data and Systems _____ 194

Chapter 12: The Social Impact of Technology: Transforming Society _____ **199**
Technology and Employment: Automation and the Changing Workforce _____ 199
Technology and Communication: Connecting People Across Distances _____ 202
Technology and Education: Expanding Access to Learning _____ 205

Chapter 13: The Digital Divide and Moral Responsibility _____ **209**
Autonomous Systems and Moral Responsibility _____ 212

Chapter 14: Emerging Technologies and Trends _____ **215**
Quantum Computing: Beyond the Limits of Classical Computation _____ 215
Artificial General Intelligence (AGI): The Quest for Human-Level Intelligence _____ 218
Biocomputing and Nanotechnology: Integrating Biology and Technology _____ 221
The Internet of Things (IoT): Connecting Devices and Data _____ 224
The Metaverse and Virtual Reality: Immersive Digital Experiences _____ 227
Anecdotes, Musings, and Recollections _____ 230

Chapter 15: Reflections on the Past, Present, and Future of Computing and Technology _____ **231**
Key Themes and Lessons from the History of Computing _____ 231

Glossary _____ 235
Index _____ 241

Acknowledgments

First and foremost, I must thank my incredibly patient muse, Patty Haines, who somehow managed to decipher my often-cryptic comments and rambling explanations. Her ability to translate my techno-babble into coherent prose borders on the miraculous. She was very instrumental in providing suggestions in structure as we hammered out ideas together. (Patty, if you're reading this, please send more coffee. Or, maybe something a little stronger?)

Many thanks to Dr. Sylvia Sydow—our greatest cheerleader, unofficial marketing department, and pre-release hype machine. Sylvia had this book sold before we'd even settled on the title. Her enthusiasm was so contagious, we briefly considered bottling it and selling it as a productivity supplement. Thank you, Sylvia, for believing in this project before it had a pulse, and for cheering louder than anyone else in the room.

A **huge** thanks also goes to my friend and co-author William (Bill) Inmon, whose original idea for writing this book, relentless enthusiasm and input to this "history" made this whole thing possible. Bill, you're a legend!

Preface

A while back, I (Bill Inmon) was at a conference having lunch with a group of fellow technicians. The attendees at the conference were all from Silicon Valley and had spent many years in the industry.

At lunch, I mentioned that Ed Yourdon had passed away. I was shocked to find out that no one at the table knew who Ed Yourdon was. Then I mentioned some other names—Grace Hopper, Gene Amdahl, John Zachman. Again, no one had ever heard these names.

It is a peculiarity that the IT profession buries its pioneers and dumps them in an unmarked grave.

The truth of the matter is that the IT profession stands on the shoulders of giants. Yet the IT profession rushes to push those giants into the shadows of time as soon as they can.

Other professions revere their giants. In medicine, notable figures include Dr. Jonas Salk, Dr. Michael DeBakey, and Dr. Christiaan Barnard. In aviation, there are Orville and Wilbur Wright. In exploration, there are Christopher Columbus and Ferdinand Magellan. Other professions respect their pioneers. The IT profession hides them in the closet as soon as possible and acts as if they never existed.

It is a crime what has happened to the pioneers of the IT profession.

This book attempts to make up in small measure what has been lost and should never have been lost.

This book has been written by two friends who have very different backgrounds, yet emerge on the same path. Dr. Roger Whatley is an academic in the field of computer science with a background in electronic engineering. He has extensive experience in systems software engineering as well as in hardware design and programming. He was intimately involved in the pioneering days of personal computers, having designed and built several of his own. I am a hard-core programmer and designer. No one has ever mistaken me for being an academic. I know very little about electronics. But I know a lot about design and data architecture. Together, Roger and I form a reasonably complete and complementary picture of technology.

Roger and I have had some shared experiences. Both of us were in Silicon Valley in the early days of the rise of the computer. In those days, nearly all of the pioneers passed through Silicon Valley. Both Roger and I had the opportunity to form personal relationships with many of those pioneers. Some of the relationships were very close and occurred over a long period of time. Some of the relationships amounted to little more than a brief handshake and the exchange of a few pleasantries.

However, Roger and I had the opportunity to get to know many of the early pioneers of technology on a personal level as they made their way through Silicon Valley.

This book is organized in an unconventional fashion. There is a deliberate separation between Roger's writing and mine. Roger has adopted a conventional narrative approach, incorporating a touch of humor for added effect. I have taken the approach of writing in the form of personal recollections. We hope that this unconventional approach is not distracting. Instead, we hope it is like visiting a smorgasbord and finding a broad and diverse selection of foods to choose from.

The topic of computing and technology is difficult to write about for no other reason than the extremely wide variety of topics that encompass technology, each of which is important in its own way.

Technology is like a musical ensemble made up of the Beatles, Mantovani, Ice Tea, Reba McIntyre, Frank Sinatra, Fleetwood Mac, and Madonna. Each has their own talent. But combining them together in a rational manner is a real trick.

It is worth noting that every topic mentioned in this book has much more depth and detail to be found elsewhere in the books and articles that have been written. This book is not an attempt to describe in depth every topic mentioned.

In any case, we hope you enjoy this book. And we hope that the book helps answer the question, "How in the world did technology arrive where it is today?"

Introduction

So, you're holding a book about the ***History of Technology and Computing***. I know, I know, it doesn't exactly scream "thrilling beach read." But fear not, intrepid reader! This isn't your grandfather's dusty tome filled with dry facts and incomprehensible diagrams. First and foremost, it is NOT a "how to" book, but rather a "How did we get from there to here?" We're diving headfirst into the wacky, wonderful, and occasionally disastrous world of technology and computing, with all its characters and unexpected twists. Think of it as a comedic opera of innovation, complete with soaring triumphs, crashing failures, and enough unexpected plot turns to make a Hollywood screenwriter blush.

We'll explore the ***evolution of computing*** from the days of room-sized mainframes that required their own cooling systems (a pre-historic data center) to the sleek smartphones we carry in our pockets that possess more processing power than the entire Apollo mission control. This book is a journey through time, filled with anecdotes, musings, surprising facts, and hopefully, a few laughs along the way. After all, who needs a stuffy lecture when you can have a good chuckle while learning about the evolution of programming languages? Settle in, grab a beverage, and prepare for a roller coaster ride through the annals of technological history.

The ***History of Technology and Computing*** is not a straight line of progress, but rather a winding path paved with brilliant insights, baffling mistakes, and sheer dumb luck. It's a story filled with characters as colorful and unpredictable as the technology they created. Think of Charles Babbage, a man whose ambition far outstripped the capabilities of Victorian-era engineering, tirelessly attempting to build a mechanical computer the size of a small car. Or Ada Lovelace, a visionary mathematician who not only understood Babbage's contraption but also wrote the first computer program, long before there were actual computers to run it on! This is the world we're exploring here: a world of ingenious inventions, frustrating setbacks, and accidental discoveries that have reshaped civilization.

We will traverse the bumpy terrain of early programming languages, where a simple typo could lead to hours of head-scratching (and maybe some hair-pulling). We'll witness the birth of the internet, a chaotic explosion of information that turned the world upside down (mostly in a good way, let's be optimistic). And, of course, we'll examine the ever-increasing power of smart devices, those ubiquitous gadgets that simultaneously simplify our lives and simultaneously make us question the very fabric of reality. This isn't just a history of machines; it's a history of human ingenuity, perseverance, and the occasional bout of utter bewilderment in the face of technological complexity. So, grab your metaphorical hard hats and prepare to delve into the thrilling chronicle of how we progressed from stones to bones, from bones to silicon, from silicon to punch cards, and from punch cards to personalized newsfeeds. It's going to be a wild ride. Buckle up, because this digital history lesson is anything but boring!

CHAPTER 1

The Dawn of Computation: From Abacus to Babbage

Ancient Calculating Devices and Their Limitations

Long before the silicon chips and sleek screens of modern computing, humanity wrestled with the fundamental problem of calculation. Ancient mathematicians and scholars sat under the stars, pondering life's great mysteries, like why they couldn't get 2+2 to equal anything other than 4. These early thinkers had no idea they were sowing the seeds for what would become one of humanity's greatest inventions: the computer. Our ancestors, lacking the digital wizardry we take for granted, devised ingenious methods to perform arithmetic operations. These methods, while primitive by today's standards, represented a crucial stepping stone in the grand narrative of computation. Let's journey back to a time when calculating wasn't a matter of tapping a key or swiping a screen, but a labor-intensive art demanding dexterity, patience, and a whole lot of counting beads. The poor souls of antiquity had to resort to moving around colored beads

Used by permission - larrywhatley.org

like some advanced version of "cat batting at a toy." But hey, at least it worked. Who needs fancy silicon chips when you've got a bunch of carefully arranged pebbles?

The evolution of ancient accounting to the abacus is akin to humanity's greatest math transformation. In the Stone Age, early humans relied on the original "pocket calculators"—fingers, rocks, and tally sticks—to keep track of quantities. Enter the **Lebombo bone** (circa 42,000 years ago), the prehistoric equivalent of a spreadsheet, complete with tally marks.

Fast-forward to around 7500 BCE, and the Mesopotamians were crushing the accounting game. They crafted clay tokens shaped like cones, spheres, and disks to symbolize grain measurements and livestock, demonstrating that they were skilled multitasking mathletes long before Excel existed. This clever system graduated to counting boards, paving the way for the big leagues: written language and numerical systems.

The **base-60 system**—shoutout to the ancient Sumerians in the 3rd millennium BCE—still rules our time and angles today. Babylonians took it to the next level, dominating mathematics and astronomy while setting the stage for modern timekeeping. Meanwhile, the Egyptians swapped clay for papyrus and inked out hieroglyphic records around 3250 BCE, showing that even in ancient times, diversification was key. And the Chinese? They leveled up with counting rods and eventually rolled out the MVP of ancient math tools—the abacus.

The abacus, arguably the most famous of the ancient calculating devices, is a testament to human ingenuity. Imagine a world without calculators, spreadsheets, or even simple adding machines. The abacus, in its various forms across different cultures, filled that void for millennia. From its humble origins in ancient Mesopotamia, possibly dating back to around 2700 BCE, it spread across the globe, adapting to regional customs and mathematical practices. Its basic design is deceptively simple: a frame holding parallel rods, each with beads that can be moved to represent numbers. This simple mechanism allows for remarkably efficient addition, subtraction, multiplication, and even division, a feat that earned it a place in the hearts (and on the desks) of countless merchants, accountants, and scholars for thousands of years.

The Roman abacus, for example, differed significantly from its Chinese or Japanese counterparts. The Roman abacus used grooves in a slab of stone or metal to hold counters that represented values of 1, 5, 10, 50, 100, 500, and 1000. This system directly reflected the Roman numeral system, making calculations easier for those familiar with this unique way of

Wikipedia, CC BY-SA 4.0

representing numbers. But the Roman abacus was limited by its physical construction.

Trying to perform large-scale calculations was incredibly cumbersome, requiring a substantial amount of physical space and many, many counters because nothing says "advanced mathematics" like a glorified Peg Board. Picture someone hunched over a slab of marble, frantically rearranging dozens of counters, trying to perform large calculations while muttering under their breath.

The Chinese abacus (Suanpan), on the other hand, presented a more compact and sophisticated design. Its rods typically held two beads above and five beads below a horizontal bar. The upper beads represented values of 5 each, while the lower beads each held a value of 1. It was like the Swiss Army Knife of calculating devices—efficient and ready for a numerical emergency.

This system allowed for more efficient calculations, particularly when dealing with larger numbers, and significantly reduced the physical space required compared to the Roman abacus. Consider trying to add Roman numerals like MCCCLXXIV (1374) and DCCCLXXXVIII (888)—the process is far less intuitive than using a suanpan, a testament to the design's effectiveness. The Suanpan, in all its bead-sliding glory, made such mathematical feats almost bearable. However, even the suanpan, with its elegant design, possessed inherent limitations. Unlike modern computers, it couldn't store complex algorithms or perform advanced mathematical operations beyond basic arithmetic. Each calculation required manual manipulation of the beads, a process prone to error, particularly when dealing with large or complex equations.

The Japanese abacus (soroban) shares a lineage with the suanpan, and yet holds a unique place in the history of calculating devices. The Japanese soroban took the abacus concept and added a touch of Asian flair. Its structure, with one bead above and four below the bar, was ideally suited to the Japanese numerical system. It was, and still is, favored for its speed and efficiency, enabling rapid mental calculations that remain astonishing to modern observers. But, even the soroban, while a refined masterpiece of mechanical calculation, still lacked the programmable nature of modern computing. Each calculation was a stand-alone event, with no possibility of storing a sequence of operations or repeating a computation automatically.

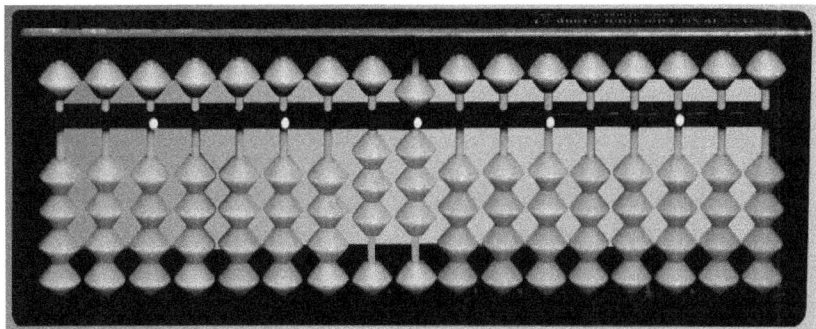

Wikipedia, CC BY-SA 4.0

Moving beyond the abacus, we encounter other ingenious calculating tools developed in various ancient civilizations. The Antikythera mechanism, a complex device discovered in a shipwreck off the Greek island of Antikythera, dates back to the 1st century BC and is considered a marvel of ancient technology. This intricate mechanical marvel is capable of tracking the positions of the sun, moon, and planets, calculating dates of eclipses and other astronomical events, and it even incorporates a sophisticated gear system that demonstrates an understanding of complex astronomical cycles. It's like someone took a grandfather clock, jammed it full of gears, and said, "You know what this needs? Astronomy!" While not a general-purpose computer by any stretch of the imagination, the Antikythera mechanism demonstrates that ancient civilizations were capable of creating incredibly complex mechanical devices to address specific calculation problems. Its design, based on intricate gear systems, required mastery of engineering and an advanced understanding of mathematics, illustrating the high level of technical skill achieved in ancient times.

However, these ancient calculating devices, regardless of their ingenuity and sophistication for their time, suffered from several fundamental limitations. First, their operations were inherently limited by their physical nature. They could only perform a relatively small set of mathematical operations, and the complexity of the calculations they could handle was restricted by their mechanical design. These limitations often resulted in lengthy and error-prone processes, particularly when handling complex or large-scale computations. There was no concept of data storage in the way we understand it; each calculation started from scratch, with no memory of previous steps or results. This contrasts sharply with modern computers, which can readily store and access vast amounts of data at lightning speed, processing complex information for extended periods.

Second, the materials used in the construction of these devices influenced their potential functionality. Bronze, wood, and stone, which were prevalent in ancient times, lacked the precision and durability of modern materials, such as silicon. This restricted the complexity of the mechanisms that could be reliably created and limited their operational lifespan. The intricate design of the Antikythera mechanism, for example, is a testament to the skill of its creators; yet, its fragility serves as a reminder of the limitations imposed by the available materials. The relative coarseness of ancient materials also led to inaccuracies in the calculations, which are often manifested as systematic errors in the computations.

Third, the lack of a standardized system of representing numbers across different cultures often hampered interoperability and the transfer of mathematical knowledge. The unique ways various civilizations represented numbers led to variations in algorithms and calculations, hindering the development of a unified system of mathematics. The Roman numerals, with their irregular and inconsistent representation, highlight the challenges of efficient computation in such a system. The adoption of the Hindu-Arabic numeral system was a crucial step in simplifying mathematical notation, facilitating more complex and efficient calculation methods.

In summary, ancient calculating devices were ingenious inventions that represented early steps toward modern computing. However, the limitations of their materials, their physical nature, and the lack of a standardized mathematical notation constrained their computational power and accuracy. Nevertheless, their legacy lives on, not only as captivating artifacts of ancient cultures but also as a testament to the enduring human desire to understand and harness the power of numbers. These early struggles with calculation laid the groundwork for the future evolution of computing, paving the way for the development of increasingly powerful and sophisticated computational tools. From the simple abacus to the astonishing Antikythera mechanism, these devices stand as a remarkable tribute to human ingenuity—and a reminder of just how far we've come. But fret not, for the story of computation doesn't end with the abacus and its ilk. Enter the Analytical Engine, the brainchild of one Charles Babbage.

The Analytical Engine: A Vision Ahead of Its Time

While the abacus and the Antikythera mechanism represented significant leaps in humankind's ability to manipulate numbers, they were, in a sense, analog precursors to the digital revolution. The next major step in this grand narrative arrived not in the bustling workshops of ancient civilizations, but in the mind of a brilliant and eccentric Victorian inventor: Charles Babbage. Babbage, a man whose ambition outstripped the technological capabilities of his time, conceived of a machine that would forever alter the course of computation: the Analytical Engine.

Wikipedia, CC BY-SA 4.0

Imagine a contraption of gears, levers, and punched cards, a mechanical behemoth dwarfing even the most imposing industrial machinery of its day. This wasn't just a calculator; Babbage envisioned a general-purpose computing machine, capable of performing any computation imaginable, provided the appropriate instructions were fed into it. This concept was so radical and far ahead of its time that its full potential wouldn't be realized for over a century.

The Analytical Engine, conceived in the 1830s, was a marvel of mechanical engineering. It was composed of several key components working in concert, each meticulously designed to perform a specific function. The "mill" was responsible for performing arithmetic operations. This wasn't simply a collection of gears adding numbers; Babbage designed it with intricate logic, allowing for complex mathematical computations. Think of it as the 19th-century equivalent of a central processing unit (CPU), a marvel of clockwork precision that executed instructions at a speed, albeit slow by modern standards, was remarkably advanced for its era.

Then there was the "store," the engine's memory, which held both the numbers being processed and the instructions that governed the mill's operations. Instead of the silicon chips that populate today's computers, Babbage's store was a mechanical marvel, capable of storing a significant amount of numerical data—a feat that astounded his contemporaries. Imagine a massive, intricate system of interconnected gears and levers, each precisely positioned to hold and retrieve specific numerical values on demand. This ingenious system, although mechanically complex, served the vital function of providing the Analytical Engine with a working memory—a critical component of any computing device.

Library of Congress https://www.loc.gov/resource

The "reader" was the device's input mechanism. It read instructions from punched cards, a technology borrowed from the burgeoning field of automated weaving (the Jacquard loom), where perforated cards controlled the patterns woven into cloth. Babbage's genius lay in realizing that this system could be adapted to control the flow of computations within the Analytical Engine. These punched cards, akin to modern software programs, contained precise instructions for each calculation, enabling the execution of complex algorithms.

Finally, the "printer" represented the output mechanism, allowing the results of computations to be recorded. In an age before digital displays or even sophisticated printing presses, the printer was a vital part of the Analytical Engine's design. It was a mechanical device capable of transferring the results of calculations onto paper, enabling the retrieval and sharing of the processed information. The printer's role solidified the Analytical Engine's capacity to not only process information but also to create a physical record of its computations.

Babbage's vision wasn't merely a theoretical exercise. He meticulously designed the engine, producing detailed blueprints and working prototypes for some of its components. He dedicated decades of his life to this ambitious project, pouring significant personal resources and seeking governmental funding—a pursuit that often tested his patience and sanity. However, the technology of his time proved to be a formidable obstacle. The precision required for constructing the engine's thousands of parts was simply beyond the capabilities of the existing manufacturing techniques. Even the slightest imperfection in a gear or lever could throw the entire system into disarray. The project's complexity and the technological limitations of the era ultimately prevented the Analytical Engine from ever being fully realized during Babbage's lifetime.

Despite the failure to construct a fully functional Analytical Engine, Babbage's legacy rests not solely on his engineering ambition but also on the profound conceptual leap he made. He wasn't just improving existing calculation methods; he was envisioning a machine capable of universal computation, a machine that could be programmed to perform any calculation imaginable. This fundamental shift in thinking laid the groundwork for the modern computer.

And then there's Ada Lovelace. The daughter of Lord Byron, Ada Lovelace, possessed a remarkable mathematical mind and a keen understanding of Babbage's work. She isn't merely a footnote in the history of computing; she's recognized as the world's first computer programmer. Her collaboration with Babbage transcended mere commentary; she went beyond explaining the Analytical Engine's function and explored its capabilities, specifically designing an algorithm that could compute Bernoulli numbers using the engine. This wasn't simply a theoretical exercise; it represented a concrete demonstration of the machine's potential to solve complex mathematical problems. This algorithm, documented in her notes, marks a watershed moment in the history of computing, representing the first published algorithm intended to be processed by a machine. Her foresight and intellectual contribution are unmatched, firmly establishing her as a pioneer in a field that wouldn't truly blossom for another century.

Wikipedia, CC BY-SA 4.0

Ada's work with Babbage highlights the crucial role of human ingenuity in shaping the development of computing. While Babbage's vision was instrumental in conceptualizing the machine, Ada's insights revealed its true potential. Her algorithm showed that the Analytical Engine wasn't simply a number-crunching machine; it was a programmable device capable of executing complex mathematical processes, a capability that would become the defining characteristic of modern computers.

The Analytical Engine stands as a testament to human ambition and the enduring power of visionary thinking. While the machine itself remained unrealized in Babbage's lifetime, its influence on the development of computing is undeniable. Its impact resonates through the evolution of programming languages, the architecture of modern computers, and the very concept of general-purpose computation. Babbage's dream, fueled by Ada Lovelace's genius, foreshadowed the digital age, paving the way for the technological marvels that define our modern world. It's a story of incredible vision, frustrating setbacks, and the enduring power of human ingenuity.

Early Punched Cards and the Birth of Programmable Machines

Before Babbage's ambitious, albeit ultimately unrealized, Analytical Engine, another pivotal technology quietly laid the groundwork for the digital revolution: the punched card. While Babbage dreamed of a mechanical marvel, the punched card offered a surprisingly effective, if less glamorous, method of programming machines. This simple technology, far from being a mere stepping stone, played a surprisingly significant role in the early development of computing, its impact echoing through decades of technological advancement. Its story isn't one of gears and steam, but of holes punched in cardboard—a testament to the often-unassuming origins of groundbreaking innovations.

The punched card's narrative begins not in the realm of computing, but in the world of textiles. Joseph Marie Jacquard, a Frenchman with a penchant for mechanical ingenuity, revolutionized the weaving industry in the early 19th century with his ingenious invention: the Jacquard loom. This wasn't just any loom; it was a programmable one. Instead of relying on a weaver to manually select the threads for each pattern, Jacquard's loom used a series of punched cards to control the process. Each card, a rectangular piece of stiff paper, had holes punched in specific locations. These holes corresponded to the selection of warp threads, thus dictating the pattern woven

Wikipedia, CC BY-SA 4.0

into the fabric. Imagine trying to create an intricate tapestry without this technological advancement; it would have been an exercise in mind-numbing tedium.

The ingenuity of the Jacquard loom lay in its ability to automate a complex process, essentially transforming a repetitive task into a programmable one. The punched cards acted as the program, feeding instructions to the loom and automatically creating the desired patterns. While simple in concept, this represented a monumental shift. For the first time, a machine's actions were being dictated not by a human operator's direct control, but by a pre-programmed set of instructions. It was a quiet revolution, but a revolution, nonetheless. Weavers, once bound by the limitations of manual control, could now create intricate designs with relative ease, allowing for increased efficiency and the creation of more elaborate textiles.

Now, the leap from weaving patterns to processing numbers might seem vast, yet the underlying principle remained the same: using punched cards to control a machine's actions. This crucial connection is often overlooked, but without the Jacquard loom's legacy, the story of punched cards in early computing would be incomplete. It's like saying the internet only started with Google—ignoring the decades of groundwork that came before. The Jacquard loom provided a practical, proven example of how punched cards could be used to automate a complex task, a template that later inventors would brilliantly adapt to the world of computation.

The next chapter in our punched card saga involves a man named Herman Hollerith, whose name might not be as familiar as Babbage's or Lovelace's, but whose contribution to early computing was equally significant. Faced with the monumental task of processing data from the 1890 United States Census, Hollerith recognized the potential of punched cards to automate this gargantuan undertaking. The 1880 census had taken seven years to process; the population growth

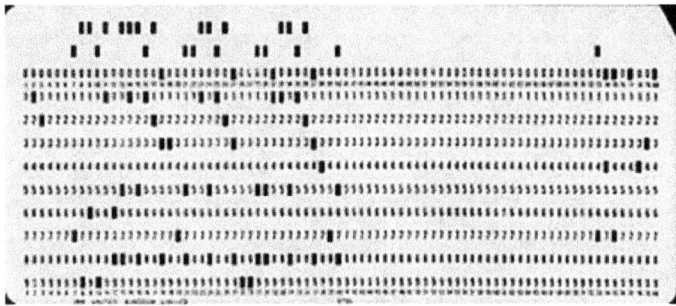

Wikipedia, CC BY-SA 4.0

between censuses meant the 1890 census promised an even more formidable data-processing challenge. Hollerith ingeniously designed a tabulating machine that used punched cards to record and process census data. Each card represented an individual, with holes punched to indicate demographic information such as age, sex, and occupation.

Hollerith's machines were mechanical marvels, but a far cry from the sleek, silent computers we use today. They were a symphony of gears, levers, and carefully calibrated mechanisms, designed to read and interpret the information encoded on the punched cards. These machines mechanically counted the holes punched on the cards, thereby tallying the responses to each question and generating summary statistics. It was a crude but effective system, a testament to Hollerith's innovative approach to data processing. Imagine the sheer scale of the undertaking: processing millions of cards, one hole at a time. It was a herculean task, but Hollerith's machines managed it significantly faster than their manual predecessors. He reduced the time it took to process the 1890 census data to just three years—a remarkable achievement considering the size of the task.

The success of Hollerith's tabulating machines in the 1890 census solidified the punched card's position as a crucial element in data processing. His company, the Tabulating Machine Company, eventually merged with others to form the Computing-Tabulating-Recording Company (CTR), which was later renamed to the behemoth we know today as IBM. From humble beginnings as a solution for the tedium of census processing, the punched card became the backbone of business data processing for much of the 20th century.

Wikipedia, CC BY-SA 4.0

The use of punched cards expanded beyond the confines of census taking. Businesses, particularly those in industries with large datasets, such as insurance and banking, rapidly adopted Hollerith's technology. Think of the sheer volume of paperwork involved in these sectors before computers—mountains of invoices, bank statements, and policy records. Punched cards offered a way to organize and process this information with significantly greater speed and accuracy than manual methods. They effectively became the digital equivalent of handwritten ledgers and spreadsheets. Each card, a small rectangle of cardboard, held a potentially significant piece of business information.

However, the punched card system wasn't without its flaws. The cards themselves were bulky and prone to damage; a single bent corner could render a card unreadable. The machines, while ingenious, were mechanical behemoths that required regular maintenance and were susceptible to mechanical failures. Furthermore, the limited storage capacity of a single card meant that processing large datasets required handling massive quantities of cards, which was both labor-intensive and prone to human error. Imagine trying to sort through millions of cards, each representing a transaction or piece of data—an error-prone and painstaking process. The limitations of punched cards are apparent, yet the technology's impact on early computing should not be underestimated.

These limitations, while significant, didn't diminish the punched card's influence. It wasn't a perfect technology, but it was a workable one, a functional solution for a time when electronic alternatives were in their infancy. It served as a vital bridge between manual computation and the electronic age, a testament to the ingenuity of finding workable solutions within the constraints of available technology. The punched card's story is a reminder that even crude technologies, when cleverly applied, can have a profound impact on the course of history. The legacy of the punched card is deeply intertwined with the rise of computing, a testament to its crucial, if often understated, role in shaping the digital world we inhabit today.

The Human Element: The Unsung Heroes of Early Computation

But the story of early computation isn't solely about ingenious machines; it's also about the tireless individuals who powered them, often operating in the shadows of the technological advancements they enabled. Long before the age of electronic computers, there existed a silent army of human "computers"—men and women who performed complex calculations by hand, their work laying the foundation for the digital revolution. Their contributions, often overlooked, are crucial to understanding the dawn of computation.

These human computers weren't working with sleek digital interfaces or powerful algorithms; their tools were far more rudimentary: pencils, paper, slide rules, and an astonishing amount of patience. Their tasks involved everything from calculating artillery trajectories for wartime efforts to painstakingly crunching astronomical data to charting navigational routes. Imagine the sheer volume of calculations required for a single celestial map – each calculation a potential source of error. The accuracy demanded of these human computers was remarkable. A minor slip of the pencil, a

NACA (NASA) – Dryden Flight Research Center Photo Collection – http://www.dfrc.nasa.gov/Gallery/Photo/Places/HTML/E49-54.html, public domain

misplaced decimal point – these could have significant consequences, especially in fields such as astronomy and navigation.

The working conditions for these individuals varied greatly depending on the institution or organization employing them. Some worked in comfortable offices, while others labored in cramped, dimly lit rooms. The meticulous nature of the work often led to long hours and eye strain. Consider the task of manually calculating a large matrix multiplication—a process that today's computers handle with ease. This involved hours of tedious calculation with the constant risk of errors. A single error could invalidate an entire set of calculations, rendering days, even weeks, of work useless. This intense focus and dedication underscore the human element in early computation.

The Role of Women in Early Computing

One particularly poignant example comes from the history of astronomical computation. Throughout the 19th and early 20th centuries, observatories around the world employed large teams of human computers, predominantly women, to analyze astronomical data. Their job involved reducing raw observational data, a process that involved numerous calculations to determine the positions and movements of celestial bodies. The data poured in from telescopes, often in vast quantities. Each observation needed to be meticulously reduced to yield meaningful scientific results. These women, usually lacking formal training in astronomy, were nonetheless responsible for critical computations that supported major scientific discoveries. Their contributions were fundamental, even if their names were rarely associated with the scientific publications resulting from their work.

Wikipedia, CC BY-SA 4.0

An example of women's contributions is Katherine Johnson. Her mathematical calculations were crucial to the success of NASA's early space missions, which ultimately helped land astronauts on the Moon. Without her calculations, who knows? Maybe we'd still be stuck trying to figure out how to get to the moon using paper airplanes. There is even a movie about the contributions of women to the early space efforts. (It's called "Hidden Figures", if you haven't seen it—highly recommend!) These women were literally performing the job that we now consider a computer's function. The work of women in computing was instrumental in shaping the field's trajectory, although their contributions were often overlooked in history for many years.

The meticulous nature of their work is highlighted by the fact that a single error could lead to significant inaccuracies in astronomical predictions and modeling. Yet, these women worked with incredible accuracy and efficiency, often under difficult conditions. Their stories deserve to be told not just as a footnote in history but as a critical piece of the narrative of scientific progress. They were the unsung heroes of scientific advancement, their quiet dedication laying the groundwork for future breakthroughs.

Another striking example of the human element in computation can be found in the realm of wartime efforts. During World War II, the Allied forces relied heavily on human computers to perform ballistic calculations. The trajectory of artillery shells, for example, involved complex mathematical computations considering factors such as wind speed, air density, and the shell's initial velocity. The accuracy of these calculations directly impacted the effectiveness of military operations. Groups of human computers, often assembled from various backgrounds and skill sets, worked tirelessly to produce these calculations, often under pressure and with limited resources.

Human Computers 1947
NASA Langley Research Center   1/28/1947   Image # EL-2001-00471

Published in Winds of Change, 75th Anniversary NASA publication, by James Schultz, public domain photo

The calculations were not simply a matter of plugging numbers into a formula. The process involved interpolating tables, making corrections for various factors, and checking and rechecking their results to ensure accuracy. The reliance on human accuracy was critical in the midst of military operations—a single miscalculation could mean the difference between success and failure. The sheer speed and accuracy required demonstrated the exceptional skills of these human computers. Their expertise was essential to the war effort.

Their contributions extend beyond the purely mathematical. Many of these human computers also possessed an innate understanding of the data they were manipulating, able to identify anomalies and potential errors. This knowledge extended beyond mere arithmetic skills; it involved an insightful understanding of the underlying scientific principles and the ability to identify outliers or inconsistencies in the data. They acted as crucial checks on the computational process, often preventing errors from propagating into significant inaccuracies.

The transition from human computation to electronic computation wasn't a sudden switch but a gradual evolution. As electronic computers emerged, they initially aided human computers rather than replacing them entirely. The early electronic machines were not particularly user-friendly; preparing the input data and interpreting the output frequently required the skills of human computers, who could ensure accuracy and identify any anomalies. The early machines required significant human intervention, not only to operate them but also to ensure the accuracy of their results.

In many cases, these human computers played a crucial role in training others to use the new machines. They possessed a deep understanding of the computational processes, allowing them to translate complex problems into forms suitable for the early electronic computers. Their expertise was invaluable in bridging the gap between established manual calculation methods and emerging electronic computation technologies. They were, in essence, the first generation of programmers, adapting their knowledge and skills to a new technological landscape.

The contributions of these unsung heroes cannot be overstated: the human "computers" who manually crunched numbers, their pencils and paper the digital equivalent of a rotary phone. They represent a crucial stage in the evolution of computation, demonstrating the human ingenuity and dedication that underpinned the development of digital technologies. Their stories are a testament to the power of human perseverance, accuracy, and the remarkable ability to adapt to technological change. Without their dedication and precision, the advancement of computation might have taken a far different course.

Their contributions remind us that even the most advanced technology relies on human intellect and effort, a fundamental truth that remains relevant even in the age of artificial intelligence (AI). Their legacy underscores the importance of acknowledging the human element—the often overlooked but always essential ingredient—in the narrative of technological progress.

Anecdotes, Musings, and Recollections

The Abacus: A Merchant's Workout. The abacus wasn't just a calculator; it was a full-body workout. Imagine ancient merchants furiously sliding beads back and forth while negotiating the price of silk. Who needs a gym when you've got daily bead-pushing marathons? And forget spreadsheets—picture someone calculating profit margins with beads while a camel nudges them impatiently. True multitasking genius.

Pythagoras: The Cult Leader of Math. Pythagoras wasn't just a mathematician; he was the head of a cult-like group that worshipped numbers. His followers were so obsessed with the purity of whole numbers that discovering irrational numbers—like the square root of 2—caused quite the scandal. Legend has it that one of his followers who revealed this "dirty secret" to the world was...well, let's just say, "permanently removed" from the group. Who knew math could be so cutthroat?

Hypatia: The Math Rebel. Hypatia, an ancient Alexandrian mathematician, wasn't just brilliant—she was fearless. In a time when women in science were about as common as unicorns, she lectured on math and philosophy, often while riding through the city in a chariot. Imagine Einstein cruising through town on a Segway, shouting about relativity. Hypatia was truly ahead of her time in every way.

Gauss: Math Prodigy with No Time for Nonsense. Carl Friedrich Gauss was a child math prodigy who, at the age of 10, supposedly outsmarted his teacher. When tasked with summing the numbers from 1 to 100 as a classroom punishment, Gauss quickly found the solution by pairing the numbers (1 + 100, 2 + 99, and so on). Instead of spending the whole day calculating, he calculated the answer in mere moments: 50 pairs of 101, totaling 5,050. His teacher, stunned by the speed and elegance of the solution, realized this boy wasn't just clever—he was operating on a different mathematical wavelength entirely.

Katherine Johnson: A First Computer. When NASA used electronic computers for the first time to calculate John Glenn's orbit around Earth, officials called on Johnson to verify the computer's calculations; Glenn had specifically requested her and had refused to fly unless Johnson verified the calculations. Smith, Yvette (November 24, 2015). "Katherine Johnson: The Girl Who Loved to Count", Sloat, Sarah (August 15, 2016). "'Hidden Figures' Gives NASA Mathematicians Long Overdue Movie."

Recollections (By Bill Inmon)

Memory is essential to human existence. There is no learning without memory.

In the earliest dawns of civilization, memory was passed down orally. The grandfather/grandmother would pass a story down to the grandson/granddaughter. Then the grandson/granddaughter would pass the story down to his/her grandsons/granddaughters and so forth. Oral tradition was one of the first forms of human memory.

These early memories were stories about the origins of mankind, the origins of animals, fables, constellations in the sky, and so forth. Then one day paper appeared, and then the printing press followed. Soon, there was the written word.

Even today, some of our earliest memories are of Jacob, Esau, David and Goliath, Jesus and Mary. These early memories were passed down through the written word of the Bible.

Memory is absolutely essential for computer processing. The computer requires a very different form of memory. The computer requires something much more reliable, precise, and speedy than oral conversations and the written word.

Memory is still memory, but the computer requires a very different form of memory.

Memory in a computer is achieved by the magnetization and demagnetization of what are called bits, or core. A bit remembers what is stored by being either magnetized or not being magnetized. The bit is either off or on. It is a "1" or a "0". A bit is best thought of as a bead—a tiny circular disk with a hole in it. The bit can be magnetized or not magnetized. The bit is either off or on, depending on its magnetization.

Bits are combined in groups of eight to create a byte. Collectively, eight bits hold the information of the byte.

To achieve the magnetization or demagnetization of the bits, three wires need to pass through the bit—the X, Y, and Z wires. An electrical current is passed through these wires to control the magnetization of the bit.

In the very earliest days of computing, it was thought that memory could be created manually by beading the bits together.

Early hardware companies sought individuals with experience in beading. The American Indian came to mind.

In most Indian cultures, beading is thought to be a task for women (although there are some very accomplished and talented male beaders).

Fairchild Industries—an early Silicon pioneer—created a plant in Shiprock, New Mexico, on the Navajo reservation to start building memory for computers in the 1960s. Fairchild Industries knew that there was an available pool of talented Navajo women who were skilled beaders, available for the task of building memory.

One of the challenges of building memory by hand was that the quality of the memory produced had to be exceptionally high. Computer memory demanded that every aspect of the beading process be done perfectly. If anything in the beading process was done incorrectly, the memory would fail.

Given that the early memory was used for such things as the Space Shot and NASA exploration, lives truly did depend on the talents of the Navajo women.

One of the challenges facing the Navajo beaders was the fact that a wire had to be passed through a frame. This took two women—one on each side of the frame, passing a wire through the board.

The testing of the final memory components was extremely important.

Needless to say, the cost of memory and its availability were real issues. In early computing, memory was one of the key limiting factors in determining the boundaries of what could be accomplished by a computer.

Today, memory is fabricated by manufacturers. Silicon Valley and its manufacturers churn out memory by the bucketloads. There are kilobytes, megabytes, gigabytes, terabytes, and petabytes of memory to be found in major corporations. Children's computers contain terabytes of memory.

If the memory that exists today had to be handwoven by Navajo women, the world would look drastically different from what it does today.

Chapter 2

The Transition to Electronic Computing: The First Steps

Mainframes: The Dawn of Large-Scale Computing

The story of computation, as we've seen, began long before the sleek silicon chips and powerful processors of today. It was a story etched in the painstaking work of human computers, individuals who wielded pencils and paper as their primary tools, meticulously performing calculations that laid the groundwork for the digital age. But the transition from this human-powered computation to the electronic marvels we know today wasn't a sudden revolution; it was a gradual, often bumpy, evolution.

Now we're getting into the fun stuff—the big, ugly machines that could fill up an entire room but still couldn't do much without the help of humans. Mainframes were the dinosaurs of computing: giant, expensive, and slow (by today's standards). But they were also capable of doing lots of calculations, as long as you had a solid set of punch cards. These machines were the go-to solution for governments, corporations, and anyone who didn't mind spending their life sitting in front of a whirring, overheating beast.

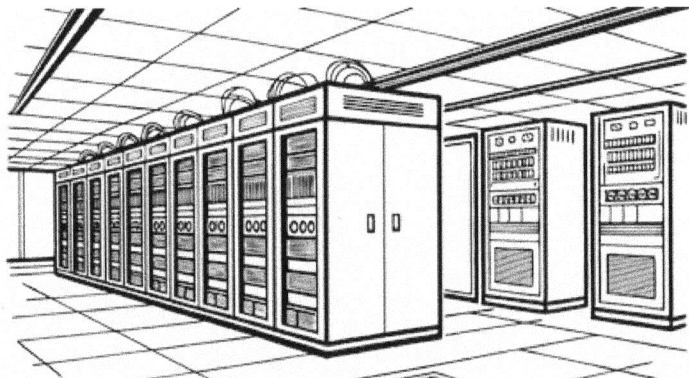

Illustration of a vintage computer server room with multiple racks and a tiled floor and ceiling By ALi STUdIO, public domain

The first steps toward electronic computing were tentative, filled with innovative ingenuity and frustrating setbacks. These early machines, though primitive by modern standards, represented a monumental leap forward in computational power and paved the way for the digital world we inhabit. And while modern tech companies may lead you to believe that they *invented* computing, they're really just the cool kids on the block. The true pioneers of computing were nerdy geeks, people doing math with their minds, and a lot of machines that could only think in binary. This is not a history of an overnight revolution but a raucous relay race where each ingenious machine passed the baton to the next.

The Early Pioneers: The ABC (Atanasoff-Berry) to the Cray

Atanasoff-Berry Computer (ABC)—1939-42

The 1940s and 1950s saw the birth of the first mainframe computers. One of the earliest contenders in this electronic race was the Atanasoff-Berry Computer (ABC), a creation born from the fertile mind of John Vincent Atanasoff and the dedicated efforts of Clifford Berry. Built during the late 1930s at Iowa State College, the ABC wasn't your typical computer. True, it wasn't solving world hunger, but it did a bang-up job as a specialized machine designed to solve systems of linear equations. While limited in its application, this focus allowed Atanasoff to pioneer several crucial concepts that would shape future computer design.

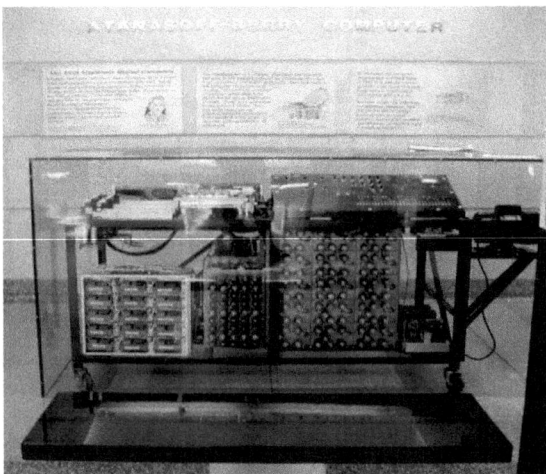

Wikipedia, CC BY-SA 4.0

The ABC's innovation lay not just in its function but in its fundamental architecture. Unlike the mechanical calculators that preceded it, the ABC employed binary numbers (zeros and ones) to represent data, a foundational element of modern computing. This binary system, inherently simpler than decimal representation, drastically simplified the design and operation of the machine. Atanasoff's intuition in adopting binary was a crucial turning point, proving remarkably efficient for electronic implementation. He cleverly used vacuum tubes—then a relatively new technology—to represent the binary digits, creating a system that could store and manipulate data electronically. This was a stark contrast to the gears, levers, and punch cards of earlier mechanical machines. The ABC's use of binary and electronic components laid the groundwork for the digital revolution.

However, the ABC's story isn't just about technological breakthroughs; it's also a cautionary tale of the challenges facing inventors. The machine, though innovative, suffered from numerous limitations. Its capacity was relatively small, capable of handling only 30 equations simultaneously. Furthermore, its reliance on vacuum tubes, though groundbreaking, resulted in a machine that was far from reliable. Vacuum tubes were notoriously prone to failure, resulting in frequent breakdowns and significant downtime. Repairing these failures required significant expertise and time, hindering the machine's overall efficiency.

The ABC's impact, despite its limitations, is undeniable. It demonstrated the feasibility of electronic computation using binary representation and laid the conceptual foundation for many subsequent designs. Yet, for a variety of reasons, including the onset of World War II and a lack of funding, the ABC was never fully completed to the level of a general-purpose machine and remained relatively unknown for many years. This relative obscurity didn't diminish its historical significance; its innovative features were undeniably influential in the subsequent development of electronic computers.

Harvard Mark I—1944

The Harvard Mark I was the original showstopper. It was a gargantuan electromechanical marvel conceived by Howard Aiken in 1937 while a graduate student at Harvard. While the idea and initial design came from Harvard, the actual construction was built in collaboration with IBM in Endicott, New York. The completed machine was delivered to Harvard. When unveiled in 1944, this colossal calculator was designed to handle complex tasks, such as calculating ballistic trajectories. Not exactly a speed demon by today's standards, the Mark I nonetheless proved that automating computation was not a pipe dream nor the fever dream of nerds with slide rules.

ENIAC - 1945

Meanwhile, across the country, another groundbreaking machine was taking shape: the Electronic Numerical Integrator and Computer (ENIAC). Developed at the University of Pennsylvania during World War II under the direction of John Mauchly and J. Presper Eckert, the ENIAC was a colossal undertaking, a far cry from the more modest ABC. The ENIAC was designed specifically to calculate ballistic firing tables for artillery, a task that was both time-consuming and crucial for the war effort. It was a machine of immense scale, comprising over 17,000 vacuum tubes, occupying a vast space, and consuming enough power to light a small town. Programming wasn't for the faint-hearted; reconfiguring hundreds of physical cables was more an exercise in patience than prowess.

Replacing a bad tube meant checking among ENIAC's 19,000 possibilities.

The sheer size and complexity of the ENIAC were staggering. Its vacuum tubes generated immense heat, requiring a sophisticated cooling system. Programming the ENIAC was a painstaking process that involved physically reconfiguring the machine's circuitry by plugging and unplugging cables, a process that could take days or even weeks. Yet despite these logistical hurdles, the ENIAC demonstrated the immense potential of electronic computation. It computed faster than any existing mechanical or electromechanical calculator.

While the ABC used binary numbers for internal calculations, the ENIAC used a decimal system. This minor difference reflects the different priorities of the two projects. The ABC, being focused on solving a specific type of mathematical problem, benefited from binary's inherent simplicity. The ENIAC, on the other hand, was built to address a pressing wartime need, and the designers opted for a decimal system more familiar to those working with the data. This choice highlights the pragmatic compromises often inherent in the development of new technologies. The choice may have slowed down the calculation speed, yet it addressed the immediate necessity during a period of war.

 So, why decimal rather than binary? ENIAC's designers, John Mauchly and J. Presper Eckert, were heavily influenced by mechanical calculators of the time, which operated in decimal. They envisioned ENIAC as an "electrical analogue" of these machines. (Project PX and the ENIAC, ds-wordpress Haverford.edu). Decimal was the standard for human computation—engineers, scientists, and military personnel were accustomed to thinking in base-10. Using decimal made it easier to verify results and align with existing workflows.

The ENIAC's impact was profound, although not without its complexities. Its sheer computational power dramatically reduced the time required for ballistic calculations, providing crucial support for the Allied war effort. However, its programming complexity and lack of stored program capability (instructions were physically wired into the machine) made it a cumbersome tool. Each new task required significant reconfiguration, which added complexity to the machine's operation.

Despite its flaws, the ENIAC stands as a landmark achievement in the history of computation. It wasn't just a more powerful calculator; it demonstrated the practical potential of electronic computation on a large scale, paving the way for more sophisticated and flexible machines. The ENIAC's impact transcended its wartime role, influencing the subsequent development of computers and inspiring generations of engineers and scientists. Its story is not only one of technological prowess but also a testament to human perseverance in overcoming immense technical challenges.

EDVAC—1949

ENIAC's success inspired others to jump on the computer bandwagon. A few years later, EDVAC (Electronic Discrete Variable Automatic Computer) emerged on the scene. Spearheaded by John von Neumann and his team, EDVAC introduced the revolutionary stored-program concept—a design in which both data and instructions reside in the same memory space. The EDVAC was the first effort to develop a computer with stored memory capability. This breakthrough laid the foundation for nearly every computer that followed, proving that the seeds of modern computing had been sown. Soon, punch cards were all the rage. These cards, with their tiny holes, resembled confetti but held the secrets of computer programs. Forget losing your keys, misplace a punch card and you'd be tearing your hair out faster than you could say "binary."

IBM 650—Early 1950s

Then came the IBM 650, the blue-collar hero of early computing. It was a workhorse with a magnetic drum memory that made computing more accessible. Engineered by IBM's bright minds, the 650 transitioned computing from colossal, exclusive machines into the realms of businesses and academic institutions. It signaled a shift where technology began to leave the hallowed halls of research and step into everyday use.

Wikipedia, CC BY-SA 4.0

UNIVAC I - 1951

No discussion of early computers would be complete without a nod to UNIVAC I—the Universal Automatic Computer developed by J. Presper Eckert and John Mauchly. Delivered in 1951, UNIVAC I was the first commercially produced computer and a veritable celebrity of its day. Its claim to fame? Accurately predicting election outcomes and crunching colossal datasets for government and business. This trailblazer proved that computers weren't just confined to labs; they were ready to tackle real-world challenges. UNIVAC I was the first commercial computer to use punch cards and magnetic tape. (pabook.libraries.psu.edu) Soon, punch cards were all the rage. These cards, with their tiny holes, resembled confetti but held the secrets of computer programs. Forget losing your keys, misplace a punch card and you'd be tearing your hair out faster than you could say "binary."

Wikipedia, CC BY-SA 4.0

IBM 1401—1961

The IBM 1401 was the mainframe you'd bring home to meet your parents: dependable, versatile, and ahead of its time. It was one of the first widely used mainframe computers. It featured magnetic core memory and its suitability for business applications cemented IBM's status as the cool kid of the computing world. IBM's influence on the computing industry during the 1960s and 1970s cannot be overstated. The company set the standard for mainframe systems, offering models like the IBM System 360. The System 360 was a major innovation, as it allowed for both large and small systems to run the same software, promoting compatibility and revolutionizing the way companies operated.

Wikipedia, CC BY-SA 4.0

The Rest of The BUNCH 1950s - 1970s

Now let's talk about the underdogs who kept IBM on its toes. The BUNCH refers to five companies—Burroughs, Univac, NCR, CDC, and Honeywell—that were significant players in the computing industry during the mid-20th century. They were often seen as competitors to IBM, which dominated the market at the time.

- **Burroughs Corporation.** Think of them as the quirky innovators. Initially known for its mechanical adding machines, it transitioned into a major player in the computer industry. Its B5000 series, released in 1961, was a standout for its use of a stack architecture and high-level programming environment tailored for business applications. The Burroughs B5000's emphasis on efficient multitasking and its support for high-level programming languages set it apart as a forward-thinking machine for its time. Eventually, they merged with Sperry in 1986 to form Unisys, proving you can be both cool and corporate.

- **Univac (Sperry Rand).** As discussed earlier, Univac created the first commercially available computer, the UNIVAC I, which was used for business and government applications. It played a pivotal role in demonstrating the potential of computers beyond scientific calculations.

- **NCR (National Cash Register).** Initially a cash register company, NCR transitioned into computing by developing early business computers. Their machines were widely used in banking and retail, helping to automate financial transactions.

- **CDC (Control Data Corporation).** If computing had a speedster, it would be Control Data Corporation. CDC was a leader in supercomputing during the 1960s and 1970s. Founded in 1957, CDC rose to prominence as a pioneer in high-level performance computing. Under the leadership of Seymour Cray, CDC produced some of the fastest computers of their time, including the CDC 6600 in 1964, often regarded as the world's first supercomputer. This machine could execute tasks faster than any of its contemporaries, setting a benchmark for performance that spurred the development of even more advanced systems. CDC's focus on scientific computing and its contributions to high-speed processing capabilities made it an indispensable force in the computing revolution.

- **Honeywell.** Honeywell, another major contributor, decided that computing was a lot hotter than thermostats and heating systems, and diversified its business into the computing world. In the 1950s and 1960s, Honeywell developed a series of mainframes, most notably the Honeywell 200 series, which gained popularity for its reliability and cost-effectiveness. These systems found applications in both business and government, reinforcing Honeywell's reputation as a dependable player in the mainframe market and ensuring that players could hop on the tech train without breaking the bank.

These companies collectively contributed to the evolution of computing technology, from mainframes to supercomputers, and helped shape the industry as we know it today. They not only expanded the reach of computing systems but also fostered competition and innovation. Together with IBM and other industry leaders, their contributions paved the way for the widespread adoption of computing technologies in various sectors. These early pioneers didn't just build machines—they built the foundation for everything from your smartphone to the cloud.

The Rise of Versatile Computing

Minicomputers (Mid-1960s and Beyond)

In the mainframe era, these machines were the playground of governments, research institutions, and large corporations. They guzzled power like they were on a never-ending buffet and filled entire rooms with linking lights and whirring tape drives. Operating one required a Ph.D., a diet of caffeine, and the patience of a saint. In short, mainframes were the regal titans of computing, intimidating and inaccessible to most mortals. Their very existence laid the groundwork for a revolution, even if they were about as portable as a dinosaur fossil.

Enter the minicomputers—smaller and ready to ruffle some technical feathers. Imagine shrinking the power of a room-sized computer into a machine small enough to grace a laboratory bench. It was as if someone had finally put computers on a diet. That's exactly what Digital Equipment Corporation (DEC) achieved with its PDP (Programmed Data Processor) series. Launching with the PDP-8 in the mid-1960s, these minicomputers were not as bulky as mainframes but still capable of performing serious calculations. Suddenly, computing wasn't reserved for a select cadre of corporate honchos; it had become available to smaller businesses, universities, and research facilities. The PDP-11, in particular, became a linchpin in the computing revolution, underpinning the development of early operating systems and fostering a new generation of interactive computing. With these machines, the computing world began to pivot from expensive, centralized mainframes to widely accessible miniature powerhouses.

The minicomputer era was marked by innovation and a healthy dose of irreverence. They were the rebellious teenagers of the computing landscape—pushing boundaries, advocating for time-sharing (allowing multiple users to interact with a single computer, a concept that evolved into modern cloud computing), and proving that even a punchy little machine could deliver a knockout performance. Their whiz-bang efficiency and affordability sparked a trend: why should the best technology be locked away in climate-controlled rooms when it could be shared and enjoyed by many?

Gene Amdahl's Mainframes

Meanwhile, Gene Amdahl was busy refining the art of mainframe computing. After making waves with IBM's System/360 designs, Amdahl launched Amdahl Corporation in 1970 and focused on plug-compatible mainframes, which could run the same software as IBM computers but at a lower cost. His mainframes balanced raw horsepower with efficiency, challenging the status quo and nudging the industry into new arenas. At its peak, his mainframes captured over a fifth of the market. His work underscored that innovation was as much about refining existing ideas as it was about inventing entirely new ones.

The Cray Legacy

No retrospective on computing evolution is complete without celebrating Seymour Cray—the high-performance virtuoso who created supercomputers built for peak speed and precision. Debuting in the mid-1970s, the Cray machines, with their aerodynamic designs and remarkable processing power, redefined what computation could achieve. They tackled some of humanity's most complex scientific problems, from climate simulations to particle physics, earning their reputation as the athletic champions of the digital arena.

A Dance Between Man and Machine

The transition from human computers to electronic machines wasn't a simple replacement. The early electronic computers, such as the ABC and ENIAC, were in many ways partners, not replacements, for human computers. The machines needed people to prepare the input data, often painstakingly converting information into a format suitable for the machines. Human computers were essential in interpreting the output, identifying anomalies, and ensuring accuracy. The early machines were not self-sufficient; they required human expertise to translate problems into machine-readable forms and validate the results.

What unites these pioneering feats—from the early Mark I, ENIAC, EDVAC, IBM 650, and UNIVAC I to the later PDP series, Amdahl's refined mainframes, and Cray's supercomputers—is a shared spirit of audacious innovation and resilient collaboration. Today, we celebrate not just cold circuits and vacuum tubes but the vibrant tapestry of human perseverance, where skilled mathematicians and engineers transformed abstract ideas into machines that redefined our world.

In essence, the human computers of the mid-20th century didn't vanish; they evolved, becoming the first generation of programmers, adapting their skills and understanding of computation to the emerging technology. They were the bridge between the meticulous world of hand calculations and the burgeoning age of electronic computation. They provided the expertise needed to operate these complex machines, ensuring the accuracy of their calculations and bridging the gap between human understanding and machine capabilities. Their role underscores the intertwined relationship between human intellect and technological advancement. Their expertise wasn't replaced; rather, it evolved, adapting to the new landscape of electronic computation. The transition to electronic computation was a dance between human ingenuity and burgeoning technology, a partnership that laid the foundation for the digital age.

Anecdotes, Musings, and Recollections

The Great Cable Jungle Escape

Imagine stepping into a room that looked less like a laboratory and more like the set of a spaghetti western—only instead of tumbleweeds, there were hundreds of writhing cables. Engineers working on the ENIAC would often joke that untangling that jungle of wires was more challenging than assembling IKEA furniture without instructions. One engineer claimed he once got so lost in the maze of cables that he considered leaving a trail of breadcrumbs, if only he had the stomach for it! Every misplaced wire was like a hidden prank from the machine itself, daring you to find the error before the next coffee break. It wasn't just about reconfiguring circuits; it was an extreme sport of patience and precision.

Punch Cards: The Original Cryptic Love Letters

Remember the days when computing meant whispering sweet nothings to a deck of punch cards? Each card was like a cryptic love letter to the machine, painstakingly filled out by human computers who took immense pride in every perfectly punched hole. Imagine the panic if one of those delicate cards went rogue—kind of like losing the secret ingredient in your grandma's legendary chili. In those moments, engineers

By Unidentified U.S. Army photographer -
ARL Technical Library, Public Domain,
https://commons.wikimedia.org/w/index.ph

might've felt like detectives in an old-time film, desperately hunting down that one missing piece that could make or break their case.

I recall some innovative individuals taking a magic marker and drawing a diagonal line across the deck of cards. If one (or several) card(s) got misplaced, one simply was able to find its location by looking at the line and finding the misplaced card.

Used by permission: larrywhatley.org

Grace Hopper and the (Literal) Bug

Picture this: It's a warm September day in 1947 at Harvard, and the engineers are deep in the throes of making the Mark II computer work its magic. Out of nowhere, they discover—yes, an actual moth—stuck in one of the relays. Instead of just dusting it off, the team taped the critter into the logbook with the caption, "First actual case of bug being found." This wasn't Grace Hopper's invention of the word "bug"—after all, folks had been complaining about "bugs" long before then— but her wit and deep involvement in the project helped popularize the idea of "debugging." That moth sparked a revolution in debugging practices. Imagine explaining that to a modern-day programmer:

Used by permission: larrywhatley.org

Recollections (By Bill Inmon)

In 1979, I left Standard Oil of California in San Francisco to go to work at Amdahl Corporation in Sunnyvale.

When I interviewed for the job at Amdahl Corporation, they indicated that I would be a database support person based in San Francisco, with a territory covering Europe. When this was said to me the first time, I didn't think twice about the logistics. (Later, I would be thinking a LOT about that statement.) I was going to be travelling to Europe, and that was exciting.

I had never travelled much before in my life, and this sounded like a great adventure.

For the first few months—six months or so—I was off to another European country every two weeks. During those six months, I was really excited about seeing a new part of Europe. Then, after six months, I began to dread the flight. It was impossible to have a personal life when you are constantly on the road. Every two weeks, I was going to a different European country. I woke up and travel began to feel like a noose around my neck.

To make matters worse, it was almost all just business. A typical trip—I went to Stockholm. I arrived at the airport. I took a taxi to the hotel. I got up the next morning, went to an office building, and worked all day. That night we went out to a nice restaurant. The next morning, I got up and headed for the airport. I might as well have been anywhere. I saw absolutely nothing of Sweden except for the airport, taxi, hotel, and office building.

And that is what it was like travelling all over Europe.

When I heard I was going to be a database support person based in San Francisco for Europe, it never occurred to me that I would be spending an inordinate amount of time on an airplane.

During my three years at Amdahl Corporation, I visited every European country except Gibraltar, Monaco, Andorra, Estonia, Latvia, and Macedonia. Every country. I had to obtain a passport extender, which involved adding pages to my passport to accommodate the necessary stamps for entry into the country.

By the time I arrived at Amdahl Corporation, it was a thriving business. Amdahl Corporation sold a plug-compatible mainframe computer that was compatible with the IBM mainframe.

Gene Amdahl was the founder of Amdahl Corporation. Gene had worked previously for IBM. Gene was an electrical engineer. At IBM, Gene had created plug compatibility of computers within the IBM line of computers.

Before plug compatibility, every computer had to have its own unique operating system. This meant that software written for a computer worked ONLY on that computer. In addition to application programs, the entire operating system had to be custom-built for each computer. A program written for one computer would not operate on another computer before plug compatibility.

Today, we take it for granted that we can run a program on one computer, then transfer the program to another computer, and the program will run properly. The interchangeability of software from one computer to the next was not the case before Gene Amdahl developed plug compatibility for IBM.

In addition to programs becoming interchangeable due to plug compatibility, data could also be exchanged freely. Before Gene Amdahl, if data was created on one computer, it was only readable and usable on that computer. There was no data exchange across different computers before plug compatibility.

Today, we take it for granted that data can be freely exchanged between computers. Thank Gene Amdahl for that convenience.

Gene Amdahl left IBM to form his own company, Amdahl Corporation, in Sunnyvale, California. Amdahl Corporation introduced competition to IBM in the sale of its mainframe computer. Before the emergence of Amdahl Corporation, IBM sold mainframes for a very high price. Once Amdahl Corporation entered the marketplace, the cost of mainframes dropped.

The impact on the business community of the lowering of computer prices was well received, but IBM Corporation was less enthusiastic about having competition.

No one had ever built operating system compatibility across computers before Gene Amdahl. The product line sold by IBM, which introduced plug compatibility, was called the 360 computer. There were small 360s, mid-size 360s, and large 360s. Software that ran on one 360 would run on all 360s.

The appearance of the 360 computer changed the marketplace entirely. Before the 360, there were a host of mainframe manufacturers, including Burroughs, Univac, NCR, CDC, and Honeywell. Before the 360, the mainframe marketplace was divided among these companies. But with the advent of the 360, IBM soon dominated the market for mainframes. And it was plug compatibility that was the factor causing the marketplace to consolidate.

In this regard, Gene Amdahl and his plug compatibility had an ENORMOUS effect on the marketplace and the way computing is done today.

While I was at Amdahl Corporation, I was a low-level technician, doing support in Europe. I had some direct contact with Dr. Amdahl in those days. Dr. Amdahl would be seen eating in the cafeteria.

(On a side note, the Amdahl cafeteria had a female Chinese cook who made hot and sour soup. Workers from all sorts of companies in Silicon Valley would come to the Amdahl cafeteria to get her soup. To this day, it was the best hot and sour soup that I have ever had.)

In the Amdahl cafeteria, you could walk up to Dr. Amdahl and chat. He was very approachable. He often ate lunch with Ken Simonds or Cliff Madden. Ken Simonds went on to become the president of Teradata. At Amdahl, Ken was responsible for marketing and sales.

The few occasions on which I actually worked with Dr. Amdahl were when a visiting company would come to visit Amdahl headquarters. Dr. Amdahl would start the presentation, then I (along with engineers and others) would dive into a technical discussion about our specialties. Of course, I talked about databases.

These meetings occurred two or three times a month, and I would go if I weren't travelling.

I left Amdahl because the travel finally got to me. I just could not take any more travel anymore. I went to work at Bank of America in San Francisco.

At Bank of America, I wrote a book dedicated to Gene Amdahl. When the book was published, I went down to Sunnyvale and spent the day with Dr. Amdahl. I presented the book to him.

The dedication in the book used lines from a song by Bob Seger—AGAINST THE WIND. Dr. Amdahl had spent his life going places where no one else had been and doing things that no one else had ever done. Dr. Amdahl spent his life running against the wind.

Dr. Amdahl showed us around the manufacturing plant, to the presentation rooms, the corporate offices, and elsewhere.

We had lunch with Dr. Amdahl and then left in the early afternoon.

It was one of the best days of my life.

Dr. Amdahl was a true genius. He was a gracious, intelligent, humble, and kind person. It was awesome to be in the presence of someone who had profoundly changed the world.

Chapter 3

The Rise of Programming Languages: From Assembly to Abstraction

The Early Days of Assembly Language: A Low-Level Approach

The dawn of electronic computing brought with it a new challenge: how to instruct these behemoths to perform the desired calculations. The elegant equations and algorithms devised by mathematicians required a translator—a language that the machine could understand. This role initially fell to assembly language, a low-level programming language that laid bare the machine's inner workings. It was a far cry from the abstract elegance of modern programming languages; it was a direct, and often grueling, dialogue with the hardware itself.

Imagine a world where programming meant wrestling with binary codes, meticulously assigning each instruction to a specific memory address. This was the reality for early programmers. Each instruction, a tiny step in a larger computation, was represented by a sequence of ones and zeros, directly reflecting the machine's architecture. There was no hiding; the programmer had to know the internal workings of the computer—the registers, memory locations, and instruction set—even to begin writing a program.

The ENIAC, for instance, presented a particularly daunting challenge. Programming was an almost physical activity, involving the painstaking connection and disconnection of thousands of cables. Each cable represented a specific instruction or data path, and rearranging them to perform a new calculation was a monumental task that could take days or even weeks. These were not the elegant keystrokes and mouse clicks of contemporary programming; this was heavy lifting, both literally and figuratively. The ENIAC's programmers were not just coders; they were circuit benders, architects of computation forged in the fires of hardware.

The emergence of stored-program computers, a pivotal development, brought a significant improvement. Instead of physically rewiring the machine, programmers could now store instructions in the computer's memory. This allowed for a degree of reusability, a monumental leap forward from the laborious process of reconfiguring the ENIAC. This still meant working directly with machine code—sequences of binary numbers—but at least the physical rewiring was eliminated. The improvement was undeniable, but the task remained inherently complex.

Assembly language, though an improvement over direct machine code, remained a low-level language, tied to the specific architecture of the computer. Each instruction directly corresponded to a single machine instruction. The programmer had to manage registers, memory, and data flow with meticulous attention to detail. A misplaced address or a single incorrect bit could lead to catastrophic errors, requiring hours, sometimes days, of debugging. The process was painstaking, unforgiving, and extraordinarily prone to human error.

To illustrate the tediousness, consider a simple task: adding two numbers. In a modern high-level language like Python, this operation is trivial: `result = number1 + number2`. In assembly language, however, the programmer would need to load the numbers into registers meticulously, issue the addition instruction, and then store the result back into memory. This would involve several instructions, each with its own binary code and memory address. This simple addition is just a single step in a larger program. Imagine the complexity of more intricate operations, algorithms, or software applications.

Furthermore, assembly language lacked the structured constructs that we take for granted today—loops, conditional statements, functions, and subroutines. The programmer had to build these essential tools from scratch, carefully managing the flow of execution using "jump" instructions to navigate between different parts of the code. This necessitated a level of mental gymnastics rarely seen in modern programming, demanding a deep understanding of computer architecture and meticulous attention to detail. Errors in managing the flow control could easily lead to crashes, unexpected results, or infinite loops that render the program useless. A single misplaced jump instruction could send the program spiraling into chaos, requiring the programmer to meticulously trace the execution flow to identify the source of the problem.

The lack of abstraction in assembly language also made programs inherently machine-specific. A program written for one computer would not work on another, unless their architectures were identical. This limited the reusability of code, forcing programmers to rewrite software for every new machine or even variations within a machine family. This significantly increased development time, cost, and effort, and represented a serious bottleneck in the expansion of computer technology.

The challenge wasn't solely the technical complexity; it was also the sheer mental strain. Working with assembly language requires an almost monastic level of concentration and an impeccable memory. The programmer had to keep track of numerous details—memory addresses, register contents, instruction sequences, and the overall flow of the program—all while painstakingly translating high-level algorithms into a language the machine could understand. This could easily lead to burnout, errors, and a significant reduction in productivity. There is a significant reason that assembly language programming is frequently described as a 'low-level' programming style. This means that programmers had to be directly familiar with the low-level details of the specific computer on which they were programming.

Debugging, or finding and fixing errors, was a particularly arduous task. Without the debugging tools available today, programmers relied on primitive techniques, like inserting extra instructions to print intermediate values or using memory dumps to examine the state of the machine. This was an incredibly slow and tedious process, often requiring hours of painstaking analysis and meticulous trial and error. The process frequently resembled detective work, tracing the flow of execution step by step, and painstakingly trying to understand why the program was behaving unexpectedly.

Despite its limitations, assembly language played a crucial role in the early development of computing. It allowed programmers to interact directly with the hardware, pushing the limits of what computers could do. It was the bedrock upon which more abstract, user-friendly languages would be built. But it was also a testament to the grit, determination, and remarkable ingenuity of the early pioneers of computer science. They were not simply programmers; they were machine whisperers, speaking the language of ones and zeros, coaxing electronic giants to perform feats of computation previously unimaginable. Their work was painstaking, demanding, and often frustrating, but it laid the foundations for the sophisticated, user-friendly programming languages that we rely on today. Their legacy extends not only to the software they created but also to the development of higher-level abstractions that made programming more accessible and productive for future generations.

The early struggles with assembly language highlight the importance of abstraction in programming. The move from low-level languages to higher-level languages was not merely a matter of convenience; it was a crucial step in making computing more accessible, efficient, and reliable. As we'll see in the following sections, the evolution of programming languages has been a continuous process of abstraction, moving away from the nitty-gritty details of hardware towards more conceptual and user-friendly approaches. This transition allowed programmers to focus on solving problems rather than wrestling with the machine's inner workings. This shift is analogous to the progression from assembly line to modern manufacturing: assembly language was akin to building a car by hand, bolt by bolt, while modern high-level languages are like using a sophisticated automated assembly line to produce a superior, more reliable, and scalable product. The history of assembly languages serves as a valuable reminder of the journey towards more abstract and powerful programming paradigms, a testament to the enduring drive of human innovation in the realm of computation. The sheer grit and perseverance of those early programmers, working with such primitive tools, lay the groundwork for our appreciation of the elegance and efficiency of modern programming. Their struggles, though arduous, were essential in forging the path towards the world of computing that we know and depend on today.

The Invention of High-Level Languages: Making Programming More Accessible

The limitations of assembly language became increasingly apparent as computers grew more powerful and the complexity of software applications soared. The sheer tedium of working with low-level instructions, the high propensity for errors, and the inherent machine-specificity of assembly code presented a significant bottleneck to the growth of the computing field. A paradigm shift was needed—a way to bridge the gap between human thought and machine execution without sacrificing efficiency or power. This necessity gave rise to the concept of high-level programming languages.

Ah, the dawn of high-level programming languages—the moment computers finally started speaking something other than cryptic, machine-specific gibberish. Imagine being a programmer in the early days, painstakingly wrangling assembly language, where a simple arithmetic operation felt like wrestling an octopus made of memory addresses and registers. It was tedious, error-prone, and frankly, not what you'd call "user-friendly." The world needed a change.

Enter the late 1950s, when programmers collectively decided they'd had enough of bending over backward just to make a computer do basic math. The breakthrough came with high-level languages—essentially, a linguistic glow-up for programming. No longer shackled by the intricate whims of hardware, these languages allowed humans to write code in something closer to, well, human language. While assembly language remained a necessary tool for specialized tasks that required intimate control over hardware, a new generation of programming languages emerged, designed to abstract away the intricate details of the machine's architecture. These languages allowed programmers to express algorithms and instructions in a manner far closer to human-readable mathematical notation or natural language. This represented a colossal leap in both productivity and accessibility.

One of the pioneering high-level languages was FORTRAN (FORmula TRANslation), developed by a team at IBM led by John Backus. First released in 1957, FORTRAN was initially conceived as a tool for scientific and engineering computations. Its syntax, heavily influenced by mathematical notation, significantly reduced the cognitive burden of programming. While assembly language required a deep understanding of computer architecture, FORTRAN allowed programmers to focus on the logical steps of their algorithm without needing constant attention to memory management or register allocation. For example, instead of wrestling with individual instructions to add two numbers and store the result, a FORTRAN programmer could simply write `RESULT = A + B`, a much more intuitive and human-friendly expression.

FORTRAN's impact on the scientific and engineering communities was transformative. Before its arrival, complex calculations that would have taken weeks, even months, to perform could now be programmed and executed much more efficiently. This led to significant advancements in research and development in areas such as aerodynamics, nuclear physics, and weather forecasting. The ease with which FORTRAN allowed scientists and engineers to express complex mathematical operations paved the way for the development of advanced simulations and models, leading to breakthroughs that would have been impossible with assembly language alone. Its ability to handle floating-point arithmetic, crucial for scientific applications, made it a powerful tool for numerical computation. This marked a significant shift; instead of worrying about register allocation and memory addresses, scientists could concentrate on solving complex mathematical problems. The computational equivalent of cave paintings no longer bogged down researchers—they had a tool that let them work smarter, not harder.

While FORTRAN was revolutionizing science, COBOL (Common Business-Oriented Language) emerged in 1959 to do the same for the business world. COBOL took a radically different approach—it looked suspiciously like English. This meant that people who weren't hardcore programmers (like accountants and business professionals) could actually make sense of it. COBOL became the darling of payroll departments, banks, and inventory management systems, helping businesses automate their operations. Before COBOL, managing massive datasets was an exercise in frustration and manual labor; after COBOL, computers could efficiently crunch numbers with ease. COBOL's English-like syntax made it relatively easier to learn and use, especially for those with little prior programming experience. This facilitated the integration of computers into the business world. Prior to COBOL, business data processing was heavily reliant on manual methods, which were slow, prone to errors, and often lacked the scalability to handle the growing volume of business transactions. COBOL's ability to efficiently manage and manipulate large datasets made it a crucial tool in automating these processes. Its impact on the business world was as profound as FORTRAN's influence on scientific research.

The creation of FORTRAN and COBOL marked a watershed moment in the history of programming. These languages provided a level of abstraction that significantly reduced the cognitive load on programmers, enabling the development of more complex software more quickly and efficiently. The shift from low-level to high-level programming was not just a matter of convenience; it was a fundamental change that unlocked the potential of computers on an unprecedented scale. The subsequent development of compilers, programs that translate high-level code into machine-executable instructions, further enhanced the accessibility and efficiency of these new languages. Compilers removed the need for programmers of FORTRAN and COBOL to manually translate their code into assembly language, automating a tedious and error-prone process.

The impact of FORTRAN and COBOL rippled across various sectors. The aerospace industry relied on FORTRAN for complex simulations and designs, while the banking and finance industries adopted COBOL for managing massive financial transactions. The availability of higher-level languages spurred the growth of these sectors, facilitating automation and innovation. The development of new software applications became feasible, resulting in increased productivity and efficiency across numerous industries. These early high-level languages demonstrated the potential for abstraction to significantly improve the efficiency and accessibility of programming. The programmer could now focus on the problem at hand, rather than the intricacies of the hardware itself.

However, the early high-level languages were not without their limitations. They lacked some of the features that are common in modern languages, such as dynamic memory allocation, powerful data structures, and sophisticated error-handling mechanisms. The syntax, while an improvement over assembly language, could still be quite verbose and inflexible. These languages were also often tied to specific computer architectures. Program portability, the ability to run the same code on different computer systems, was often a significant challenge. For instance, a COBOL program written for one IBM mainframe might not run without modification on another manufacturer's computer.

Despite these limitations, the invention of FORTRAN and COBOL represented a monumental step forward. They paved the way for the development of increasingly sophisticated and powerful high-level languages, including ALGOL, PL/I, and ultimately, the wide array of languages we use today, such as C, C++, Java, Python, and many others. The story of high-level languages is one of continuous refinement and improvement, a testament to the enduring human quest for more efficient and accessible tools for computation. The creation of these languages not only increased programmer productivity but also democratized programming, making it accessible to a far wider range of individuals and opening up opportunities for innovation across multiple fields. The transition from assembly language to high-level languages is a powerful illustration of how abstraction can unlock tremendous potential, simplifying complexity and enabling progress on an unprecedented scale.

So, if you've ever enjoyed the ease of modern programming languages or marveled at how effortlessly software operates today, tip your hat to FORTRAN and COBOL. These pioneers didn't just make computing more powerful—they made it bearable.

The Evolution of Programming Paradigms: Different Approaches to Problem Solving

The evolution of programming paradigms is like a software soap opera, full of drama, intrigue, and the occasional twist that makes us say, "Wait, what?" Let's take a wry dive into this riveting tale.

Once upon a time, FORTRAN and COBOL came along, speaking the high-level language of computers and shaking up the procedural scene. They were basically the nerdy kids who thrived on step-by-step problem-solving—a programming style resembling a recipe for software soufflé. It worked fine until programs grew larger and developers found themselves tangled in an ominous bowl of spaghetti code. Imagine trying to untangle that mess—utterly unenviable.

But the story doesn't end there. These early languages, while revolutionary, were fundamentally *procedural*. Their step-by-step approach to problem-solving mirrored the linear execution of a computer processor. The program was essentially a long sequence of instructions, executed one after another. This "recipe-like" approach proved effective for many tasks, but it began to reveal its limitations as software systems expanded in scale and complexity. Managing large, intricate programs written in a purely procedural style became a logistical nightmare. Spaghetti code—a tangled, confusing mess of interconnected routines—became a common, and dreaded, phenomenon.

Enter *object-oriented programming* (OOP), the knight in shining armor. OOP introduced the idea of objects—tiny, self-contained units of data and functionality—a bit like software Lego® blocks. Instead of one giant pile of linear instructions, OOP brought structure, modularity, and a sanity-saving approach to coding. Objects could act like little specialists: the pistons, crankshaft, and carburetor of the software world. Put them together, and voilà—a functioning car (or program, but you get the idea). Think of an object as a miniature, encapsulated computer program within a larger program. This paradigm shift moved away from a linear, procedural approach to a more modular, organized structure. Instead of a single, monolithic program, OOP allowed for the creation of many smaller, interacting objects, each responsible for a specific aspect of the overall functionality.

One of the key benefits of OOP is *encapsulation*. The encapsulation principle of OOP further enhanced code reliability. An object's internal workings are hidden from the outside world, accessible only through a defined interface. By hiding the internal details of an object, OOP minimized the risk of unintended modifications. Changes within one object were less likely to cause ripple effects throughout the entire system. Encapsulation improved code stability and predictability, reducing the frequency of bugs and making debugging significantly easier. Instead of sifting through a tangled web of code, developers could focus on the specific object exhibiting problematic behavior, making the problem identification and resolution process significantly more efficient. This promotes modularity, making it easier to understand, maintain, and modify individual components without affecting the rest of the system. Using the car analogy used earlier: instead of having a single, massive engine block, you have various components—the pistons, the crankshaft, the carburetor—each working independently but interconnected to form a functioning whole. OOP allows for similar compartmentalization within software, making large-scale development vastly more manageable.

Another crucial aspect of OOP is *inheritance*. This allows for the creation of new objects (classes) based on existing ones, inheriting their properties and functionalities. This significantly reduces redundancy and promotes code reuse. Instead of rewriting code from scratch, developers could leverage existing code components, adapting and extending them to meet new requirements. For example, if you have an object representing a "vehicle," you can easily create new objects representing "cars," "trucks," or "motorcycles," each inheriting the common properties of a vehicle (like having wheels and an engine) but adding their own unique characteristics. This capability streamlines development and reduces the likelihood of errors through code duplication. The elegant simplicity and efficiency offered by inheritance proved revolutionary in streamlining the software development process.

Polymorphism, another cornerstone of OOP, introduced flexibility and adaptability. It allows objects of different classes to respond to the same method call in their own specific ways, enhancing the extensibility and maintainability of software. For example, a "draw" method could be applied to both a "circle" object and a "square" object, each producing a different visual output based on its own internal data. This flexibility allows for greater code adaptability and extensibility, as new object types can be introduced without altering existing code. The ability to modify and extend software without disrupting its existing functionality was a significant advancement in software engineering.

The rise of OOP coincided with the development of powerful new programming languages like C++, Java, and Smalltalk. These languages provided the tools and structures needed to implement OOP principles effectively. C++, in particular, emerged as a highly influential language, combining the power and performance of procedural languages with the organizational benefits of OOP. Java, with its platform independence and robust features, further cemented OOP's position as a dominant paradigm in software development. Smalltalk's influence on design patterns and programming methodologies remains significant. These languages, coupled with the power of OOP principles, were instrumental in the creation of the software-rich world we inhabit today.

However, the journey of programming paradigms doesn't end with OOP. *Functional programming* (FP), another significant approach, rose in prominence. FP emphasizes the use of functions as the primary building blocks of programs, emphasizing immutability—no changing data willy-nilly, thus avoiding side effects. Instead of modifying data in place, FP focuses on transforming data through functions, creating new data structures without altering the originals. By treating functions as first-class citizens, FP embraced a declarative style, allowing programmers to specify *what* the program should do rather than *how* it should do it. This approach fosters cleaner, more predictable code, reducing the likelihood of subtle bugs caused by unexpected data modifications. With FP, 2 + 2 is always 4, no matter how grumpy your compiler feels. Languages like Lisp, Scheme, and Haskell embraced FP. Even trendy newcomers like Scala and Clojure hopped on the FP bandwagon.

The core principle of FP is that a function, given the same input, will always produce the same output. This property, known as *referential transparency*, simplifies program reasoning and makes it easier to test and debug. FP seeks to apply a similar predictability to software development, resulting in code that's easier to understand, maintain, and scale.

Functional programming also utilizes concepts like *higher-order functions*, which take other functions as arguments or return functions as results. This enables a powerful level of abstraction and code reuse, allowing for concise and expressive solutions to complex problems. For instance, a higher-order function could be designed to apply a specific operation (like sorting or filtering) to any data collection, regardless of the data type.

The adoption of functional programming is driven, in part, by the rise of concurrent and parallel computing. FP's emphasis on immutability and lack of side effects makes it easier to write programs that can run concurrently without interfering with each other, a crucial factor in harnessing the power of multi-core processors. Modern programming increasingly blends paradigms, integrating aspects of functional programming into object-oriented languages and vice versa. Languages like Python and JavaScript, for instance, incorporate elements of both paradigms, allowing programmers to choose the most suitable approach for a given task.

Another noteworthy paradigm, though less dominant than OOP and FP, is *logic programming*. Prolog, the most prominent example, represents programs as a set of logical statements, and the program's execution involves proving or disproving these statements. Prolog is well-suited for tasks involving symbolic reasoning, such as AI, expert systems, and natural language processing. Logic programming provides a declarative style, where the programmer specifies *what* the program should achieve, rather than *how* it should achieve it. The underlying inference engine handles the "how," making it suitable for problems where the solution path isn't immediately apparent.

The evolution of programming paradigms is not a linear progression, but rather a dynamic landscape where various approaches coexist and influence one another. *Procedural* programming laid the groundwork, OOP revolutionized software organization, *functional* programming brought clean code and concurrency benefits, and *logic* programming offered a unique declarative perspective. Modern programming often involves a combination of these paradigms, offering a rich toolbox for tackling increasingly complex software challenges. The future will likely see continued refinement and the potential emergence of new paradigms altogether, as programmers continually strive for more efficient, elegant, and scalable solutions. The quest for the perfect programming paradigm, like the quest for the perfect programming language, is an ongoing journey.

The impact of OOP extended beyond efficiency. It enabled the creation of more sophisticated and user-friendly software applications. The modularity and organization inherent in OOP facilitated the development of larger, more complex systems, exceeding the capabilities of procedural programming. It played a pivotal role in the rise of graphical user interfaces (GUIs), which revolutionized user interaction with computers. OOP's contributions to the development of sophisticated software systems continue to shape the digital landscape today.

In reflecting on this evolution, it's clear that abstraction in programming does more than simplify the process. It unleashes our capacity to innovate. Just as stepping away from literal translations of thought can reveal a broader, more expressive worldview, high-level languages have made the digital realm both accessible and dynamic.

The Impact of Programming Languages on Software Development Efficiency and Innovation

Programming languages serve as the fundamental instruments through which software developers articulate solutions, express logic, and innovate in countless domains. The impact of these languages on software development efficiency and innovation is profound—they influence not only the ease and speed with which code is produced but also determine the paradigms and architectures that drive technological breakthroughs. This discussion explores the multifaceted roles that programming languages play in software engineering and examines how their evolution has driven both efficiency gains and transformative innovations.

The shift from assembly language to higher-level languages marked a quantum leap in software development efficiency. Assembly, with its painstakingly detailed instructions that mirror the processor's architecture, was incredibly time-consuming and prone to errors. A simple task might require hundreds of lines of code, each prone to subtle errors that could cascade into significant problems. The debugging process was arduous, often involving tracing the execution flow through memory dumps—a process akin to searching for a specific grain of sand on a vast beach. The resulting software was typically limited in scope and functionality, reflecting the sheer effort required to produce it.

FORTRAN, COBOL, and their contemporaries dramatically changed this landscape. These languages introduced higher-level abstractions, allowing programmers to express complex operations with far fewer lines of code. Suddenly, tasks that previously demanded hundreds of assembly instructions could be accomplished with a handful of statements. This increased productivity was not merely incremental, it was transformative. It enabled the development of significantly larger and more sophisticated software applications than previously imagined. The impact on scientific computation, business data processing, and other domains was profound. As computing needs diversified, newer languages began to offer higher levels of abstraction and better tools for managing complexity.

For instance, C brought low-level control with system-level efficiency during system programming, while advanced languages like C++ introduced object-oriented concepts to manage growing software complexity. The emergence of languages such as Java and Python in the 1990s and early 2000s signaled a paradigm shift toward readability, robustness, and platform independence. This historical shift highlights how programming languages have continuously addressed evolving developer needs and the challenges imposed by increasingly complex problem domains.

By providing higher levels of abstraction over machine code, modern languages reduce the cognitive load on developers, thereby enhancing productivity and efficiency. This evolution has not only reshaped the way developers perceive and tackle problems but has also laid the groundwork for innovative methodologies, such as Agile development and continuous integration.

Modern languages are often designed to let developers express complex ideas succinctly without getting bogged down in low-level details. For instance, high-level constructs such as list comprehensions in Python or pattern matching in functional languages like Haskell minimize boilerplate code and reduce the risk of defects. By increasing expressiveness, these languages allow developers to translate models of real-world problems into code with greater clarity and lower error rates. Programming languages not only streamline existing development practices but also often act as catalysts for groundbreaking innovations. The design and popularity of a language can give rise to entirely new programming paradigms and approaches to solving problems.

The continued refinement and evolution of programming languages and paradigms are a testament to the ongoing effort to improve software development efficiency and innovation. Each new paradigm builds upon its predecessors, learning from their strengths and addressing their limitations. Modern software development often employs a combination of procedural, object-oriented, and functional paradigms, reflecting the diverse needs and challenges of contemporary software projects. The journey continues, with new approaches and refinements continuously emerging to meet the ever-evolving demands of the digital world. The future of programming language development will likely involve even more sophisticated paradigms and techniques, driven by the need for ever more efficient, powerful, and reliable software.

The Ongoing Evolution of Programming Languages: Meeting the Demands of Modern Computing

The landscape of programming languages has continued to evolve at a breathtaking pace, spurred by the relentless march of technological advancements. The rise of cloud computing, for instance, demanded languages and frameworks capable of handling distributed systems, scalability, and massive datasets. This led to the prominence of languages like Java, with its robust platform independence and extensive libraries designed for enterprise-level applications often deployed across cloud infrastructures. Python, with its simple syntax and extensive ecosystem of libraries for data science and machine learning (ML), also saw a dramatic surge in popularity, becoming a cornerstone of cloud-based analytics and AI applications. Its ease of use and vast community support made it an ideal choice for rapid prototyping and development in the dynamic cloud environment. The ability to rapidly deploy and scale applications across geographically distributed servers became paramount, and languages like Go, known for their efficiency and concurrency features, emerged as a strong contender for building highly scalable and performant cloud services. Go's built-in concurrency mechanisms allowed developers to easily leverage the power of multi-core processors and distributed systems, a critical advantage in the demanding world of cloud computing.

The emergence of the Internet of Things (IoT) presented another significant challenge. The sheer volume and diversity of connected devices, ranging from tiny sensors to sophisticated embedded systems, necessitate languages and frameworks that can handle resource constraints, real-time processing, and interoperability across disparate platforms. This led to the continued relevance of C and C++, languages known for their fine-grained control over hardware resources and efficient execution. These languages, often used in embedded systems programming, enable developers to extract maximum performance from resource-limited devices while maintaining real-time responsiveness, which is essential for many IoT applications. Languages like Rust, which focus on memory safety and concurrency, have also gained traction, offering a more modern and secure approach to low-level programming while mitigating common issues such as buffer overflows that plague systems with limited memory. The need for seamless communication across different IoT devices and platforms fostered the development of standardized communication protocols and message formats, further shaping the choice of programming languages and frameworks used in this space.

The explosion of data, fueled by the internet and connected devices, placed immense pressure on data processing and analysis capabilities. Languages such as Python, R, and Scala have become crucial tools for data scientists and analysts, providing powerful frameworks and libraries for data manipulation, statistical modeling, and ML. Python's ease of use and vast ecosystem of data science libraries, such as Pandas and Scikit-learn, have made it incredibly popular for data analysis and ML tasks. R, specifically designed for statistical computing, continued to be a mainstay in statistical modeling and data visualization. Scala, with its blend of object-oriented and functional programming paradigms, provided a powerful platform for building large-scale data processing pipelines, often used in conjunction with frameworks like Apache Spark. The ability to efficiently process and analyze massive datasets had become a fundamental requirement, leading to the development of highly optimized distributed computing frameworks, such as Hadoop and Spark, which in turn influenced the choice and design of programming languages used in this domain.

The demands of mobile computing led to the rise of languages like Swift for iOS development and Kotlin for Android development. These languages were designed to streamline mobile app development, offering features such as type safety, ease of use, and seamless integration with the respective mobile operating systems. Swift, developed by Apple, aimed to provide a safer, more expressive, and easier-to-learn alternative to Objective-C, while Kotlin emerged as a modern and concise language for Android development, gaining significant traction due to its interoperability with Java and its enhanced developer productivity. The focus on user experience in mobile apps demanded languages and frameworks capable of creating visually appealing and highly interactive applications, leading to continuous innovation in mobile development tools and languages.

Furthermore, the increasing complexity of software systems necessitated new approaches to software development. The rise of agile methodologies and DevOps practices emphasized iterative development, continuous integration, and rapid deployment. Languages and frameworks that supported these practices gained prominence. This led to a focus on modularity, testability, and maintainability in programming languages and frameworks, allowing for faster development cycles and more robust software.

The quest for greater security in software also impacted programming language design. Languages like Rust, with its focus on memory safety and concurrency control, emerged as a viable option for building secure systems. Increased awareness of cybersecurity threats prompted a shift toward safer programming practices, leading to the development of languages and tools designed to minimize vulnerabilities and improve security.

The evolution of programming languages is not just about creating new languages but also about refining and extending existing ones. Many established languages have undergone significant updates and improvements to meet the demands of modern computing. Java, for example, has continuously evolved with new features and improvements. Similarly, C++ has undergone significant revisions to enhance its capabilities. This continuous improvement of existing languages demonstrates the iterative and incremental nature of the programming language evolution process.

The future of programming language evolution is likely to see an increased focus on several key areas. AI will play a growing role in software development, possibly leading to the development of tools that can automatically generate code or assist programmers in writing more efficient and robust code. Quantum computing, though still in its nascent stages, will ultimately require new programming languages and paradigms capable of harnessing the power of quantum computers. The increasing use of AI in software development itself is leading to the exploration of new approaches, like automated code generation and sophisticated code analysis tools that can identify potential bugs and vulnerabilities more effectively. This will, undoubtedly, influence the design and features of future programming languages.

The constant interplay between hardware advancements, software development methodologies, and the ever-growing demands of various applications continues to drive the evolution of programming languages.

Anecdotes, Musings, and Recollections

JAVA's Coffee Connection. Java was named after the coffee bean, and its logo features a steaming cup. Legend has it that copious amounts of coffee fueled the developers during its creation. So, the next time you debug Java code, remember you're sipping on the essence of caffeine-powered brilliance.

PYTHON. Python isn't named after the snake but rather the British comedy group Monty Python. The creators wanted a name that was short, unique, and a little whimsical. So, every time you write Python code, you're channeling the spirit of absurd humor.

GRACE HOPPER was a visionary force in computing who reimagined how humanity interacts with machines. In an era when coding involved wrestling with intricate assembly instructions, she dared to dream of a world where computers could understand human language—at least in part. She developed the first-ever compiler in the early 1950s. This breakthrough was the literal springboard for COBOL.

Recollections (By Bill Inmon)

Grace Hopper

Wikipedia, CC BY-SA 4.0

It was the 1970s, and I was working in San Jose, California. Silicon Valley was a good place to be if you wanted to rub shoulders with the leaders in technology in those days. For a variety of reasons, almost every pioneer in technology passed through Silicon Valley. Some made themselves publicly accessible, while others didn't.

It was with great interest that I saw a posting for a speaking event featuring Grace Hopper. It was an evening event in San Mateo at a very nice, mid-sized restaurant. I believe it was an Italian restaurant. There were probably 50 people at the event. It was nice and intimate, and we all had dinner together. Then Grace Hopper made her appearance.

Grace was a slight, small person. She probably was not 5 feet four inches. She had grey hair, and she wore her naval uniform. I believe she was an admiral, but I am not sure of her rank.

One of the most remarkable things she said was that her military occupational specialty (MOS) was amphibious landings. The thought of this slight, elderly, frail woman charging up a beach with a rifle in one hand and a hand grenade in the other was very humorous. This conjured up an unforgettable image.

But her small stature belied the mind that she had.

Grace Hopper emancipated programming from its early days. Before Grace, there were these gruesome languages—machine language, assembler language, and a variety of other languages. Trying to write and debug code in the early languages was like walking on a beach of broken glass without slicing your foot open. The early languages were very error-prone. Programming them could be done, but the effort was just enormous. The early computer languages had a million ways for you—the programmer—to fall off the cliff. And everyone at one time or another fell off the programming cliff.

It was one thing for an experienced person to program. But to the novice, programming was like trying to navigate through a maze blindfolded. The complexity factor was out of sight.

Trying to learn how to cope with these languages bruised the ego and minds of the early programmers—all of them.

The idea that Grace Hopper brought to the world was that there ought to be an easier, more efficient, less error-prone path to creating code. Enter COBOL—Common Business Oriented Language. The intent of COBOL was to unlock the computer from the tyranny of the early computer languages.

And COBOL was an outrageous success. Soon, banks, insurance companies, government agencies, retailers—everyone—were writing code. In an earlier day, these organizations did minimal coding. With COBOL, the floodgates of business were opened.

There is no question that COBOL—Grace Hopper's contribution—had an emancipating effect on the world of computing. One shudders to think what the world would be like if programming still had to be done as it once was.

Today, there are many more advanced computer languages. The newer languages have features and sophisticated techniques. But the newer languages today ALL stemmed from the pioneering work done by Grace Hopper.

One of the statements that has been attributed to Grace Hopper (and I don't know if she really said this or not) is that COBOL makes programming so easy that even secretaries will be doing coding.

That statement goes a little bit too far. I don't think many secretaries actually did programming. (I knew exactly one secretary in my life who really did programming.) But COBOL opened the door to a whole new profession: programmers.

One of Grace Hopper's signature trademarks was giving her audience a wire that was the length that electrons could travel in a unit of time. Her point was that over time, the wire was getting shorter.

She gave anyone in the audience a wire for their amusement.

At the end of her talk, I went up to her, shook her hand, and had a short conversation. It was one of the honors of my life. Her impact on computing is evident everywhere around the world, every day.

Ed Yourdon

In the very earliest days of the advent of the computer, in the early 1960s, it was recognized that software programs were needed. A computer by itself does nothing. The computer requires software to perform any meaningful tasks.

Programs were how businesses connected business value to the computer. And in the earliest days, there were few, if any, packages of software. Organizations hired programmers and set out to program their own corporate computers.

When programming first began, there were no best coding practices. There were no rules of thumb. Everything started from scratch, and no one had any real experience to rely upon. People just sat down and started coding.

Programming in the very earliest days was akin to the Wild West—anything went.

One of the watchwords of the day was that the end user wants to discuss the possibility of a new system. Bring your coding pads.

The thought was that there was a direct path from the statement of user requirements to the production of code. No design. No flowchart. No diagrams. No structure. No thought given to such topics as:

Performance of the system

The changing requirements over time

The maintenance of the code

The integration of code with already existing code

Who might need the system other than the direct users?

And so forth.

It was thought that nothing happened from the statement of end-user requirements until coding commenced. Just start coding as fast as possible.

Another coding mantra of the day was 'code it quickly now, and we will tune in performance later.' Time would prove this to be a very foolish thing to do.

The entire focus of the coder was on the speed of the production of code in the very early days.

The notion of quality of code, code that could be maintained or code that had to satisfy multiple requirements, never entered the mindset of the developer.

It is into this burgeoning world of coding that Ed Yourdon made his entrance. Ed had an idea that was heretical for the day and age. Ed had the revolutionary idea that code and system design ought to be produced in an orderly, well-organized manner. People should be able to read the code, understand what it does, and maintain it if necessary.

Ed Yourdon coined the term structured programming and design. Ed's concept included both programming practices and the design of systems. Ed laid out the structure and practices that would provide organization to computer programs.

At the time Ed Yourdon did his seminal work, his thoughts were considered heretical. But quickly, people began to realize that just throwing code into the computer led to some real disasters. Yourdon recognized the need for discipline and organization in a world of the complexities of computer code.

Thus was born the discipline of structured programming and design. Structured programming and design were the handiwork of Ed Yourdon.

Yourdon's focus was mainly on coding and coding practices, but he also included system design.

Yourdon wrote articles, books, and spoke at conferences. Ed was well recognized in the high-tech industry.

I was a burgeoning writer at the time. I wrote a weekly column for a journal called Computerworld. I had written my first two books by then.

One day, Ed Yourdon invited me to one of his conferences. This one was held in Ft Lauderdale, Florida. I was more than happy to attend. It was cold in Denver and Florida seemed like a good place to be.

When I first started writing the material, my focus and viewpoint were controversial. I had a different perspective on the world than the one dictated by conventional wisdom. In particular, I had views that did not comply with the technical giant of the industry at the time: IBM.

As a result, people who IBM influenced had more than one professional conflict with me. I had been disinvited to more than one conference.

Ed Yourdon, on the other hand, became a sort of mentor to me. And at that time in my life, I needed a mentor and someone who would let me express my unconventional ideas.

In many ways, Ed fostered my start in the IT profession.

I remember my first Yourdon conference well. Tom DeMarco spoke. Tom caught the audience's attention by throwing candy bars, frisbees, and other objects to the audience during his talk. To say that Tom would catch people's attention was an understatement. Some of the other speakers at the first Yourdon conference that I attended were Larry Constantine, as well as Lois Zells and Steve McMenamin.

But Ed did not just invite me to his conference. I got to have some extended conversations with Ed at the conference. After the conference, Ed and I had a long correspondence, exchanging ideas. In addition, Ed opened doors for me that would otherwise be closed.

Programmers today take it for granted that there is an orderly way to do coding and database design. Programmers can all thank Ed Yourdon for his seminal work.

Ed Yourdon was my friend and mentor (of sorts). In addition to being really smart, he was a genuinely friendly person.

CHAPTER 4

Data Storage and Management: From Punch Cards to the Cloud

Early Data Storage Methods, Limitations, and Innovations

Imagine a world where storing data meant meticulously punching holes in stiff cardboard. Each card had a series of tiny holes punched in it, representing different pieces of information. This wasn't some quaint hobby; punched cards were the digital workhorses of the late 19th and early 20th centuries. Used in everything from Jacquard looms (automatically weaving intricate patterns) to early tabulating machines (processing census data), they represented information as a binary code: a hole meant "1," no hole meant "0." The sheer scale of operation sometimes involved millions of these cards, painstakingly punched, sorted, and processed. Think of the logistical nightmare! Imagine the card jams, the misreads, the sheer physical bulk of it all. One can almost smell the dust and hear the clatter of those early machines. Early applications relied heavily on the accuracy of the

punched card system, and errors were costly both in terms of time and effort. The painstaking process of checking, re-punching, and sorting made error correction a laborious process. Many a computer scientist lost sleep over the fear of a misplaced hole. Punch cards ruled the data kingdom for decades. They were so important that losing one was akin to misplacing the crown jewels. Entire rooms were dedicated to storing these vast card decks. The photo is of the IBM Card Storage Center.

Wikipedia, CC BY-SA 4.0

The limitations were many and obvious. The cards themselves were bulky, fragile, and prone to damage, and reading the data was slow and error-prone. Storing large amounts of information meant huge amounts of physical space. The sheer physicality of it all underscored the crucial distinction between "data" and "information" in those early days. Data was physical; information was extracted from it after considerable time and effort. But the punched card, in its simple elegance, laid the foundation for the digital age. It took four days to load the five megabyptes of punched cards in this photo. However, it demonstrated the feasibility of representing and processing information mechanically, a concept that would soon be revolutionized by electronic technologies.

Los Alamos National Lab. Copyright Triad National Security, LLC. All Rights Reserved.

As the 20th century progressed, humanity craved more efficient ways to store and manage data. So, the next act in our data storage saga is the magnetic tape. Magnetic tape offered a significant leap forward in storage capacity and speed compared to punched cards. It allowed for sequential access to data, a marked improvement over the random-access limitations of cards. Imagine reels of

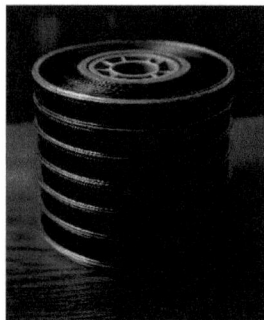

magnetic tape, resembling oversized cassette tapes, storing vast quantities of data—a true technological marvel of its time. Data was recorded onto the magnetic tape in a series of magnetic pulses. Early magnetic tape systems were used extensively in mainframe computers and for storing large datasets. These tapes were crucial for backing up large databases, ensuring against catastrophic data loss. However, this was not a painless transition. Magnetic tape, while a monumental improvement, still suffered from significant limitations. Its sequential access meant that retrieving specific data points could take a considerable amount of time. The tape had to be read from the beginning until the required information was found, often resulting in significant delays. Finding a specific data point within a giant reel was akin to finding a particular grain of sand on a vast beach, a metaphor made all the more literal by the sheer physical size of the storage medium.

Fast forward to the 1970s and data storage took a stylish turn with the advent of the floppy disk. The first commercial floppy disk drive was introduced by IBM in 1971 as an 8-inch model. This breakthrough innovation replaced clunky alternatives like magnetic drums, providing a flexible (literally) and portable storage (also literally) solution that fundamentally changed how data was handled and distributed.

Improvements quickly followed the initial 8-inch floppy drive. By 1976, the industry welcomed the 5¼-inch floppy disk. These sleek, square disks were the epitome of cool, fitting snugly into the floppy drive of your computer. Eventually, they came in two sizes: the 5.25-inch disk, which was a bit flimsy and had a capacity of 1.2 MB, and the legendary 3.5-inch disk, introduced in the early 1980s, which had a hard plastic shell for added protection. These hard-shell disks could store a whopping 1.44 megabytes of data, which, at the time, felt like an infinite amount of space. You could save your entire collection of text files and maybe even a couple of pixelated images. This new design quickly came to dominate the market. The sound of the floppy drive whirring to life was music to the ears of computer enthusiasts everywhere. Despite their limited capacity, floppy disks were celebrated as the height of technological advancement. They were the perfect medium for sharing files, installing software, and trading games with friends. Just be sure to keep them away from magnets—one wrong move, and your precious data could vanish into the digital Never Land.

The search for faster data access led to the development of hard disk drives (HDDs). The first hard drives, in the 1950s, were behemoths, boasting a mere 5 MB, occupying entire rooms, and costing a fortune. These early systems utilized rotating platters coated with magnetic material to store data. The read/write heads, the tiny marvels that danced above the spinning platters, were marvels of miniaturization and engineering for their time. Their introduction marked a crucial shift towards random access storage, allowing for significantly faster data retrieval. This development drastically altered the landscape of computing, enabling more interactive and responsive applications. However, the early hard drives were far from perfect. They were expensive, had limited storage capacity by today's standards, and were mechanically complex, resulting in frequent breakdowns. Consider the sheer weight and size of those early drives; moving one required multiple people and specialized equipment. And data recovery? Let's just say it was a job best left to specialists, often involving tweezers, magnifying glasses, and a healthy dose of patience.

As we moved into the 1990s, the era of the floppy disk began to wane, and the hard drive rose to prominence. While early hard drives were the size of large suitcases and, in some cases, filled entire rooms, their storage capacities were measured in megabytes. Over time, they shrank in size and grew in capacity, eventually reaching the gigabyte and terabyte realms. And guess what, you could actually put one on your desk! These spinning platters of data became the backbone of computers everywhere, providing the stability and reliability that floppy disks could only dream of.

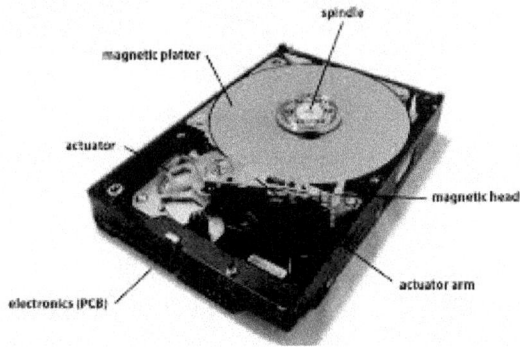

Wikipedia, CC BY-SA 4.0

The evolution from punched cards to magnetic tape, then to floppy drives, and finally to hard drives represents a remarkable journey in terms of storage capacity, access speed, and cost efficiency. Each technology was built upon its predecessors, overcoming limitations while introducing new challenges. The simplicity and robustness of the punched card paved the way for the larger scale of magnetic tape, which in turn prepared the ground for the random-access capabilities of the hard disk. This incremental progress, driven by both technological advancements and the ever-increasing demands for data processing, laid the groundwork for the sophisticated and diverse storage technologies we utilize today.

Consider the impact of these early data storage methods on various sectors. In science, for example, early hard drives allowed researchers to store and process vast quantities of experimental data, accelerating the pace of scientific discovery. In business, the advent of magnetic tape revolutionized record-keeping and accounting, enabling more efficient data management for large organizations. The processing of census data, once a tedious task involving mountains of paperwork, was radically transformed by punched card machines, which sped up the process and improved accuracy. The story of early data storage is inextricably linked to the broader evolution of computing, marked by a constant interplay of innovations and challenges.

The limitations of these early technologies were, in many ways, as significant as their achievements. Storage capacity was extremely limited by today's standards, the cost was prohibitive for most, and reliability issues were rampant. But these limitations also spurred innovation. The desire for greater capacity, faster access, and improved reliability fueled the relentless pursuit of more efficient and robust storage solutions. The history of data storage isn't just about the technology itself; it's also about the creative solutions humans devised to overcome the constraints of the available technology. It's a testament to our ingenuity and determination in our quest to manage and utilize ever-increasing amounts of information efficiently.

Before the internet "paved the way to the cloud", computing was literally limited by what you could physically hold in your hand. Floppy disks, while the workhorse data carriers, were laughably tiny by comparison. Then came the CD-ROM, a shiny disc that contained around 700 MB of storage capacity. This was a quantum leap that meant entire operating systems, software suites, multimedia presentations, and interactive encyclopedias could now be delivered on a single, reliable disc—no more juggling a bundle of floppies. The CD wasn't just a storage medium; it was a passport to a richer, multimedia-infused computing experience.

As computing demands grew, so too did our need for heftier carriers of data. DVDs answered that call by increasing the storage capacity to between 4.7 and 8.5 gigabytes (GB) per disc. Suddenly, the medium wasn't only about crunching software into neat packages; it was also the delivery vehicle for full-length movies, robust educational content, and complex applications. With built-in DVD drives becoming standard on many computers, these discs assumed a crucial role in installing operating systems, running applications with multimedia content, and even facilitating data backups in an era when the internet was still finding its digital footing.

Then Blu-Ray entered the stage like the dazzling high-definition headliner we all needed. Boasting 25 GB per layer (and often even more with dual layers), Blu-ray discs provided the storage necessary for ultra-high-definition video, immersive gaming experiences, and data-rich multimedia projects. In computing terms, Blu-Ray signaled a move toward precision and performance—whether it was for archiving vast amounts of data, running high-performance applications, or delivering cinematic experiences right from your desktop.

Today, while digital downloads and streaming have largely taken over, the legacy of these optical marvels is undeniable. CDs, DVDs, and Blu-Ray not only elevated the storage capacity available to the average computer user but also revolutionized how media and software were distributed and experienced. They helped transition computing from a text-and-number world to an era rich in graphics, sound, and interactive content—a transformation that continues to influence our digital lifestyles.

But wait! There's more! Enter the flash drive. Flash drives revolutionized computer storage by making data transfer faster, more portable, and more durable than previous magnetic and optical storage methods. Before their arrival, people relied on floppy disks, hard drives, CDs, and DVDs—each with its own limitations in terms of capacity, speed, and reliability. Flash drives changed the game by offering solid-state storage, meaning no moving parts, which made them far more resilient and efficient.

The first USB flash drives emerged in the late 1990s, with Israeli company M-Systems introducing the DiskOnKey in 1999. Around the same time, other companies, including PNY and SanDisk, developed similar devices. Early flash drives had 4 MB and 8 MB of storage, which was a massive leap from floppy disks but tiny compared to today's standards. Over the years, capacities skyrocketed, reaching gigabytes and eventually terabytes, with modern flash drives exceeding four terabytes (TB).

Flash drives quickly replaced floppy disks and CDs, and in some cases, even tabletop hard drives, for everyday file transfers, backups, and even bootable operating systems. Their plug-and-play functionality made them indispensable, and their durability ensured they could withstand frequent use without the wear and tear of older storage media. Today, while "cloud" storage has taken over much of the data-sharing landscape, flash drives remain a reliable, offline solution for quick and secure file transfers.

The transition to each new storage method involved considerable technical hurdles and logistical challenges. Think about the transition from the bulky punched cards to the unwieldy reels of magnetic tape. Training staff in new equipment, adapting software to the latest technology, and ensuring data compatibility all presented significant obstacles. The transition to hard disk drives presented a similar set of problems. This shift necessitated changes in operating systems, data management software, and even the physical infrastructure of computer rooms. Each step forward involved not just technological advancements but also substantial organizational and logistical adjustments.

The development of new error correction techniques and improved data compression algorithms further contributed to the evolution of data storage. Early systems had limited error correction capabilities, making data loss a persistent concern. As the density of data storage increased, so did the importance of effective error correction methods. The development of advanced algorithms helped minimize data loss and enhance the reliability of storage systems. Similarly, the development of data compression techniques enabled more efficient storage and transmission of data, thereby maximizing the utilization of available storage capacity.

The Rise of Databases: Organizing and Managing Information Efficiently

The dawn of the digital age, while marked by the impressive feats of ever-faster processors and increasingly sophisticated software, would have been utterly crippled without a parallel evolution in how we organized and accessed the exploding volume of data. The punched cards, magnetic tapes, and hard drives we've discussed provided storage, but they lacked the crucial element of *management*. This is where the database management system (DBMS) comes into play, a true hero of the technological revolution.

Before the advent of DBMS, imagine the chaos: thousands, even millions, of punched cards representing diverse information, haphazardly sorted or, worse, jumbled in a chaotic mess. Finding specific data was a laborious, time-consuming process, akin to searching for a particular grain of sand on a beach, only exponentially more frustrating. Magnetic tapes offered sequential access, an improvement, but searching remained a linear, slow process. Even the early hard drives, with their random-access capabilities, lacked the sophisticated tools to efficiently manage, query, and analyze the ever-growing volumes of data being generated.

The need for a more efficient way to organize and retrieve information was undeniably acute. Enter the database management system (DBMS). These systems provided a structured way to organize, store, and retrieve data. Early DBMS were relatively simple affairs, often custom-built for specific applications. Imagine the databases behind, say, the early airline reservation systems—a testament to the ingenuity of programmers grappling with the limitations of the technology. They were a crucial step towards effectively managing the growing demand for data storage and retrieval. This represented a paradigm shift; data was no longer just stored—it was *managed*.

The first DBMS were largely file-based systems, utilizing flat files that lacked the sophistication of later relational models. This means that data was organized in simple tables, with each record containing information on a single entity. While functional for small datasets, these systems quickly became unwieldy as the size and complexity of datasets grew. The challenge of managing relationships between data items in separate files, say, linking customer records to order records, was a major hurdle, leading to redundancy and inconsistencies. Imagine the complexities of tracking a customer's order history across multiple disparate files; the potential for errors was immense, mirroring the challenges of managing millions of punched cards without a systematic organization.

The next breakthrough was the emergence of the relational database model, a paradigm shift that dramatically changed how data was structured and managed. Introduced by Edgar F. Codd in his seminal 1970 paper (A Relational Model of Data for Large Shared Data Banks), the relational model organized data into tables with rows (records) and columns (fields), related through shared attributes or keys. This structured approach ensured data integrity, consistency, and reduced redundancy. The relational model made querying data infinitely easier thanks to Structured Query Language (SQL). SQL became the lingua franca of database interaction, offering a standardized way to retrieve, insert, update, and delete data. The standardization provided by SQL was, and continues to be, a vital force in the evolution of database technology.

The adoption of relational databases has transformed various industries. Consider the banking sector: managing millions of accounts, transactions, and customer details requires a robust and reliable system. Relational databases provided exactly that, ensuring data integrity and consistency across large datasets. The same transformation occurred in various other sectors: airlines, retail, manufacturing—any industry dealing with significant data volumes benefited immensely from the efficiency and reliability offered by relational DBMS.

The success of relational databases led to the development of numerous commercial systems, from giants like Oracle and IBM DB2 to smaller, niche players. These systems boasted sophisticated features for data management, including concurrency control (allowing multiple users to access and modify the database simultaneously), transaction management (ensuring data integrity in complex operations), and security features to protect sensitive information. The development of these commercial systems spurred innovation in both hardware and software, resulting in improved performance and scalability. The era of mainframe computers, with their massive storage and processing capabilities, became perfectly suited to hosting these sophisticated database systems.

However, the relational model, despite its revolutionary impact, had its limitations. As data volumes exploded in the digital age, the rigid structure of the relational model proved to be a bottleneck. The "one-size-fits-all" nature of relational databases struggles to handle the unstructured or semi-structured data increasingly common in areas such as social media, sensor networks, and the IoT. This limitation provided the impetus for the rise of NoSQL databases.

NoSQL databases challenged the dominance of the relational model by offering alternative approaches to data modeling and storage. Instead of the rigid structure of relational databases, NoSQL databases provide greater flexibility in handling diverse data types and structures. These databases, often distributed across multiple servers, offered improved scalability and resilience compared to their relational counterparts. Different NoSQL database models, including key-value stores, document databases, graph databases, and column-family stores, cater to specific needs and use cases.

Key-value stores are simple, fast, and highly scalable, making them ideally suited for applications that require fast read-write operations. Document databases, such as MongoDB, utilize JSON-like documents for storing data, offering flexibility in managing semi-structured information. Graph databases are well-suited for managing relationships between entities, like social networks or knowledge graphs. Column-family stores, such as Cassandra, excel in managing massive datasets with high-throughput requirements. The choice of NoSQL database depends on the specific requirements of an application, reflecting the increasing diversification of data types and use cases.

The rise of cloud computing, which will be discussed in more detail later, further revolutionized the database landscape. Cloud-based database services offer scalability, flexibility, and cost efficiency compared to on-premise solutions. Major cloud providers, such as Amazon Web Services (AWS), Microsoft Azure, and Google Cloud Platform (GCP), offer a wide range of database services, including relational, NoSQL, and other specialized options, enabling businesses to select the best solution for their specific needs. The flexibility offered by cloud-based databases is particularly crucial for organizations that need to scale their database infrastructure to meet fluctuating demands rapidly.

The evolution of database management systems is a continuous journey, mirroring the ever-increasing demands of data management. From the simple file-based systems of the early days to the sophisticated relational and NoSQL databases of today, the evolution reflects the ingenuity and problem-solving abilities of countless programmers, engineers, and data scientists. The future will likely involve hybrid approaches, combining the strengths of relational and NoSQL databases to handle the diverse data needs of modern applications.

Data Warehousing Building Centralized Repositories of Information

The journey from managing data with punch cards to the sophisticated database systems of today wouldn't be complete without discussing the pivotal role of data warehousing. Imagine our previous examples—the airline reservation system, the banking behemoth juggling millions of transactions—those are just glimpses of the data explosion. To truly harness the power of this data, something more than simple relational or NoSQL databases was needed: a centralized repository, a single source of truth, a data warehouse.

Think of a data warehouse as a massive, meticulously organized library dedicated solely to business intelligence. Instead of novels and encyclopedias, its shelves are stocked with structured and curated data, ready to be accessed and analyzed for strategic decision-making. Unlike operational databases that focus on real-time transactions, data warehouses are designed for analytical processing. This distinction is crucial. Operational databases prioritize speed and efficiency in handling daily transactions; a data warehouse prioritizes comprehensive analysis across potentially vast datasets spanning months, years, or even decades.

When discussing the origins and evolution of data warehousing, specifically the creation of centralized data repositories, the conversation is almost always framed around two pioneering approaches. Bill Inmon is celebrated as the "Father of Data Warehousing" for his top-down, comprehensive strategy that emphasizes establishing an enterprise-wide, integrated, and time-variant "single source of truth," a framework reflected in his Corporate Information Factory model.

Equally influential is Ralph Kimball. In contrast to Inmon's approach, Kimball popularized the bottom-up methodology. His work on dimensional modeling, particularly the use of star schemas and the concept of data marts, enabled organizations to create more agile, user-friendly analytical environments. Kimball's techniques have become synonymous with making business intelligence accessible; they simplify complex queries and reporting processes, enabling companies to quickly translate vast amounts of data into actionable insights.

Beyond Inmon and Kimball, the evolution of data warehousing drew on broader contributions from industry innovators. Early architects at companies like IBM played foundational roles in defining the architecture that would support decision support systems. Their work on integrating diverse data sources and optimizing systems for analytical queries helped shape modern practices, even if their names are less frequently cited in discussions dominated by Inmon and Kimball. Later figures—such as Dan Linstedt, known for developing the Data Vault modeling approach in the early 2000s—built on these concepts, further advancing how businesses manage, extract, and analyze large datasets.

Together, these pioneers established the frameworks and methodologies that not only addressed the data explosion of their time but also paved the way for today's hybrid solutions—integrating on-premise and cloud-based systems, and combining the flexibility of data lakes with the rigor of structured warehouses. Their contributions continue to inspire innovations in business intelligence and data analytics, enabling organizations to transform ever-growing digital deluges into strategic assets.

The challenges in data warehousing are substantial. *Data volume* is a major hurdle. Modern businesses generate colossal amounts of data, requiring massive storage capacity and powerful processing capabilities. *Data velocity* is another issue; data arrives at a rapid pace, demanding near real-time processing capabilities. The sheer *variety* of data formats and types adds to the complexity. Integrating structured data from databases with semi-structured data from social media and unstructured data from text documents requires sophisticated tools and techniques.

Finally, *veracity*, or data quality, is paramount. Inaccurate, incomplete, or inconsistent data can lead to flawed analyses and poor decision-making. Dealing with these challenges necessitates a well-defined strategy, robust infrastructure, and a skilled team of data professionals.

The term "Data Lake" was coined by James Dixon in 2010. It describes a centralized repository for storing raw, unstructured, semi-structured, and structured data in its native format, offering flexibility for big data analytics and ML. However, managing and analyzing data in a data lake requires more sophisticated tools and techniques than the relatively structured star schema model.

Furthermore, the increasing adoption of cloud-based solutions has transformed data warehousing. Cloud-based data warehouses offer scalability, flexibility, and cost-effectiveness compared to on-premise solutions. Major cloud providers offer a wide range of data warehousing services, allowing businesses to choose the option that best suits their needs. The ability to scale resources up or down based on demand is particularly valuable for businesses with fluctuating data requirements. Cloud-based solutions are often complemented by cloud-based ETL tools, providing a seamless and integrated data warehousing solution.

The ongoing evolution of data warehousing reflects the ever-increasing complexity and volume of data generated by businesses. Future developments will likely involve further integration of data lakes and data warehouses, creating a hybrid approach that balances the flexibility of data lakes with the structured analysis capabilities of data warehouses. Furthermore, the increasing adoption of AI and ML in data warehousing promises to automate data management tasks, improve data quality, and enhance analytical capabilities. The ongoing developments in data warehousing are critical for enabling businesses to extract valuable insights from their data and make data-driven decisions, which are increasingly essential for success in the modern business environment. The future of data warehousing is indeed dynamic, a reflection of our unceasing quest to make sense of the ever-growing digital deluge.

Cloud Computing and Data Storage: The Modern Approach

The evolution of data storage didn't stop with the sophisticated data warehouses we've just explored. The sheer scale and velocity of data generated in the 21st century demanded a paradigm shift—a move towards *cloud computing*. So, what exactly is cloud computing? The cloud is like an invisible storage space for your data and programs. Instead of saving files on your computer or phone, they're stored on powerful computers somewhere else—often in big data centers run by companies like Microsoft, Google, or Amazon. You access them over the internet. So, in essence, you shift the heavy lifting of data processing and storage from your local device to networks of powerful, remote servers housed in large data centers. Think of it as a cosmic filing cabinet, available anytime, anywhere, if you have an internet connection.

Cloud computing wasn't just a technological leap; it was a fundamental change in how we think about data ownership, management, and access. Instead of investing heavily in physical infrastructure—such as servers, storage arrays, and dedicated IT staff—businesses can leverage the vast resources of cloud providers, paying only for what they use. This pay-as-you-go model offered unprecedented flexibility and scalability, particularly beneficial for startups and rapidly growing companies unable to afford the upfront costs of traditional data centers.

The transition to cloud computing for data storage wasn't without its growing pains, of course. Security concerns were, and remain, paramount. Entrusting sensitive data to a third-party provider requires rigorous vetting and robust security protocols. Data breaches, while thankfully relatively rare among reputable providers, carry significant financial and reputational risks. Furthermore, reliance on a cloud provider introduces a degree of vendor lock-in, making it potentially difficult and costly to switch providers should the need arise. The "cloud" often masks a complex infrastructure and understanding the nuances of service level agreements (SLAs) and the intricacies of data governance within a cloud environment is essential.

However, the advantages of cloud computing for data storage and management are undeniable. Scalability is perhaps the most significant benefit. Businesses can easily increase or decrease storage capacity and processing power based on their needs, avoiding the costly over-provisioning often associated with on-premise solutions. This elasticity is especially crucial for businesses experiencing seasonal fluctuations in data volume, such as e-commerce companies during the holiday season or streaming services during peak viewing hours. Imagine the logistical nightmare of procuring and configuring additional hardware to meet a sudden surge in demand—the cloud eliminates this challenge.

Cost-effectiveness is another compelling driver. The pay-as-you-go model significantly reduces capital expenditure (CAPEX) compared to the substantial upfront investment required for on-premise infrastructure. Instead of purchasing and maintaining expensive hardware, businesses only pay for the computing resources they consume, potentially leading to significant savings in the long run. This is particularly attractive for smaller businesses or those with limited IT budgets. The operational expenditure (OPEX) model also allows for better budget planning and forecasting, as costs are directly tied to usage.

Geographic distribution is yet another advantage of cloud computing for data storage. Cloud providers typically maintain data centers across multiple geographic regions, allowing businesses to store data closer to their users, improving performance and reducing latency. This is particularly important for applications that require low latency, such as online gaming or real-time collaboration tools. This global reach also enhances disaster recovery capabilities, as data can be replicated across multiple regions, ensuring business continuity even in the event of a localized outage.

The choice of cloud provider is a crucial decision, with each offering its unique strengths and weaknesses. Amazon Web Services (AWS), the market leader, provides a vast array of services, including storage solutions like Amazon S3 (Simple Storage Service) for object storage and Amazon EBS (Elastic Block Store) for block storage. Microsoft Azure offers comparable services with Azure Blob Storage and Azure Disk Storage, integrating seamlessly with other Microsoft products. Google Cloud Platform (GCP) competes with its Google Cloud Storage and Persistent Disk options, known for its robust analytics capabilities. Each provider has its own ecosystem of tools and services, making the selection process dependent on a business's specific needs, existing infrastructure, and expertise.

Cloud storage solutions are not one-size-fits-all. The choice between object storage, block storage, and file storage depends on the type of data being stored and how it will be accessed. Object storage, exemplified by Amazon S3, is ideal for storing unstructured data, such as images, videos, and documents, offering scalability and cost-effectiveness. Block storage, such as Amazon EBS, is well-suited for applications that require high performance and low latency, including databases and virtual machines. File storage, often used for shared file systems, provides a more familiar interface for users accustomed to traditional file management systems. Understanding these distinctions is crucial for selecting the most suitable storage solution for a specific application.

The integration of cloud computing with AI and ML further enhances data management capabilities. Cloud-based AI and ML services can be used to automate data cleansing, anomaly detection, and predictive modeling, freeing up data professionals to focus on higher-level analytical tasks. The combination of cloud computing and AI promises to revolutionize data management, enabling businesses to extract more value from their data than ever before. Moreover, cloud-based solutions provide a pathway to advanced analytics, including real-time data processing and predictive modeling, capabilities that were previously inaccessible to many organizations due to cost and complexity.

However, the cloud isn't a panacea. Data governance and compliance remain crucial considerations. Businesses need to establish clear policies and procedures to ensure the security, privacy, and compliance of their data stored in the cloud. This involves understanding relevant regulations, such as the General Data Protection Regulation (GDPR) and the California Consumer Privacy Act (CCPA), two major data privacy laws designed to protect individuals' personal information, and implementing appropriate security measures to protect data from unauthorized access and breaches. Furthermore, effective monitoring and auditing are crucial for maintaining compliance and identifying potential security vulnerabilities. The shared responsibility model of cloud security, where responsibility is shared between the provider and the user, underscores the importance of proactive security measures.

The future of cloud computing for data storage promises even greater advancements. The rise of edge computing, which brings computation and storage closer to data sources, will improve latency and bandwidth efficiency, especially crucial for applications such as IoT devices and autonomous vehicles. Serverless computing, where applications run without requiring server management, further simplifies development and deployment, thereby reducing operational overhead. Advancements in data analytics, driven by AI and ML, will continue to unlock unprecedented insights from the vast amounts of data stored in the cloud.

The Future of Data Storage: Emerging Technologies and Trends

But the story of data storage, even with the cloud's impressive capabilities, is far from over. We've moved from punch cards to petabytes (PB), but the relentless growth of data demands even more radical solutions. The future of data storage promises a fascinating array of technologies, each with the potential to rewrite the rules of how we handle information. Let's explore some possibilities, acknowledging that the technological landscape is constantly evolving.

One of the most intriguing frontiers is DNA storage. Yes, the very building blocks of life are considered a next-generation storage medium. This might sound like science fiction, but the concept is surprisingly grounded in scientific reality. DNA (discovered by James Watson and Francis Crick in 1953) boasts an incredibly high storage density. A single gram of DNA can theoretically hold the equivalent of several petabytes of data—a truly staggering amount. This density makes DNA storage a compelling solution for archiving vast quantities of data, particularly for long-term storage needs. Imagine storing the entire internet on a few vials of DNA! The potential for archival storage is enormous, particularly as we confront the exponential growth of digital information. Of course, there are significant challenges to overcome. Currently, DNA synthesis and sequencing are relatively slow and expensive processes. Error correction and data retrieval are also complex issues that require further research and development. But the potential payoff is so immense that numerous research teams worldwide are actively pursuing solutions.

The process, in essence, involves translating digital data into a DNA sequence. Each bit of data, a 0 or a 1, is represented by a specific nucleotide base (A, T, C, or G). This sequence is then synthesized using biological techniques. To retrieve the data, the DNA is sequenced, and the sequence is translated back into its digital equivalent. While still in its infancy, DNA storage has already demonstrated significant progress, with successful experiments storing terabytes of data in DNA molecules. The key advancements needed involve speeding up the writing and reading processes, reducing the costs, and improving overall reliability. Yet, even with the current challenges, the potential to store immense volumes of data for centuries, essentially creating a digital library on the scale of the Library of Alexandria but far more compact, is a compelling vision.

Moving beyond biological solutions, *quantum computing* (discussed in more detail in subsequent chapters) offers another transformative possibility for data storage. Quantum computers, which leverage the principles of quantum mechanics, have the potential to dramatically enhance data processing capabilities. While not directly a storage medium itself, quantum computing could revolutionize how we manage and access data stored using traditional methods. Imagine algorithms that can instantly search and retrieve information from massive datasets, or systems that can identify and correct errors in data storage far more efficiently than current techniques allow. Quantum computing could unlock the door to previously inaccessible levels of data analysis and management.

The benefits, however, come with significant technical hurdles. Quantum computers are incredibly complex and expensive to build and operate. The technology is still in its early stages of development, with numerous practical and theoretical challenges to overcome before it can be widely adopted. Maintaining the delicate quantum states required for computation is extremely challenging, leading to significant difficulties in error correction and scalability. But the sheer potential of quantum computing to drastically change our data management practices is undeniable. The ability to perform highly complex calculations with previously unimaginable speed could lead to more efficient data compression, improved error detection and correction, and entirely new approaches to data security. This could transform not only how we store data but also how we process, analyze, and utilize it.

Beyond these cutting-edge technologies, several other trends are shaping the future of data storage. The rise of edge computing, as previously mentioned, brings processing and storage closer to the data source. This is crucial for applications that require immediate access to data, such as autonomous vehicles or industrial IoT devices. This decentralized approach reduces latency, improves efficiency, and enhances data security by reducing the reliance on centralized data centers.

Furthermore, advancements in data compression techniques continue to improve. More efficient compression methods enable the storage of the same amount of information in a smaller space, thereby reducing storage costs and improving access speeds. These advancements, although less dramatic than the potential of DNA or quantum technologies, contribute significantly to improving the overall efficiency and practicality of data management.

Ultimately, the evolution of data storage is closely tied to advancements in data management. The convergence of cloud computing, AI, and ML continues to refine our ability to organize, analyze, and derive insights from our ever-growing digital universe. AI-powered systems can automate tasks such as data cleansing, error correction, and security monitoring, freeing human analysts to focus on higher-level, strategic work. The efficient organization and analysis of data are just as important as the storage methods themselves.

In conclusion, the future of data storage isn't simply a continuation of present trends. It's a vibrant landscape of innovation and exploration. From the biological precision of DNA storage to the mind-bending potential of quantum computing, coupled with continual improvements in edge computing, data compression, and AI-powered management systems, the next chapter in this ongoing saga promises to be even more efficient and transformative than the last.

CHAPTER 5

Problem Solving Techniques in Computing: Algorithms and Beyond

The Fundamentals of Algorithmic Thinking: Breaking Down Complex Problems

Having journeyed through data storage, we now turn our attention to the very brains of the operation: algorithms. These aren't some mysterious, esoteric entities lurking in the depths of silicon; they're the step-by-step instructions that tell computers how to do…well, pretty much everything. From sorting your emails to recommending your next Netflix binge, algorithms really are the heroes of the digital age. Understanding them is key to understanding how computers solve problems—and the limitations of that problem-solving.

Think of an algorithm as a recipe. A culinary recipe tells you, step-by-step, how to create a delicious dish. Similarly, an algorithm provides a precise sequence of instructions for a computer to follow, leading it to a desired outcome. The ingredients in our computational recipe are data—the raw materials the algorithm manipulates. The "chef" is the computer, diligently following each instruction to perfection (or as close to perfection as its programming allows).

But unlike a cake recipe, which typically has a relatively straightforward set of instructions, the problems computers tackle often have a complexity that rivals the most elaborate Michelin-starred meals. This is where the art of algorithmic thinking comes into play. Algorithmic thinking isn't simply about writing code; it's a systematic approach to solving problems, breaking them down into smaller, more manageable components that a computer can process. It's a skill that transcends the specific programming language used; it's a mindset.

The first crucial step in algorithmic thinking is problem *decomposition*. This involves breaking down a large, intricate problem into smaller, more manageable sub-problems. Imagine you're trying to build a search engine. That's a massive undertaking. However, you can break it down into smaller tasks such as indexing web pages (creating a searchable database of web content), processing user queries (understanding what the user is searching for), ranking search results (determining the most relevant pages), and displaying the results (presenting the information to the user in a user-friendly format). Each of these sub-problems can then be tackled individually, with simpler algorithms developed to handle each piece.

Once the problem is decomposed, the next step is to design the individual algorithms for each sub-problem. This involves selecting appropriate data structures (ways to organize and store data) and designing the specific sequence of instructions that will transform the input data into the desired output. For example, consider the sub-problem of ranking search results. This often involves using algorithms that take into account factors such as the frequency of keywords on the page, the website's authority, and the page's relevance to the user's query. Different algorithms exist, each with its strengths and weaknesses, and the choice of algorithm often depends on the specific application and the available resources.

One popular algorithm design technique is *recursion*. Recursion is like a set of Russian nesting dolls—a function that calls itself within its own definition. It's a powerful approach for solving problems that can be broken down into smaller, self-similar sub-problems. A classic example is the factorial calculation. The factorial of a number (denoted by !) is the product of all positive integers less than or equal to that number. For instance, 5! = 5 4 3 2 1 = 120. A recursive algorithm would calculate 5! by calling itself to calculate 4!, then multiplying the result by 5. This continues until it reaches the base case (the factorial of 1, which is 1).

Another important technique is *dynamic programming*, a method used to solve optimization problems by breaking them down into smaller overlapping sub-problems. Instead of solving each sub-problem repeatedly, dynamic programming stores the solutions to the sub-problems and reuses them when needed. This significantly improves efficiency, especially when dealing with problems that have many overlapping sub-problems. Consider the problem of finding the shortest path between two points in a network. Dynamic programming would systematically explore all possible paths, storing the shortest paths to intermediate points and reusing this information to find the shortest path to the final destination efficiently.

Iteration, in contrast to recursion, involves repeatedly executing a set of instructions until a specific condition is met. This is arguably the most common algorithmic design technique, as it's simple to understand and implement. Consider a simple program that calculates the sum of numbers from 1 to 100. An iterative approach would use a loop that repeatedly adds the next number to a running total until it reaches 100.

Beyond these core techniques, many other algorithm design paradigms exist, tailored to specific problem types. Greedy algorithms, for instance, make locally optimal choices at each step in the hope of finding a global optimum. This is often faster but doesn't guarantee finding the absolute best solution. Divide and conquer algorithms break a problem into smaller sub-problems, solve them recursively, and then combine the solutions to solve the original problem. This is particularly effective for problems that can be easily divided into smaller, independent sub-problems.

However, the choice of algorithm is not arbitrary. It depends on several crucial factors. Firstly, the efficiency of the algorithm is often measured by its time and space complexity. Time complexity refers to how the running time of the algorithm scales with the input size. Space complexity refers to the amount of memory required by the algorithm. A highly efficient algorithm will have low time and space complexity, meaning it will run quickly and require minimal memory, regardless of the input size.

Secondly, the correctness of the algorithm is paramount. An algorithm is only as good as its ability to produce the correct output. Rigorous testing and validation are essential to ensure that an algorithm produces the desired results for all valid inputs.

Thirdly, the readability and maintainability of the algorithm are important considerations. A well-written algorithm is easy to understand, debug, and modify. This is crucial for collaboration and for long-term maintenance.

Finally, the suitability of the algorithm to the specific hardware and software environment must be considered. Some algorithms may be optimized for certain architectures, while others may be more suitable for parallel processing environments.

The development of efficient and effective algorithms is a continuous process of refinement and improvement. As new problems emerge and computing technology evolves, new algorithms are constantly being developed and optimized. The ability to design and implement algorithms effectively is a crucial skill for computer scientists, programmers, and anyone working with computers to solve real-world problems. From the simple task of sorting a list of numbers to the incredibly complex challenge of predicting stock market trends, algorithms are the engine that powers the digital world. Understanding their underlying principles opens a world of possibilities, enabling us to tackle increasingly complex challenges with computational ingenuity and finesse.

Data Structures: Efficiently Organizing and Accessing Information

Having established the fundamental principles of algorithmic thinking and design, we now delve into a crucial element that underpins the efficiency and effectiveness of any algorithm: data structures. Think of algorithms as the recipes, the step-by-step instructions; data structures are the kitchens, the organization of ingredients and tools that determine how smoothly and efficiently the recipe can be executed. Without a well-organized kitchen, even the best recipe can become a chaotic mess. Similarly, a poorly chosen or implemented data structure can severely hamper the performance of even the most cleverly designed algorithm.

Data structures are essentially ways of organizing and storing data in a computer's memory so that it can be accessed and manipulated efficiently. The choice of data structure depends heavily on the specific problem being solved and the types of operations that will be performed on the data. Using the wrong data structure can lead to algorithms that are slow, cumbersome, and resource-intensive. Conversely, a well-chosen data structure can significantly improve an algorithm's performance, making the difference between a program that runs in seconds and one that takes hours or even days to complete. The selection process isn't a random guess; instead, it requires a deep understanding of both the problem domain and the properties of various data structures.

Let's start with one of the simplest and most fundamental data structures: the array. Imagine a row of neatly organized drawers in a filing cabinet. Each drawer corresponds to a specific location within the array, and each location holds a single piece of data—perhaps a number, a character, or even a more complex data structure. Arrays provide direct access to any element using its index (its position in the array). This makes them exceptionally fast for retrieving individual elements. To access the fifth item in the array, simply use index 4 (indexing usually starts at 0). This constant-time access is a key advantage. However, arrays are static in size; once you've created an array of a certain size, it's difficult to increase or decrease its size. This inflexibility can be a significant drawback when dealing with dynamically changing data sets. Adding or deleting elements often requires creating a new array and copying the data, which can be time-consuming for large arrays. Picture trying to rearrange a full filing cabinet—it's a significant undertaking.

Linked lists offer a more flexible alternative. Instead of storing data in contiguous memory locations like an array, linked lists store data in individual nodes, each containing the data itself and a pointer (a reference) to the next node in the sequence. This structure allows for dynamic resizing—adding or removing elements is relatively straightforward, involving only changing a few pointers. Think of a train; each carriage represents a node, and the couplings between carriages represent the pointers. Adding or removing a carriage only requires adjusting the couplings. This dynamic nature is particularly beneficial when the size of the data set is unknown or changes frequently. However, accessing a specific element in a linked list is less efficient than in an array. To access the fifth element, you need to traverse the list from the beginning, following the pointers until you reach the desired node. This linear search can be quite slow for large lists, making linked lists less suitable for scenarios where frequent random access is needed.

Trees provide a hierarchical way of organizing data, with elements arranged in a parent-child relationship. The root is the top-most element, and each node can have zero or more child nodes. There are many types of trees, each with different properties and applications. Binary trees, for example, are trees where each node has at most two children (a left child and a right child). Binary search trees (BSTs) are a particularly useful type of binary tree where the left subtree contains only nodes with values smaller than the parent node, and the right subtree contains only nodes with values larger than the parent node. This structure allows for efficient searching, insertion, and deletion of elements, with an average time complexity of $O(\log n)$, significantly faster than the linear time complexity of a linked list for large datasets. Imagine a hierarchical organizational chart, where the CEO is at the top, and each subsequent level represents different managerial positions. This hierarchical organization allows for efficient searching of specific individuals.

Graphs, on the other hand, are more general and powerful data structures that consist of nodes (vertices) connected by edges. Unlike trees, graphs can contain cycles (paths that lead back to the starting node) and multiple paths between nodes. Graphs are widely used to model relationships between entities, such as social networks, transportation networks, or computer networks. The algorithms used to traverse and analyze graphs are more sophisticated than those used for trees, often employing techniques such as depth-first search (DFS) and breadth-first search (BFS). Consider a map of roads and cities; each city is represented as a node, and each road is represented as an edge. Graph algorithms can then be used to find the shortest route between two cities. The complexity and efficiency of graph algorithms depend significantly on the nature of the graph (dense versus sparse, directed versus undirected) and the specific algorithm employed.

Beyond these fundamental structures, numerous specialized data structures exist, each tailored for specific applications. Heaps, for example, are tree-based structures that satisfy the heap property (the value of a node is greater than or equal to the values of its children), making them ideal for priority queue implementations. Hash tables utilize hash functions to map keys to indices in an array, allowing for constant-time average-case performance for insertion, deletion, and retrieval operations. Tries (pronounced "try") are tree-like structures used for efficient string searching and prefix matching. The choice of data structure is often a delicate balance between speed, memory usage, and the complexity of implementation. A programmer must carefully consider the trade-offs involved in selecting the most suitable data structure for a specific task.

Moreover, the efficiency of a data structure often depends on factors beyond its intrinsic properties. The size of the dataset, the frequency of various operations (search, insertion, and deletion), and the specific hardware and software environment all play a crucial role. A data structure that performs well for small datasets might perform poorly for huge ones. Similarly, a data structure optimized for frequent searches may be less efficient for frequent insertions. The art of choosing the right data structure is about understanding these trade-offs and selecting the structure that best balances the competing requirements of the application.

Finally, the implementation of a data structure can also significantly impact its performance. An inefficient implementation of even a fundamentally efficient data structure can lead to poor performance. Factors like memory management, pointer manipulation, and algorithm design within the data structure itself all contribute to its overall efficiency. A skilled programmer understands the nuances of data structure implementation and can optimize the code to minimize overhead and maximize performance. The choice and implementation of data structures are critical elements in the art of efficient programming, often directly impacting the speed and scalability of software applications, particularly in scenarios involving large datasets or complex operations.

Data Architecture: Designing the Blueprint for Information Flow

If data structures are the organization of ingredients in the kitchen and algorithms are the recipes, then **data architecture** is the blueprint for the entire kitchen—and often, the house itself. It dictates not just where ingredients are stored, but how they arrive, where they go after use, and how the kitchen connects to the rest of the building. In the context of computing, data architecture is the high-level design and structure that governs how data is collected, stored, managed, and utilized across an organization or system.

Data architecture is the overarching framework that defines the standards, policies, models, and rules for data collection, storage, integration, and usage. It ensures that data flows smoothly and securely from source to destination, supporting business processes, analytics, and decision-making. Just as a well-designed kitchen anticipates the chef's needs and workflows, a solid data architecture anticipates the needs of business users, applications, and future growth.

John Zachman's contribution to data architecture is foundational and transformative. Zachman was instrumental in developing IBM's Business Systems Planning (BSP) methodology, which helped organizations analyze and design their information architectures. The Zachman Framework is a pioneering model for enterprise architecture that provides a structured way to view and define an enterprise's systems and processes. It's not a methodology but an ontology, a classification system for organizing descriptive representations of an enterprise. The framework uses a matrix of six interrogatives (What, How, Where, Who, When, Why) across six perspectives (Planner, Owner, Designer, Builder, Subcontractor, and Functioning Enterprise), creating a comprehensive grid for understanding complex systems. Zachman's work laid the groundwork for modern enterprise architecture practices and influenced other frameworks, such as The Open Group Architecture Framework (TOGAF)—one of the most widely adopted frameworks for Enterprise Architecture. It provides a comprehensive approach for designing, planning, implementing, and governing enterprise information systems. In short, Zachman didn't just contribute to data architecture, he helped define the discipline itself.

As big data, cloud computing, and ML continue to reshape the digital landscape, data architecture is undergoing a profound transformation. Cloud-native architectures now enable organizations to harness scalable, on-demand resources and data services with unprecedented flexibility. Meanwhile, emerging paradigms such as data mesh and data fabric decentralize data ownership and seamlessly connect distributed sources, thereby fostering greater agility and collaboration. Real-time processing capabilities are becoming essential, allowing enterprises to support streaming data and deliver instant analytics. At the same time, AI-driven data management is revolutionizing how data is handled—automating tasks such as data quality assurance, integration, and discovery to enhance efficiency and insight.

Data architecture is the silent enabler behind every successful digital initiative. It is the thoughtful planning and design that transforms raw, scattered data into a powerful, unified asset. In a world where data drives innovation and competitiveness, investing in a sound data architecture is not just a technical necessity—it is a strategic imperative.

Algorithm Analysis: Measuring Efficiency and Performance

Having explored the crucial role of data structures in shaping algorithm performance, we now turn our attention to the equally vital task of analyzing algorithms themselves. Just as a chef needs to understand cooking times and ingredient ratios, a programmer must be able to assess how efficiently an algorithm utilizes resources, time, and memory, before deploying it in a real-world application. This assessment is conducted through algorithm analysis, a process that enables us to predict an algorithm's behavior under various conditions and compare its performance with that of other potential solutions.

The cornerstone of algorithm analysis is the concept of asymptotic analysis, which focuses on the algorithm's behavior as the input size grows very large. We're not concerned with minor differences in execution time for small inputs; instead, we're interested in the overall trend as the input scales. This is crucial because an algorithm that is efficient for small datasets might become utterly impractical when dealing with millions or billions of data points.

The most widely used notation for describing the efficiency of an algorithm is Big O notation. It's a mathematical way of describing how an algorithm's runtime or space requirements grow relative to the size of the input. Big O provides an upper bound on the growth rate of an algorithm's resource consumption (typically time) as the input size (n) increases. It expresses this growth in terms of dominant factors, ignoring constant factors and lower-order terms. For instance, if an algorithm's execution time is described as $O(n)$, it means that the time taken increases linearly with the input size. Doubling the input size roughly doubles the execution time. This is considered a relatively efficient growth rate.

Let's illustrate with a simple example: searching for a specific element within an unsorted array. The most straightforward approach is a linear search: we examine each element one by one until we find the target value or reach the end of the array. In the worst-case scenario (the target element is at the end or not present), we examine all 'n' elements. Therefore, the time complexity of this linear search is O(n).

Now, consider the same search problem, but this time, the array is sorted. We can leverage a much more efficient algorithm: binary search. Instead of checking each element sequentially, binary search repeatedly divides the search interval in half. We start by comparing the target value to the middle element of the array. If the target is smaller, we continue the search in the left half; otherwise, we search in the right half. We repeat this process until we find the target or the search interval becomes empty. In binary search, the number of comparisons needed is approximately proportional to the base-2 logarithm of the input size ($\log_2 n$). This means its time complexity is O(log n), making it far more efficient than O(n), particularly when dealing with large datasets. Imagine searching a phone book—a linear search would be agonizing, but a binary search (opening to the middle, then adjusting based on the name) is remarkably efficient. Big O notation doesn't provide the exact execution time; instead, it gives a general idea of how the runtime scales with input size.

Beyond time complexity, algorithm analysis also considers space complexity, which refers to the amount of memory an algorithm uses. A similar Big O notation can be used to express space complexity. An algorithm with O(1) space complexity uses a constant amount of memory regardless of the input size. In contrast, an algorithm with O(n) space complexity uses memory proportional to the input size.

Software Engineering Principles: Building Reliable and Maintainable Systems

Building upon our exploration of algorithms and their analysis, we now delve into the crucial realm of software engineering principles. While elegant algorithms form the heart of efficient programs, it's the application of robust software engineering practices that transforms these algorithms into reliable, maintainable, and scalable systems. Think of algorithms as the individual ingredients of a culinary masterpiece—essential, yes, but ultimately needing a skilled chef (the software engineer) to combine them harmoniously into a delectable final product.

One of the cornerstones of good software engineering is the concept of **modularity**. Instead of writing monolithic, gigantic blocks of code, we strive to break down complex systems into smaller, self-contained modules. Each module has a specific responsibility and interacts with other modules through well-defined interfaces. This approach is akin to constructing a building with prefabricated components rather than laying each brick individually. The benefits are numerous: increased readability and understandability, easier debugging and maintenance, and the ability to reuse modules in different parts of the system or even in entirely separate projects. Imagine trying to maintain a program where everything is intertwined—a nightmare! Modularity allows for manageable complexity, even in very large software systems. For example, a modern operating system comprises thousands of modules, each handling specific tasks like memory management, file systems, or network communication.

Another powerful concept is the use of **design patterns**. These are reusable solutions to common software design problems. They are not specific algorithms or code snippets but rather templates or blueprints that guide the design process. Over the years, experienced software engineers have identified recurring design challenges and developed proven patterns to address them. Examples include the Model-View-Controller (MVC) pattern, commonly used in web applications to separate data handling, presentation, and user interaction logic; the Singleton pattern, which ensures that only one instance of a particular class exists; and the Factory pattern, which encapsulates the object creation process, promoting flexibility and maintainability. Using established design patterns enables engineers to build upon the collective wisdom of the community, resulting in more robust and well-structured systems. These patterns serve as a common language, making the code easier to understand and collaborate on among developers.

The principle of **abstraction** is another vital aspect. Abstraction hides complex implementation details behind simple interfaces, simplifying interaction and reducing the cognitive load on developers. Think of driving a car: you don't need to understand the intricate workings of the engine to operate it effectively. Similarly, in software, abstraction allows programmers to use pre-built functionalities without needing to comprehend their internal mechanisms. This promotes efficiency and reusability. The development of high-level programming languages and the proliferation of software libraries exemplify the power of abstraction, allowing us to build upon existing functionalities without reinventing the wheel for every task. Libraries handle much of the tedious detail, allowing programmers to focus on the higher-level logic and design of their application.

The importance of proper **documentation** often gets overlooked, but it is undeniably essential. Comprehensive documentation, including clear comments within the code, detailed design specifications, and user manuals, facilitates maintainability, collaboration, and knowledge transfer. Imagine trying to understand a complex system without any documentation—it's like trying to decipher an ancient hieroglyphic script. Good documentation is crucial for long-term support and ensures the system remains easily understandable and modifiable even years after its initial development.

The process of **refactoring** is an iterative improvement process that enhances the internal structure of the code without altering its external behavior. It's like tidying up your workspace—you're not changing the final output, but the improved organization makes future tasks significantly easier. Refactoring helps reduce code complexity, enhance readability, and address technical debt (accumulated inefficiencies). It is an ongoing process throughout a project's lifespan, making sure the codebase remains healthy and maintainable. Regular refactoring sessions can prevent the code from becoming a tangled mess over time. This is particularly crucial in larger projects where many developers work on the codebase concurrently.

Another significant principle is **version control**, often implemented using systems like Git, a control system that tracks changes in source code during software development. Git was created by Linus Torvalds in 2005 to support the development of the Linux kernel, and since then, it has become an essential tool in almost every software project. Version control allows multiple developers to collaborate effectively, track changes over time, and easily revert to earlier versions if necessary. It's akin to keeping a detailed history of edits in a document, allowing you to see every change made, undo mistakes, and collaborate effortlessly with others. It's impossible to imagine large-scale software development without the robust version control systems available today. They're instrumental in managing the complexity inherent in collaborative development projects.

Finally, remember that software engineering is an ever-evolving field. New technologies and techniques are continuously emerging. Continuous learning and adaptation are crucial for staying relevant and building high-quality software. The field requires creativity, problem-solving skills, and attention to detail—not just mastery of algorithms.

Advanced Problem-Solving Techniques, Artificial Intelligence, and Machine Learning

These AI and ML technologies represent a paradigm shift in problem-solving, moving beyond the explicitly programmed instructions of traditional algorithms to systems that learn and adapt from data. Think of it as graduating from meticulously following a recipe to becoming a culinary innovator, creating dishes based on experience and experimentation. An in-depth analysis of AI and ML is covered in a subsequent chapter, but in the meantime, let's do an intro to this fascinating area.

The core of AI and ML lies in their ability to tackle problems that are too complex or ill-defined for traditional algorithmic approaches. Consider the task of image recognition. While we could conceivably write algorithms to identify specific features in an image, such an approach would be incredibly brittle and prone to failure when faced with variations in lighting, angle, or background. ML, on the other hand, allows us to train a system on a vast dataset of images, allowing it to learn the underlying patterns and features that distinguish different objects. This approach yields far more robust and adaptable solutions. The system not only identifies objects but can also generalize to new, unseen images—a capability far beyond the reach of traditional programming. This is the magic of ML—the ability to learn from data rather than being explicitly programmed.

Several key techniques underpin the power of AI and ML. One prominent approach is **supervised learning**, where the algorithm is trained on a dataset of labeled examples. Imagine teaching a child to identify different types of animals. You show them pictures of cats, dogs, and birds, labeling each image accordingly. Over time, the child learns to associate visual features with each animal category. Similarly, in supervised learning, the algorithm learns to map inputs (e.g., image pixels) to outputs (e.g., animal labels) based on the provided labeled data. This training process allows the algorithm to build a model that can predict the labels of new, unseen examples. Applications span diverse fields, from medical diagnosis (identifying cancerous cells in images) to spam filtering (classifying emails as spam or not spam).

Conversely, **unsupervised learning** tackles the challenge of finding patterns in unlabeled data. Consider clustering customers based on their purchase history, without needing to know their demographics. The algorithm identifies inherent groupings or structures within the data without any pre-defined categories. This technique is invaluable for exploratory data analysis, uncovering hidden relationships and insights that might otherwise remain undetected. For example, recommendation systems often leverage unsupervised learning to group users with similar tastes, suggesting products or services they might enjoy. Market segmentation, anomaly detection, and dimensionality reduction are all areas where unsupervised learning shines.

A third major category is **reinforcement learning**, where an agent learns to interact with an environment and maximize a reward signal. This is akin to training a dog with treats—rewarding desired behaviors and discouraging undesired ones. The agent explores the environment, learns the consequences of its actions, and progressively refines its strategy to achieve its goals. This technique has led to breakthroughs in robotics, game playing (AlphaGo famously defeating a world champion Go player), and resource management. The challenges of reinforcement learning lie in designing effective reward functions and handling the exploration-exploitation trade-off—balancing the need to explore new actions with the need to exploit known successful strategies.

The choice of AI/ML technique depends heavily on the nature of the problem and the available data. Supervised learning excels when labeled data is plentiful, while unsupervised learning is ideal for exploratory data analysis or when labels are unavailable. Reinforcement learning shines when the problem involves sequential decision-making within an interactive environment. However, regardless of the chosen technique, data quality and quantity are paramount. "Garbage in, garbage out" holds particularly true in the realm of AI/ML. A biased or incomplete dataset will inevitably lead to flawed models and unreliable predictions. Data preprocessing, cleaning, and feature engineering are crucial steps in ensuring the robustness and accuracy of the resulting AI/ML system.

The ongoing development of AI and ML necessitates a multidisciplinary approach. Computer scientists, mathematicians, statisticians, and domain experts must collaborate to build effective and ethically sound solutions. AI/ML is not a magic bullet but a powerful tool that must be wielded responsibly and thoughtfully. By understanding the underlying principles, limitations, and ethical considerations, we can harness the transformative potential of these technologies while mitigating their potential risks, ensuring that AI/ML serves humanity's best interests.

Anecdotes, Musings, and Recollections

Recollections (By Bill Inmon)

John Zachman

Ed Yourdon recognized the need for organization and discipline in the creation of computer code. Ed Yourdon provided the first step toward an organized approach to building systems.

Following Ed Yourdon was John Zachman. John Zachman also recognized the need for a more systematic approach to building systems. The difference between Ed Yourdon and John Zachman lay in the level of development each addressed. Ed Yourdon's work was primarily aimed at a low level of producing computer code. John Zachman focused on a more comprehensive level of the system.

Both John Zachman's and Ed Yourdon's approaches were necessary in the evolution of system design and development. In fact, the Yourdon and the Zachman approaches were complementary to each other.

The steps outlined in John Zachman's approach to system development are analogically equivalent to the steps found in the construction of a home or other edifice. There are many aspects to the building of a home—a blueprint, the laying of the foundation, the electrical wiring, the sewage, the water piping, and so forth. There is an order in which the steps should be addressed. There is a right way and a wrong way to do construction. Just like construction, Zachman addressed the right way to do system development and the wrong way. Zachman recognized the need to bring together many aspects of technology to build a system. Zachman recognized the need for the selection of a platform, database design, the gathering and assimilation of requirements, the need for a plan of construction, the identification of the parties involved in the construction, and so forth.

The primary objective of the Zachman Framework is to minimize or eliminate system design rework. Before Zachman, it was a common practice to rewrite systems repeatedly. The system would be built. Then, after the system went into production, flaws would be discovered. Then the system would be rebuilt.

CHAPTER 6

The Personal Computer Revolution: From Hobbyists to Households

The Early Days of Personal Computing: The Rise of Hobbyist Culture

The story of the personal computer is a story of garages, basements, and late nights, fueled by lukewarm pizza and the intoxicating glow of cathode-ray tubes. It's a story of hobbyists, the sometimes-unrecognized heroes who, armed with little more than ingenuity, soldering irons, and a fervent desire to build something amazing, laid the groundwork for the digital revolution.

These weren't your buttoned-down, tie-wearing engineers toiling away in climate-controlled offices. (More like thick-rimmed or horn-rimmed glasses, and don't forget the pocket protector.) These were enthusiasts, tinkerers, and mavericks who saw the potential of computing power beyond the confines of massive, room-sized mainframes and the exclusive domain of universities and corporations. They saw a future where computing power was accessible, affordable, and, most importantly, *fun, fun, fun.*

The 1970s witnessed the emerging stages of this revolution. The price of electronic components, particularly microprocessors, began to decline, making them increasingly affordable for individuals. This accessibility, coupled with the mushrooming popularity of electronics hobbyist magazines like *Popular Electronics, Creative Computing,* and *Byte,* fostered a vibrant community of enthusiasts eager to explore the escalating world of personal computing. These magazines weren't just repositories of technical specifications; they were vessels of innovation, brimming with articles, schematics, and code snippets that empowered readers to build their own computers from scratch.

They fostered a collaborative environment where individuals could learn from one another, share their successes (and failures), and contribute to the collective knowledge base that was vital to the growth of personal computing. They bridged the communication gaps between enthusiasts across different geographical locations. Imagine a world where your monthly magazine subscription was essentially a DIY (Do-It-Yourself) computer kit, complete with instructions and a hefty dose of encouragement (and maybe a few troubleshooting tips!). It was an authentic grassroots movement, fueled by shared passion and an unwavering belief in the potential of personal computing.

Heathkit, one of the go-to DIY computer stores, was originally an aircraft company that transitioned into electronics after World War II. It sold kits to hobbyists and engineers. Some of its influential computers of the era were the Heath H-8, H-89, and H-11. They came with building instructions, diagrams, electronic components, and a sense of satisfaction when you finished building one of their kits. Sadly, for the hobbyists, it stopped making kits in 1992. Another popular electronics retailer was Radio Shack. It began as a mail-order business for amateur radio equipment.

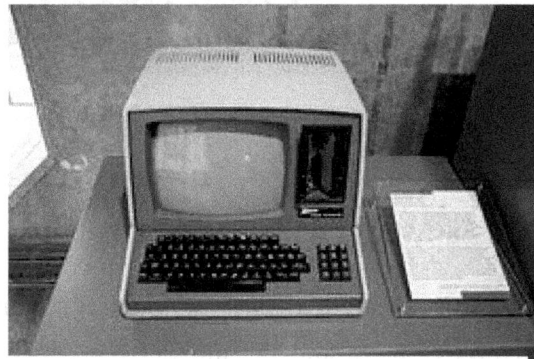

Heathkit H89 – Also known as Zenith Z-89, Kit version with 1 floppy drive, 1979, external diskette drive connector, ran CP/M, RAM: 16 KB – 48 KB on main board, Wikipedia, CC BY-SA 4.0

Over the decades, it became a go-to store for consumer electronics, including radios, computers,

Tandy Radio Shack TRS-80, August 3, 1977, , CPU Zilog Z80, Memory: 4-48KB, Mono 12-inch CRT, By Dave Jones - EEVblog, Wikipedia, CC BY-SA 4.0

and accessories. In 1962, it was acquired by the Tandy Corporation, shifting focus to hobbyist electronics. In 1977, it introduced the TRS-80 (lovingly referred to by some hobbyists as the "Trash 80"). The TRS-80 (Tandy Radio Shack 80) was one of the first mass-market personal computers. By 1979, the TRS-80 had the largest selection of software in the microcomputer market. [Welch, David and Theresa (2007). Priming the Pump: How TRS-80 Enthusiasts Helped Spark the PC Revolution] Until 1982, the TRS-80 was the bestselling PC line, outselling the Apple II by a factor of five according to one analysis. [McCracken, Harry (August 3, 2012). "Please Don't Call It Trash-80: A 35th Anniversary Salute to Radio Shack's TRS-80"] In the 1990s, it shifted focus to wireless phones, moving away from hobbyist electronics.

One pivotal moment was the introduction of the Intel 4004 microprocessor in 1971, the world's first commercially available microchip. While not incredibly powerful by today's standards (it could execute roughly 60,000 instructions per second, a speed a modern smartphone exceeds by several orders of magnitude!), its significance lay in its size and its cost-effectiveness. Suddenly, the building blocks of a computer were small enough and affordable enough to be incorporated into a project that fit comfortably on a workbench. The 4004 marked a significant shift, ushering in the era of affordable microprocessors that could be integrated into personal computing systems. More about this later.

This technological leap forward was rapidly followed by the introduction of more powerful microprocessors, such as the Intel 8008 and the Zilog Z80. Each new iteration brought increased processing power and capabilities, fueling the creativity of hobbyists who continually pushed the boundaries of what was possible. These early machines weren't exactly user-friendly by modern standards. Forget sleek interfaces and intuitive touchscreens. We're talking about blinking cursors, cryptic commands entered via clunky keyboards, and the constant threat of system crashes.

The Altair 8800, featured on the cover of *Popular Electronics* in January 1975, often serves as a symbolic milestone in the personal computer revolution. This kit-based computer, built around the Intel 8080 microprocessor, ignited a firestorm of excitement within the hobbyist community. It was far from user-friendly. Programming it involved painstakingly toggling switches to input machine code—a tedious process that demanded significant patience and technical prowess. Although primarily a bare-bones machine consisting of circuit boards, lights, switches, and a front panel, the Altair represented a significant leap toward accessibility. For the first time, individuals could purchase a computer kit, assemble it at home, and experience the thrill of building and programming their own machine. It wasn't just about the hardware; it sparked a rapid development of software, fostering a burgeoning software community and creating opportunities for others to participate in the creation and development of software solutions. While programming it often involved meticulously toggling switches to input

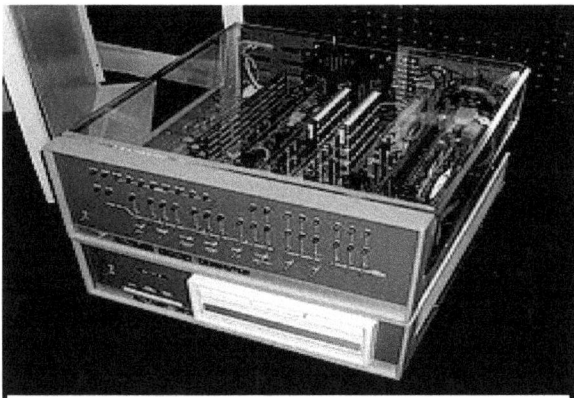

Altair 8800 Computer with 8-inch floppy disk system- Dec 19, 1974, Wikipedia, CC BY-SA 4.0

machine code, its presence marked a definitive move towards personal computing becoming a more readily attainable reality for the average person with sufficient curiosity and technical ability.

The success of the Altair spawned a flurry of imitators, competitors, and innovations, further fueling the growth of the hobbyist culture. Companies like Commodore, IMSAI, and Apple (with the Apple I) all released their own versions of personal computers, each vying for a slice of the growing market. This competitive landscape fueled rapid advancements in technology, driving down prices and improving usability. It fostered rapid innovation, with companies constantly pushing the boundaries of

Commodore C64, August 1982, Memory-64KB, CPU-MOS 6510/8500, Wikipedia, CC BY-SA 4.0

performance, affordability, and user experience. The Apple I, for instance, while still requiring considerable technical expertise to assemble and operate, represented a step towards increased usability compared to the Altair. Although it was initially offered with a bare-bones circuit board, it eventually came with a keyboard and a

IMSAI Manufacturing Corporation. Hobbyist computer, 256/4K bytes on a 4K board (static), 16K, 32K, 64K DRAM Intel 8080/8085. Author's archives.

video output, features absent in the Altair, making it easier to interact with and program. This was a significant upgrade, demonstrating a slow but important shift towards making personal computing less of a niche hobby for technical experts and more accessible to a larger audience.

However, it wasn't just about the hardware. The hobbyist culture also fostered a thriving community of software developers. These early programmers, many of whom were self-taught, wrote programs for everything from simple games to sophisticated utilities. This collaborative spirit, facilitated by publications and early computer clubs, was crucial to the development of software that would eventually propel personal computing into the mainstream. They shared code, swapped tips, and helped each other overcome the inevitable challenges of debugging and troubleshooting. This collaborative effort played a crucial role in fostering a collective understanding of these new technologies and significantly accelerated the advancement of personal computing. The community's sense of mutual support and shared enthusiasm served as a powerful catalyst for innovation. (More about this in the Hobbyist's Club anecdote at the end of this chapter.)

The early personal computers, while rudimentary compared to today's machines, were significant steps in the broader evolution of technology. They were powerful enough to perform tasks unimaginable just a few years earlier, and they inspired a whole generation of programmers, engineers, and entrepreneurs. They weren't just machines; they were gateways to a new world of possibilities, where individuals could build, create, and explore the emerging digital frontier.

The Birth of the Microprocessor: The Heart of the Personal Computer

The genesis of the personal computer revolution wasn't a singular "Eureka!" moment, but rather a gradual accumulation of breakthroughs, each building upon the last. At the heart of this transformation lay the microprocessor, a tiny marvel of engineering that shrunk the processing power of a room-sized mainframe onto a single chip. Before its arrival, computers were behemoths, accessible only to large corporations, universities, and government agencies. Their sheer size, complexity, and exorbitant cost placed them firmly beyond the reach of the average individual. Remember the earlier discussions on mainframes?

The year 1971 marked a turning point. Intel, then a relatively young company, unveiled the Intel 4004 microchip. While its processing power might seem laughably meager by today's standards, its significance transcended its raw speed. The 4004 was a game-changer because of its size and

Intel C4004 processor 11/15/71 -Data width 4 bits, Transistors 2,300 - from the author's archives.

affordability. For the first time, the computational power previously confined to massive machines was miniaturized and made accessible to a wider range of individuals and institutions. The 4004 was a 4-bit processor, meaning it could handle four bits of data at a time, severely limiting its computational prowess. Yet, its impact was monumental, symbolizing the start of the miniaturization trend that would define the future of computing.

This wasn't just a technological achievement; it was a cultural shift. Suddenly, the dream of building one's own computer, once relegated to science fiction, became a tangible possibility for dedicated hobbyists. Prior to the 4004, building a computer required a considerable investment of time, money, and technical expertise. Individuals essentially had to assemble their own computers from discrete components, a complex undertaking that often tested the limits of their patience and skills. The advent of the microprocessor simplified this considerably, providing a pre-built core component that significantly reduced the technical hurdles of computer construction.

The 4004, though groundbreaking, was just the beginning. Intel quickly followed up with the Intel 8008 in 1972, an 8-bit processor representing a significant improvement in processing power. This jump from 4-bit to 8-bit processing significantly increased the amount of data the microprocessor could handle simultaneously, resulting in a considerable boost in performance. The 8008, while still rudimentary by today's standards, laid the foundation for more advanced processors to come. It paved the way for the creation of more sophisticated and functional personal computers, laying the groundwork for even more advanced microprocessors.

The Zilog Z80, introduced in 1976, emerged as a strong competitor to Intel's offerings. It was an 8-bit processor, but its architecture was more efficient and offered several improvements over the Intel 8080. Plus, it was cheaper. The Z80's enhanced instruction set and superior memory management capabilities made it incredibly popular among hobbyists, particularly in the development of home computers. The Z80 was adopted by several prominent home computer manufacturers such as Tandy, Commodore, and Kaypro. It formed the basis of the CP/M (Control Program for Microcomputers) operating system. This further fueled the development of software and the overall evolution of personal computing. Since it could run CP/M, it became widely used in business and home computing. The Z80's popularity stemmed from its versatile design, offering a wide range of applications and functionalities. The Z80 was also widely used in arcade machines, gaming consoles, and embedded systems, making it one of the most influential microprocessors of its time.

Zilog Z80 July 1976 Data width 8 bits, Transistors 8,500 - From author's archive.

These early microprocessors weren't just about raw processing speed; they were also about efficiency and affordability. As manufacturing techniques improved and the demand increased, the cost of these chips plummeted. This price decrease made them increasingly accessible to a broader segment of the population, allowing individuals and small businesses to explore the possibilities of

personal computing. The cost reduction accelerated the growth of the personal computer market. Its affordability was instrumental in the mass adoption of personal computers. A significant number of hobbyists and companies started building systems around these affordable processors. This led to a surge in the personal computer market.

The impact extended beyond the realm of hardware. The availability of affordable microprocessors spurred a parallel revolution in software development. Before the widespread adoption of microprocessors, software development was a highly specialized field, confined mainly to academic institutions and large corporations. The appearance of these microprocessors changed this profoundly. The availability of inexpensive microprocessors enabled individuals to build their own computers. This democratized the process of computing, thus creating opportunities for a large number of people to develop their own software. This led to a surge in software development as more people became involved in creating software programs.

The Software Revolution: Operating Systems and Applications

The hardware revolution, fueled by the miniaturization of the microprocessor, was only half the battle. The other, equally crucial, component was the development of user-friendly software. Early personal computers, like the Altair 8800, were notoriously difficult to use. Programming them involved interacting directly with machine code. This severely limited their appeal to a small community of dedicated hobbyists and technically adept individuals. To reach a wider audience, the experience had to be drastically simplified. This is where operating systems and applications stepped in, bridging the gap between the machine's intricate inner workings and the user's desire for intuitive interaction.

The early operating systems were a far cry from the sleek, visually appealing interfaces we're accustomed to today. They were, by modern standards, remarkably Spartan. One of the earliest and most influential was CP/M, developed by Gary Kildall of Digital Research, Inc. in the early 1970s. CP/M wasn't tied to a specific hardware platform; it was designed to run on a variety of 8-bit microprocessors, a crucial factor in its widespread adoption. Its command-line interface, where users typed commands to interact with the computer, might seem antiquated now, but it was a giant leap forward. Before CP/M, interacting with a computer often involved flipping switches and directly manipulating memory addresses—a process demanding a near-encyclopedic knowledge of the machine's architecture. CP/M, while still requiring some technical know-how, offered a level of abstraction that made interacting with the computer significantly more manageable. It provided a standard way for programs to interact with the hardware, making it easier for developers to write software compatible across different machines using the Z80 processor. This standardization greatly stimulated software development, as programmers were no longer tied to the idiosyncrasies of individual computer models.

However, CP/M had its limitations. Its command-line interface was a barrier for the average user. The cryptic commands and lack of visual feedback made it challenging for those without programming experience to navigate. This is where the graphical user interface (GUI) began to show its potential. While the concept of a GUI had been around for some time, its implementation in personal computers was a more recent development. The Xerox PARC Alto, a pioneering research computer developed in the 1970s, showcased the potential of the GUI, using windows, icons, and a mouse to provide a more intuitive and user-friendly experience. This technology laid the groundwork for the GUI revolution that would transform personal computing. However, the PARC Alto was a highly expensive research machine, far beyond the reach of the average person. It was the vision, not the hardware, that proved truly influential.

The transition to user-friendly software wasn't a smooth, linear process; it was an iterative evolution marked by both brilliant breakthroughs and frustrating setbacks. Early applications were often limited in functionality and prone to crashes. The memory limitations of early personal computers were a significant constraint, restricting the complexity and size of the programs that could be run. A simple spreadsheet application might have required several floppy disks to store, and its capabilities were relatively limited. Data storage was also a major hurdle; early computers relied heavily on floppy disks, which were notoriously unreliable, prone to data corruption, and had small storage capacities. The process of loading and saving data could be incredibly time-consuming. Imagine waiting minutes, or even tens of minutes, for a program to load or for a file to save.

Despite these challenges, the development of early applications paralleled the rise of operating systems. Simple word processors, spreadsheet programs, and basic games were among the earliest applications that made computers more accessible to a broader audience. These initial applications were far from polished, often lacking the features we take for granted today. However, they demonstrated the potential of the personal computer for both productivity and entertainment.

Word processors, for example, enable users to create and edit documents without needing a typewriter. This simple act of being able to edit text on screen and make revisions easily marked a significant shift in how people worked and communicated. Spreadsheets have transformed the way businesses manage finances and analyze data, providing tools that simplify complex calculations. Similarly, simple games, though limited graphically, show the entertainment potential of these machines. They demonstrated the potential of the personal computer as a versatile tool, opening doors for both work and leisure.

The rise of Microsoft played a pivotal role in this evolution. While the company's early years weren't immediately focused on personal computer software, its transition into this arena would profoundly change the industry's landscape. Their partnership with IBM to provide the operating system for the IBM PC in the early 1980s, arguably the most important computer in the history of personal computing, was a pivotal moment. The IBM PC's success was primarily due to its compatibility and the availability of a substantial software ecosystem. The use of MS-DOS, Microsoft's Disk Operating System, made it a commercially viable system, allowing for significant expansion of the overall personal computer market. MS-DOS, while also a command-line interface, was far more robust than CP/M, and its compatibility with the IBM PC allowed for a much larger software ecosystem. Its adoption marked a watershed moment, establishing the PC as the dominant personal computer architecture and shaping the future of the industry.

The limitations of command-line interfaces ultimately spurred further innovations in software design. The intuitive and user-friendly nature of the GUI, initially showcased at Xerox PARC (Palo Alto Research Center) in the 1970s, finally began to make its way into commercially viable systems. Steve Jobs and his team were inspired by what they saw at Xerox. The GUI included features like windows, icons, and a mouse-driven interface—a revolutionary concept at the time. Jobs arranged a deal in which Xerox invested in Apple in exchange for a demonstration of its technology. Apple then refined and popularized the GUI with the Lisa and later the Macintosh, making it accessible to the masses. So, while Xerox pioneered the idea, Apple perfected and commercialized it. Apple's Macintosh, launched in 1984, is often credited with bringing the GUI to the mainstream. Its iconic mouse-driven interface, featuring windows, icons, and pull-down menus, made computers significantly easier to use, even for individuals with little or no technical expertise. The Macintosh offered a visually appealing and intuitive way of interacting with the computer, enabling a much wider range of individuals to use computers for both personal and professional tasks. The

Macintosh's success demonstrated that computers didn't have to be the exclusive domain of programmers and tech enthusiasts. It opened the door for a truly mass market.

The transition to GUIs also spurred the creation of more sophisticated applications, with richer visual interfaces and more intuitive functionalities. Word processors have evolved into powerful tools with advanced features, including spell-checking, grammar-checking, and WYSIWYG (What You See Is What You Get) editing. Spreadsheets became far more capable, enabling complex data analysis and the creation of intricate charts and graphs. Game development took off, producing increasingly immersive and visually stunning titles. The evolution of software paralleled the advancements in hardware. As processors became faster and memory increased, more complex and powerful applications became possible. This continuous interplay between hardware and software development is a key theme in the evolution of the personal computer, with each advancing and shaping the development of the other.

In retrospect, the software revolution of the 1970s and 1980s was as much about usability as it was about technological innovation. The transition from arcane command-line interfaces (think MS-DOS) to user-friendly GUIs (think Windows) was a landmark achievement, enabling the personal computer to move from a niche hobbyist pursuit into an indispensable tool for homes and businesses. The development of sophisticated applications broadened the capabilities of these machines, opening a world of possibilities and fundamentally altering how we work, communicate, and entertain ourselves.

The Rise of Personal Computer Manufacturers: Competition and Innovation

The shift from cryptic command-line interfaces to user-friendly GUIs and powerful applications paved the way for an explosion in personal computer manufacturing. The success of early operating systems, such as CP/M and MS-DOS, and the increasing appeal of computers equipped with intuitive graphical interfaces, created fertile ground for a burgeoning industry. No longer were computers the sole domain of hobbyists and tech wizards; they were poised to become ubiquitous tools for homes and businesses alike. This created a competitive landscape unlike any seen before, driving innovation and pushing the boundaries of what personal computers could achieve.

This burgeoning market wasn't a free-for-all, though. It was a battleground where companies clashed, each vying for a piece of the ever-expanding pie. IBM, a giant in the world of mainframes and business computing, entered the fray with a strategic move that would reshape the industry. Their 1981 introduction of the IBM PC wasn't just a machine; it was a declaration of intent, a signal that even the most prominent players recognized the potential of the personal computer market. The genius of the IBM PC wasn't necessarily in its innovative hardware. In fact,

IBM Personal Computer with keyboard and monitor - August 12, 1981, CPU- Intel 8088, Memory-256kb max, 5.25 floppy drive, 5153 color display, Wikipedia, CC BY-SA 4.0

it was primarily based on off-the-shelf components. The real brilliance lay in its open architecture. IBM made its design specifications publicly available, allowing third-party manufacturers to create compatible hardware and software. This decision, a deliberate departure from the proprietary approach of many other computer manufacturers, created a vast ecosystem of peripherals, add-ons, and applications that dramatically enhanced the value proposition of the IBM PC. Suddenly, the possibilities were practically limitless. The IBM PC wasn't just a computer; it became a platform, a foundation upon which an entire industry could be built.

This open architecture approach dramatically increased competition. While IBM set the standard, other manufacturers quickly jumped in, offering IBM-compatible PCs at often lower prices or with

The Compaq LTE was the first commercially successful Notebook computer on its release in 1989, Wikipedia, CC BY-SA 4.0

enhanced features. This "clone" market boomed, creating an era of fierce competition that drove prices down, improved performance, and fostered rapid innovation. Companies like Compaq, Dell, and Gateway emerged as significant players, leveraging the open architecture to challenge IBM's dominance. Compaq, particularly, was notable for its early success in producing near-perfect IBM PC clones, often at competitive pricing, eating into IBM's market share. Hewlett-Packard (HP) became a prime player in the laptop computer market as well. It leveraged its expertise in computing and expanded its product line in the early 1980s to include portable devices. The company initially focused on business-oriented aptops, offering reliable and powerful machines for professionals. Over time, HP diversified its lineup to include consumer-friendly models, gaming laptops (like its Omen brand), and ultrabooks. Eventually, HP acquired the Compaq brand in 2002 through a $35 billion stock swap, creating one of the world's largest technology companies at the time. However, like its other competitors, HP faced intense competition from several major brands, including Lenovo, Samsung, ASUS, and Acer.

This competition wasn't just about price; it was also about features and innovation. Manufacturers vied to create machines that were faster, more powerful, and easier to use. The race for better processors, larger memory capacity, and improved graphics capabilities pushed technological boundaries. The introduction of the hard disk drive, offering vastly more storage than floppy disks, significantly increased the functionality of PCs and enabled the development of more complex software applications. This was a critical step towards making personal computers useful for tasks beyond simple word processing and rudimentary games. Hard drives represented not only a storage revolution but also a significant leap in user experience, eliminating the constant chore of swapping floppy disks. This simple enhancement revolutionized workflows, making computers a much more usable tool.

Apple, taking a different approach, focused on user experience and design. While IBM embraced the open architecture, Apple maintained a proprietary approach, meticulously controlling every aspect of its hardware and software. This allowed for a highly integrated and user-friendly experience, embodied by the legendary Macintosh. The Macintosh, launched in 1984, wasn't just a computer; it was a cultural phenomenon. Its innovative graphical user interface, coupled with its elegant design, was a game-changer. It made computers accessible to a much broader audience than ever before. The iconic mouse, the intuitive interface, and the aesthetically pleasing design all contributed to the Macintosh's success, demonstrating that a computer could be both powerful and user-friendly. The "Think Different" campaign was more than just a marketing slogan; it encapsulated Apple's approach to the market, one that emphasized design, usability, and a unique user experience.

Macintosh- January 24, 1984, CPU Motorola 68000, memory 128KB, 3.25 floppy, built-in screen & mouse. The first successful mass-market all-in-one desktop PC with a graphical user interface, Wikipedia, CC BY-SA 4.0

The success of the Macintosh highlighted a crucial element of the competition: the user experience was as important as the technological specifications. Apple's strategy contrasted sharply with IBM's, demonstrating that multiple paths to success existed within this rapidly expanding market. While IBM focused on openness and compatibility, resulting in a vast ecosystem and fierce competition, Apple prioritized user experience and design, cultivating a devoted user base. Both strategies proved successful, albeit in different ways. This demonstrates that the computer market was diverse, appealing to different customer segments with varying needs and preferences.

The rivalry between Apple and IBM—the champion of openness and the champion of design—shaped the personal computer landscape for years to come. Their different approaches, each with its own strengths and weaknesses, created a vibrant and dynamic market. This competition, characterized by both collaboration and conflict, ultimately benefited consumers, driving innovation, lowering prices, and expanding the capabilities of personal computers. The choices consumers faced, between open systems and highly integrated ones, as well as between affordability and cutting-edge design, contributed significantly to the rapid expansion of the personal computer market. This was a market where multiple ecosystems coexisted and thrived, each catering to different customer needs.

The competition extended beyond Apple and IBM. Numerous other companies entered the market, each attempting to carve out its niche. Some focused on specific sectors, developing computers optimized for business applications, educational settings, or home use. This specialization further fueled innovation, as companies tailored their products to meet the unique needs of different user groups. The competition also spurred the development of various operating systems, creating an environment where consumers could choose between different platforms, each with its strengths and weaknesses. This wasn't just a race for the best hardware or the most sophisticated operating system; it was a race to understand and satisfy diverse customer needs. The constant quest for improvement, driven by the competitive pressures of a thriving market, led to ever-faster processors, improved graphics, larger memory capacities, and more user-friendly interfaces.

The competitive pressure also pushed software developers to create better and more efficient applications. As the PC market expanded, so did the demand for software. This led to a boom in the software industry, with numerous companies developing applications for everything from word processing (WordPerfect) and spreadsheets (Lotus) to games and graphic design. This symbiosis between hardware and software development was crucial to the personal computer revolution.

Improved hardware facilitated the development of more complex and powerful software, which, in turn, created a demand for even more powerful hardware. This positive feedback loop sustained the rapid pace of innovation, resulting in the phenomenal growth and development of the industry.

The Societal Impact of Personal Computers: Changing the Way We Live and Work

The proliferation of personal computers didn't merely reshape the technological landscape; it fundamentally altered the fabric of society, impacting how we live, work, and interact. The transition wasn't instantaneous, of course. It was a gradual yet powerful shift, a digital tide that swept across homes, offices, and schools, leaving an indelible mark on human experience. One of the most immediate effects was felt in the workplace. Suddenly, tasks once performed manually or with cumbersome machinery could be accomplished with unprecedented speed and efficiency. Word processors replaced typewriters, spreadsheets revolutionized accounting, and databases organized information in ways previously unimaginable. This surge in productivity wasn't just about efficiency; it fundamentally altered the nature of work itself. The rise of telecommuting, once a futuristic fantasy, has become a tangible reality, allowing individuals to work remotely and fostering flexibility, thereby blurring the lines between home and office.

The impact on businesses was equally transformative. Personal computers empowered entrepreneurs, providing them with the tools to manage their operations, market their products, and connect with customers globally. Small businesses, previously hampered by resource constraints, suddenly gained access to sophisticated software and technologies once the exclusive domain of large corporations. This democratization of technology leveled the playing field, fostering competition and innovation across all sectors of the economy. Businesses can analyze data, develop sophisticated marketing strategies, and streamline their operations, thereby significantly boosting their bottom line. The power of personal computing unlocked opportunities previously unavailable, changing the face of business permanently.

The effect on education was equally profound. Personal computers transitioned classrooms from lecture-centric environments into interactive learning spaces. Educational software offered students new avenues to explore subjects, fostering collaboration and creativity in ways traditional methods couldn't match. Students could access information readily, conduct research independently, and develop critical thinking skills by utilizing these new digital tools. This educational revolution continues to shape the academic experience, enriching and empowering the learning process.

Beyond the workplace and the classroom, the personal computer permeated everyday life. Home computers revolutionized entertainment, providing access to a vast array of games, educational software, and creative tools. Families could connect digitally, share information, and experience entertainment in ways previously unheard of. The ability to effortlessly connect with loved ones across geographical distances via email and early forms of instant messaging fostered greater family connectivity across the globe. Home computers were no longer just tools; they were centers for family engagement and entertainment. The societal impact of this shift from solitary pastimes to collaborative, digitally-mediated experiences was substantial.

However, the personal computer revolution wasn't without its challenges. The digital divide emerged as a significant societal concern, highlighting the unequal access to technology across socioeconomic strata. This disparity created a gap in opportunities, affecting education, employment, and overall quality of life for those lacking access. Addressing this digital divide has remained a persistent and complex issue demanding social action and ongoing technological investment. The rise of personal computers wasn't simply a technological advancement; it was a complex social phenomenon with far-reaching consequences.

Moreover, the shift towards a digitally-mediated world brought about new challenges to privacy and security. The ease with which information could be stored and transmitted created new vulnerabilities, raising concerns about data protection and personal safety. The increasing dependence on digital technologies also amplified anxieties about the misuse of personal data and the potential for cybercrime. This new reality necessitated the development of innovative security measures and responsible data management practices. The ongoing conversation surrounding data security, privacy legislation, and digital ethics underscores the complexities introduced by the pervasive influence of personal computers.

The personal computer also significantly impacted communication. Email has become a ubiquitous tool, allowing for near-instantaneous communication across geographical boundaries and impacting both interpersonal relationships and professional collaborations globally. The speed and convenience of email altered the dynamics of business communications, offering rapid feedback and improved workflow coordination. However, this newfound efficiency also brought challenges—the constant barrage of emails can lead to information overload and decreased productivity if not managed effectively.

The rise of personal computers also fueled the growth of the internet, creating a symbiotic relationship that profoundly impacted society. The internet expanded the accessibility of information, allowing individuals to access a wealth of knowledge, news, and entertainment instantly. This unprecedented access to information empowered individuals, fostering greater awareness, engagement, and participation in global affairs. The democratizing effect of the internet, facilitated by personal computers, enabled open dialogue, knowledge sharing, and global connectivity on an unprecedented scale. This led to a dramatic increase in global participation in various social and political issues.

However, the internet, fueled by personal computers, also introduced challenges. The spread of misinformation and disinformation became a significant concern, necessitating critical thinking skills to navigate the abundance of information available online. Cyberbullying and online harassment also became pervasive concerns, highlighting the need for responsible online behavior and effective moderation strategies. The societal impact of the internet underscores the importance of developing digital literacy and promoting responsible online citizenship to mitigate the negative consequences associated with this technology.

The impact of personal computers extended to the creative world as well. Software applications such as image editing programs, audio recording and editing software, and video production tools allowed individuals to create and share their work with unprecedented ease. This democratization of creative tools empowered independent artists, musicians, and filmmakers, allowing them to bypass traditional gatekeepers and distribute their work globally. The ease of sharing content also fostered collaboration and community-building among creatives, leading to the emergence of new artistic forms and innovative creative projects.

In conclusion, the societal impact of the personal computer revolution is multifaceted and far-reaching. It transformed the workplace, the classroom, and the home, altering the way we live, work, and interact with each other. While the benefits of increased productivity, enhanced education, and global connectivity are undeniable, the challenges associated with the digital divide, privacy concerns, and online safety remain significant issues demanding ongoing attention and effective solutions. The legacy of the personal computer is not simply a technological advancement;

it is a profound social transformation, shaping the present and continuously influencing the future of human society.

Anecdotes, Musings, and Recollections

The Homebrew Computer Club was less of a formal organization and more like a nerdy potluck for anyone who thought "circuit board" sounded tastier than "cheese board." Picture a bunch of tech-savvy tinkerers swapping software secrets, spare parts, wild schematics, and the occasional groan-worthy programming joke. Most of us had backgrounds in electronic engineering, software sorcery, or the ancient art of computer programming—basically, we were the people your parents called to fix the VCR.

Many of the early discussions centered around the newly introduced Altair 8800, circuit diagrams were traded the way other people swap baseball cards, and programming tips flew across the room like confetti at a New Year's bash.

The club itself was the brainchild of Gordon French and Fred Moore, who first crossed paths at the Community Computer Center in Menlo Park. Both were on a noble quest: to make computers as accessible as pizza delivery. They launched a regular, open forum where anyone with a soldering iron and a dream could show up, show off, and occasionally short-circuit something important.

Early meetings took place in the hallowed halls of the Stanford Linear Accelerator Center (SLAC)—because if you're going to talk about fast chips, you might as well do it next to a particle accelerator. By 1978, the group had outgrown its subatomic stomping grounds and moved to the Stanford Medical School.

And who graced these gatherings? Just a few future legends: Steve Jobs and Steve Wozniak (who would one day build Apple Computers in a garage, like true tech MacGyvers), Todd Fischer (IMSAI), George Morrow (Morrow Designs), Adam Osborne (Osborne Computer), Paul Terrell (Byte Shop), and a whole cast of others who'd go on to change the world—or at least make it run a little faster.

The **Altair 8800** is a microcomputer introduced in 1974 by Micro Instrumentation and Telemetry Systems (MITS), based on the Intel 8080 CPU.[1] It was the first commercially successful personal computer.[2] Interest in the Altair 8800 grew quickly after it was featured on the cover of the January 1975 issue of Popular Electronics.[3] The Altair 8800 had no built-in screen or video output, so it would have to be connected to a serial terminal or teletype to have any output. To connect it to a terminal, a serial interface card had to be installed. Alternatively, the Altair could be programmed using its front-panel switches.

The **Macintosh**, later rebranded as the **Macintosh 128K**, is the original Macintosh personal computer from Apple. It is the first successful mass-market all-in-one desktop personal computer with a graphical user interface, built-in screen, and mouse. It was pivotal in establishing desktop publishing as a general office function.[4]

Steve Wozniak, often called "Woz", was the technical genius behind Apple's early success. He co-founded Apple Computer in 1976 alongside Steve Jobs and Ronald Wayne. He single-handedly built the Apple I computer, which laid the foundation for Apple's future. His Apple II became one of the first mass-market personal computers, revolutionizing the industry. The "Woz" left Apple in 1985, although he remained an employee in a ceremonial role and continued to support tech innovation.

Ronald Wayne helped draft the original partnership agreement and was instrumental in designing Apple's first logo, featuring Isaac Newton under an apple tree. He also wrote the Apple I operations manual. Interestingly, however, just 12 days later, Wayne sold his 10% stake in Apple for $800, fearing financial risk. Had he kept his shares, they would have been worth billions today.

---

[1] Rojas, Raúl (2001). Encyclopedia of computers and computer history. Chicago [u.a.]: Fitzroy Dearborn. ISBN 1-57958-235-4.

[2] Dorf, Richard C., ed. The engineering handbook. CRC Press, 2004.

[3] Copyright catalogs at the Library of Congress. January 1975 issue of Popular Electronics was published on November 29, 1974.

[4] Polsson, Ken (July 29, 2009) "Chronology of Apple Computer Personal Computers". Archived from the original on August 21, 2009. Retrieved August 27, 2009).

CHAPTER 7

The Internet and the World Wide Web: Connecting the World

Early Networking Technologies: ARPANET and the Precursors to the Internet

The personal computer revolution, as transformative as it was, wouldn't have reached its full potential without a parallel revolution in networking. The ability to connect these individual machines to create a vast, interconnected web of information and communication, was the missing piece that unlocked the true power of the personal computer. This interconnectedness didn't emerge overnight; it was the culmination of decades of research, development, and, let's be honest, a fair amount of trial and error. The story begins not with sleek servers and high-speed fiber optics, but with a far more humble, yet incredibly important, ancestor: the ARPANET.

ARPANET, short for the Advanced Research Projects Agency Network, wasn't conceived as the precursor to the internet we know today. Its origins lie in the Cold War paranoia of the 1960s, a time when the threat of a Soviet nuclear attack loomed large in the minds of American strategists. The U.S. Department of Defense, specifically the Advanced Research Projects Agency (ARPA), recognized the vulnerability of centralized communication systems. If a single point of failure, like a central telephone exchange, were destroyed, the entire communication network could collapse. This was clearly unacceptable in a potential wartime scenario. The solution, as conceived by visionary researchers, was to create a decentralized network, a system where the failure of one node wouldn't bring down the entire system. This innovative approach, now commonplace, was revolutionary at the time.

The early stages of ARPANET were far from elegant. Imagine the internet in its infancy, sputtering to life like a recalcitrant engine. The technology was cutting-edge but incredibly limited by today's standards. The initial network consisted of only four nodes, connecting research institutions at UCLA, Stanford Research Institute (SRI), the University of California, Santa Barbara, and the University of Utah. These nodes were connected via 56 kbps leased lines, a speed that would make today's internet users weep with laughter (or possibly rage). Transmission speeds were agonizingly slow, and data transfer was far from reliable. Network outages were common, and troubleshooting these issues often involved a combination of brute force, ingenuity, and lots and lots of patience. The challenges were immense, mirroring the early days of aviation—lots of crashes, but each failure brought valuable lessons.

One of the crucial technological advancements that enabled ARPANET was the development of packet switching. Before packet switching, data was transmitted as a continuous stream. If any part of the transmission was interrupted, the entire message was lost. Packet switching, however, broke down data into small packets, each with its own routing information. These packets could travel independently across the network, and even if some were lost or delayed, the remaining packets could still arrive at their destination, allowing for a surprisingly robust system. This was a monumental leap forward in networking technology, a concept that remains central to the internet's architecture. It's like sending a letter via many different postal routes. Even if some routes are blocked, the letter can still arrive, albeit potentially in a slightly jumbled order. The receiving end then reassembles the packets to reconstruct the original message—a testament to the ingenuity of early network engineers.

The protocols used in ARPANET were also pioneering. Network Control Protocol (NCP) was the primary protocol used for communication between nodes. While rudimentary by today's standards, NCP established fundamental communication protocols that would later evolve into the Transmission Control Protocol/Internet Protocol (TCP/IP), the backbone of the modern internet. This transition to TCP/IP was a watershed moment, effectively standardizing communication across different networks, paving the way for the interconnected internet we know today. It's like transitioning from individual languages to a universal translator, allowing different computer networks to finally communicate fluently.

Beyond the technological innovations, ARPANET fostered a vibrant community of researchers and engineers who pushed the boundaries of networking. They didn't just build networks; they built a community of shared knowledge and collaboration. The collaborative spirit was crucial; it fostered a culture of open communication and shared learning, a key element in the rapid advancement of networking technology. This early community was instrumental in shaping the culture of the internet, a culture of innovation, experimentation, and collaboration that persists to this day. Think of it as a digital equivalent of the Renaissance workshops, where masters and apprentices pushed the boundaries of what was possible.

However, ARPANET wasn't without its limitations. It was primarily designed for research purposes, and its accessibility was limited. The early internet wasn't the open, freely available network we're familiar with now. It was a carefully managed system with limited access and strict controls. This restricted nature contrasts sharply with the expansive and largely unregulated internet that evolved from it. This restricted access reflects the constraints of the technology and the priorities of its funders at the time.

Preceding ARPANET were a series of smaller, less interconnected networks, each contributing crucial elements to the eventual internet. These earlier networks, although less sophisticated, experimented with concepts such as packet switching and decentralized communication, paving the way for the more ambitious project that was ARPANET. They provide a fascinating glimpse into the incremental progress that led to the interconnected world we know today. These were the tinkering stages, the trial-and-error phase before the big breakthrough.

One noteworthy example is the work done at the RAND Corporation, which explored the concept of distributed networks in the late 1950s and early 1960s. Their research on message routing and network design had a significant influence on the development of ARPANET. RAND's contributions highlight the often-forgotten work that takes place before a groundbreaking innovation emerges. It was the groundwork, the preliminary experiments that proved certain concepts were viable. It is these quieter contributions, the unseen work of countless researchers, that often pave the way for major technological advancements. It is similar to the story of the Wright Brothers. They were not the first to attempt flight, but they were the first to succeed. Their success was built on the shoulders of countless others who came before them, experimenting and learning from their failures. As Orville might have said when their first plane took off: "Well, Wilbur, I guess this idea has finally taken flight!"

The transition from these early networks to ARPANET was not a sudden leap but a gradual evolution, building upon existing technologies and expanding upon previous research. Each step, each incremental improvement, brought the vision of a connected world closer to reality. It's a testament to the power of incremental progress and the enduring value of persistent experimentation. It's a reminder that groundbreaking discoveries rarely happen in a vacuum; they are the culmination of years, sometimes decades, of research, development, and countless hours of dedicated work. The story of the early internet is not a story of singular genius, but a story of collective ingenuity and collaboration.

The Invention of the World Wide Web: Making the Internet Accessible

Before diving deep into the software and hardware that propel modern computing, it's essential to spotlight the humble workhorses—the Internet Service Providers (ISPs)—the backbone of modern computing. Think of ISPs as the friendly gatekeepers of the digital realm. They transformed the dial-up screeches of the early internet into the smooth, ultra-fast connections we now take for granted. Without ISPs laying down these vital digital highways, all the brilliant software and hardware innovations would have remained stranded on a desolate island of isolated computers.

ISPs made internet access widely available, starting with dial-up connections, in the late 1980s and early 1990s. This allowed homes and businesses to connect to the digital world, fueling the rise of online communication, commerce, and entertainment. ISPs have continuously improved internet speeds, enabling cloud computing, which has allowed businesses and individuals to store, access, and process data remotely. ISPs help manage cybersecurity by offering firewalls, encryption, and VPN services to protect users from cyber threats.

In the days when waiting for a page to load felt like watching paint dry, ISPs were the pioneers driving the evolution from snail-paced dial-up to lightning-fast broadband. They weren't just about data delivery; they were the architects behind the scenes, constructing bridges that connect our homes to the vast expanse of cyberspace. Whether ushering in the era of streaming cat videos or enabling global video conferences, ISPs have quietly ensured that every byte has a smooth ride to its destination.

While you might grumble about buffering videos or data caps, ISPs were the ones who turned the internet from a chaotic, disjointed collection of pages into a seamlessly organized digital metropolis. They built the highways of data that let us stream, share, and connect with unprecedented ease.

Every seamless video call and uninterrupted Netflix binge is a nod to those tireless data wranglers, diligently converting raw bandwidth into a smooth, well-oiled online experience.

In short, ISPs transformed computing by evolving from the crackly era of dial-up to the stable, high-speed networks we depend on today—making the internet not just a tool for the few, but a vibrant, indispensable part of everyday life. Their journey is a testament to how far we've come, all while quietly ensuring that our digital world continues to thrive, one byte at a time.

Every innovation—from the simple "You've Got Mail" of AOL to the cutting-edge cloud infrastructures—rests on the robust foundations that ISPs continue to build. Their evolution is a testament to how the digital world has become increasingly connected and reliable with every technological advancement.

The story of the internet, however, doesn't end with ARPANET. While ARPANET demonstrated the feasibility of a decentralized network, it remained largely inaccessible to the public. It was a tool for researchers, a playground for academics and government agencies, not the global communication hub it would eventually become. This is where the World Wide Web (WWW) enters the stage, a transformative invention that would finally make the internet accessible to a global audience.

The key figure in this transformation is Tim Berners-Lee, a British computer scientist working at CERN, the European Council for Nuclear Research. In the late 1980s, Berners-Lee recognized the potential of hypertext—a system of linking documents—to create a more user-friendly and interconnected web of information. He envisioned a system where researchers could easily share information and collaborate across geographical boundaries, transcending the limitations of ARPANET's primarily text-based interface.

Berners-Lee's insight wasn't simply a technical breakthrough; it was a conceptual leap. He understood that the real power of the internet lay not just in its ability to connect computers, but in its potential to connect people. This shift in perspective is what fundamentally distinguishes the World Wide Web from its predecessors. ARPANET was primarily concerned with the technical aspects of networking; Berners-Lee, on the other hand, focused on creating a system that was both technically robust and user-friendly.

His creation wasn't some stroke of genius born overnight in a lightning bolt of inspiration. It was a meticulously crafted solution to a specific problem, built upon years of research and development. He didn't invent the underlying network technologies; instead, he created a system that harnessed the power of those existing technologies in a revolutionary way. This is often overlooked; it's easy to think of groundbreaking inventions as single acts of creation, but they are often the culmination of years of work, building upon prior innovations.

The heart of Berners-Lee's invention lies in three fundamental components: HTML (HyperText Markup Language), HTTP (HyperText Transfer Protocol), and URLs (Uniform Resource Locators). HTML provides the structure for web pages, defining how text, images, and other elements are displayed. HTTP is the protocol that allows web browsers to communicate with web servers, requesting and receiving web pages. Finally, URLs provide unique addresses for each web page, allowing users to navigate seamlessly across the internet. These three components, working in concert, created a system that was both elegant and remarkably simple—at least in its core design. In its early stages, URLs were not that user friendly and difficult to remember. Web developers often use URL rewriting to make complex URLs appear user friendly. This means the browser shows a simple address, while the server handles the messy logic invisibly.

The initial implementation of the World Wide Web at CERN in 1989 was decidedly low-key. It wasn't a flashy launch with a marketing campaign and press releases. It began as a simple information-sharing system for researchers, enabling them to organize and access documents more efficiently. There were no flashy graphics or interactive elements; it was primarily text-based, but the underlying architecture was incredibly powerful. This humble beginning underscores the power of simple, elegant design; sometimes, the most transformative technologies begin with unassuming origins. It's a testament to the principle of starting small, testing thoroughly, and iterating towards a larger vision.

However, the implications of Berners-Lee's invention were far-reaching. By making the internet accessible through a simple, graphical user interface, the Web made information more accessible to a wider audience. No longer was the internet a domain exclusively for technical experts; it became a tool for everyone. This had a profound impact on the way information was shared, accessed, and consumed. This is an often-overlooked aspect of the Web's impact: its accessibility extended far beyond just technical expertise; it made information widely available irrespective of technical skills. This created a more level playing field in the information landscape.

The spread of the Web was initially slow, facilitated by the gradual adoption of personal computers and the expansion of the internet infrastructure. As more people gained access to computers and the internet, the Web's popularity surged exponentially. The visual nature of the Web, with its images and hyperlinks, made it far more engaging than the text-based interfaces of earlier network systems. This visual appeal was crucial in its widespread adoption. This wasn't just about information; it was about experience.

The growth of the Web wasn't solely determined by technology; social and cultural factors also played a significant role. The emergence of the commercial internet in the mid-1990s fueled the rapid expansion of the Web. Businesses saw the potential of the Web to reach customers globally, leading to a massive investment in developing web-based applications and services. The introduction of e-commerce further accelerated the Web's growth, transforming the way people shopped and interacted with businesses.

The advent of search engines wasn't just about collecting data—it fundamentally reshaped our digital landscape. In the early days of the Web, tools like Netscape—along with pioneering platforms such as Excite, AltaVista, and Lycos—helped transform a chaotic jumble of disconnected pages into a navigable resource. Netscape made its grand entrance into the internet world in 1994 with the release of Mosaic Netscape, which was soon renamed Netscape Navigator. These early search efforts laid the groundwork for later giants like Yahoo! and Google, and Microsoft's Internet Explorer, which refined the process of finding information with unprecedented speed and efficiency.

Before these developments, exploring the Web was an arduous task, with information dispersed across countless static sites. The introduction of search engines turned the internet from a wild frontier into an organized, user-friendly platform, making it truly accessible for the average person. With just a few keystrokes, users could now unlock a vast amount of knowledge—a transformation that revolutionized how we interact with the digital world.

The continuing evolution of the World Wide Web is a story still being written. The advent of mobile devices and social media has further transformed how we use the Web. The Web is no longer just a place to access information; it's a platform for communication, collaboration, and social interaction. The challenges of ensuring security, privacy, and accessibility remain, but the ongoing development of the Web continues to shape the way we live, work, and interact with the world. The ongoing innovations—from enhanced search algorithms to virtual reality—reflect the enduring power of Berners-Lee's original vision.

The Rise of E-commerce and Online Services: Transforming Industries

The late 1990s and early 2000s witnessed an explosion of activity on the World Wide Web, far exceeding even the most optimistic predictions of its early pioneers. This wasn't merely an increase in the number of websites; it was a fundamental shift in how businesses operated and how consumers interacted with the world. This period marks the rise of e-commerce and online services, a transformation that would irrevocably alter countless industries. Suddenly, the internet wasn't just a repository of information; it became a vibrant marketplace, a global storefront, and a revolutionary platform for service delivery.

The initial incursions into e-commerce were tentative, often characterized by clunky websites and cumbersome payment systems. Early adopters, however, recognized the enormous potential. They saw the possibility of reaching customers beyond geographical limitations, expanding their market reach exponentially. This wasn't simply about convenience; it was about access. Businesses that once were confined to a local customer base could now operate on a global scale. This was particularly transformative for smaller businesses that lacked the resources for extensive brick-and-mortar operations. The internet leveled the playing field, allowing smaller companies to compete with industry giants on a more even footing.

One of the most significant impacts of e-commerce was on the retail industry. Companies like Amazon, initially an online bookstore, quickly demonstrated the power of online retail. Their ability to offer a vast selection of products, competitive pricing, and convenient delivery revolutionized the shopping experience. The rise of Amazon wasn't merely a technological triumph; it represented a fundamental shift in consumer behavior. Consumers, increasingly comfortable with online transactions, embraced the convenience and choice offered by online retailers. This shift, in turn, forced traditional brick-and-mortar retailers to adapt, many integrating online sales channels into their business models. This competitive pressure drove innovations in logistics, supply chain management, and customer service, resulting in a more efficient and customer-centric retail environment.

The impact extended far beyond retail. Online booking platforms significantly transformed the travel industry. Websites like Expedia and Travelocity allowed users to compare prices, book flights and hotels, and plan entire itineraries online. This eliminated the need for travel agents, offering consumers more control and transparency in their travel arrangements. The ease of comparison shopping also increased competition among airlines and hotels, benefiting consumers with lower prices and better deals. The industry's reliance on physical agencies was effectively replaced by a global network of online platforms, demonstrating the internet's power to disrupt traditional business models.

The financial services industry also experienced a dramatic transformation. Online banking became increasingly commonplace, offering consumers the convenience of managing their finances from anywhere with an internet connection. This increased accessibility also led to innovations in financial products and services, with online-only banks offering competitive interest rates and fees. Online brokerage platforms further democratized access to investment opportunities, reducing the cost and complexity of investing. The ability to trade stocks, bonds, and other securities online enabled more involvement in the financial markets, fundamentally altering how individuals managed their wealth.

The rise of online services extended beyond retail and finance. Online education platforms offered new ways to access educational materials and courses. This was particularly beneficial to students in remote areas with limited access to traditional educational institutions. The flexibility and accessibility of online classes also catered to adult learners and those seeking professional development opportunities. The ability to learn at one's own pace and on one's own schedule further enhanced the appeal of online education. This transformation of the education sector is still unfolding, with the ongoing development of virtual classrooms and innovative learning technologies.

The impact of the internet on communication was equally profound. Email became the primary mode of communication for both personal and professional purposes. Instant messaging and social networking platforms fostered new forms of communication and social interaction, connecting people across geographical boundaries. The emergence of social media has changed the way businesses interact with customers and engage in marketing. Companies could now interact directly with their customer base, garnering instant feedback and building relationships more dynamically. The shift towards social media marketing fundamentally altered the marketing landscape, forcing businesses to adapt to this new, more interactive environment. The emphasis shifted from one-way communication to a more engaged, multi-directional flow of information and feedback.

However, the rise of e-commerce and online services wasn't without its challenges. Concerns about online security and privacy emerged as a significant hurdle. The increasing reliance on online transactions made users vulnerable to fraud and data breaches. The need for robust security measures and data protection has become paramount. The establishment of secure payment gateways and encryption protocols helped alleviate these concerns, but the ongoing battle to maintain online security remains a constant challenge. Similarly, the digital divide—the gap between those with access to the internet and those without—presented an ongoing societal challenge. The unequal access to the internet created disparities in access to information, education, and economic opportunities. Bridging this digital divide became a crucial social and economic objective, requiring significant investment in infrastructure and digital literacy programs.

The transformation driven by e-commerce and online services continues to evolve. The rise of mobile commerce (m-commerce) has further expanded the reach of online retail, allowing consumers to shop from anywhere using their smartphones. The use of AI and ML in e-commerce has enhanced personalization and customer service, improving the overall shopping experience. The ongoing development of augmented reality and virtual reality technologies is poised to revolutionize online shopping further, enabling more immersive and engaging online experiences. These technologies allow customers to "try on" clothes virtually, examine products in three dimensions, and even interact with a virtual sales representative from the comfort of their homes.

In conclusion, the rise of e-commerce and online services has irrevocably changed countless industries. The convenience, accessibility, and global reach offered by the internet have transformed how businesses operate and how consumers interact with the world. While challenges remain, such as security concerns and the digital divide, the ongoing evolution of e-commerce and online services promises a future of even greater innovation and transformative impact.

The Social Impact of the Internet: Connecting People Globally

Back when the internet was still a frontier, AOL's melodic "You've Got Mail" wasn't just a notification; it was a digital shout-out declaring, "Hey, your inbox is alive!" In an era when computers greeted you like a friendly neighbor (albeit one with a really monotone voice), that simple phrase turned checking your email into an event. It was as if your PC leaned over and said, "Good news: a message has arrived to brighten your day!"

In a time before snappy text messages and omnipresent push notifications, AOL's signature greeting was both a calling card and a cultural catchphrase, symbolizing the dawn of our online social lives. It was the sound of connectivity, a reminder that the digital realm was here, and it had opinions. Not unlike an old friend eagerly anticipating your response, "You've Got Mail" encapsulated the excitement of instant communication, turning an otherwise mundane digital process into a pleasant ritual. As an aside, a romantic comedy titled by the same iconic AOL email notification, starring Tom Hanks and Meg Ryan, was released in 1998, making it a nostalgic piece of internet history.

The internet's democratizing effect on communication is perhaps its most profound social impact. Before its widespread adoption, connecting with someone across the globe often involved expensive and time-consuming methods like international calls or snail mail. (In case you may have forgotten, that's an envelope with a postage stamp.) The internet, however, collapsed geographical distances, rendering them virtually irrelevant for many forms of communication. Email, initially a niche technology for academics and researchers, became a ubiquitous tool for personal and professional communication, connecting individuals and businesses across continents. The speed and efficiency of email revolutionized correspondence, fostering faster collaborations and more immediate feedback loops. This accelerated pace of communication had a ripple effect across various sectors, from international trade to personal relationships.

The rise of instant messaging further intensified this connectedness. Platforms like Skype, an application that allowed users to make voice and video calls, send instant messages, and share files over the internet, were launched in 2003. It became known for its VoIP (Voice over Internet Protocol) technology, which enabled free or low-cost calls worldwide. It was retired in 2025 in favor of Microsoft Teams. Other platforms, such as MSN Messenger, Yahoo! Messenger, and later, WhatsApp and Viber, allowed for real-time conversations, fostering a sense of immediacy and intimacy that transcended geographical boundaries. The ability to instantly share thoughts, feelings, and information with loved ones across the world forged new kinds of relationships, enriching lives in ways previously unimaginable. Families separated by continents could now maintain daily contact, bridging physical distance and fostering stronger bonds.

However, this enhanced connectivity wasn't without its complexities. The instantaneous nature of online communication could lead to misinterpretations, misunderstandings, and even conflict. The lack of non-verbal cues inherent in written communication often resulted in ambiguity and the potential for miscommunication. The internet's ability to amplify emotions, both positive and negative, also contributed to the rise of cyberbullying and online harassment, raising significant concerns about online safety and well-being. The ease of anonymity on many platforms exacerbated these issues, creating a breeding ground for negative interactions.

Social media platforms dramatically altered the social landscape, accelerating the pace of information dissemination and transforming the way people interacted with each other. Platforms like Facebook, Twitter (now rebranded as 'X'), and Instagram have connected individuals on a global scale, fostering communities built around shared interests, hobbies, and identities. LinkedIn transformed professional networking, recruitment, and business communication. Since its launch in 2003, it has evolved into a robust platform that leverages data analytics, AI, and cloud computing to connect professionals worldwide. This ability to connect with like-minded individuals, regardless of geographical location, created a sense of belonging and community, particularly for individuals who might have felt isolated or marginalized in their local communities.

Social media also empowered marginalized voices and provided platforms for social and political activism. The Arab Spring, for instance, demonstrated the power of social media in organizing protests and mobilizing support for political change. Activists utilized social media platforms to circumvent government censorship, share information, and coordinate protests, resulting in significant political upheaval in several countries. This capacity for social media to facilitate political mobilization highlighted its potential as a tool for social change, challenging traditional power structures and empowering ordinary citizens.

However, social media also presented its own set of challenges. The spread of misinformation and disinformation, often referred to as "fake news," became a major concern, impacting everything from political elections to public health crises. The algorithms that drive many social media platforms often reinforce echo chambers, exposing users primarily to information that confirms their existing biases. This phenomenon contributed to polarization and the erosion of trust in credible information sources. The addictive nature of social media also raised concerns about its impact on mental health and well-being, particularly among young people. The constant pressure to create an idealized online persona and the relentless stream of content tailored to individual tastes by data-driven algorithms contributed to feelings of inadequacy and anxiety. Furthermore, privacy concerns remained a significant issue, with users often unaware of the extent to which their data was being collected and used.

The internet also transformed the way businesses interacted with their customers. E-commerce, as previously discussed, revolutionized retail and provided businesses with unprecedented opportunities to reach global markets. However, social media platforms offered a new level of customer interaction, enabling companies to engage directly with their customers, foster brand loyalty, and gather immediate feedback. This shift towards a more direct and interactive relationship between businesses and consumers fundamentally changed marketing strategies and customer service practices.

The internet also facilitated the emergence of global online communities built around shared interests, hobbies, and identities. Blogs, a term derived from "weblog," a phrase coined in the late 1990s, are widely used for marketing, education, entertainment, and personal expression. YouTube, launched in 2005, has played a monumental role in shaping the internet, transforming how people consume, create, and share content. It gave anyone with a camera and an internet connection the ability to create and share videos, breaking the monopoly of traditional media. Online forums, gaming communities, and online fan groups connected individuals across geographical boundaries, fostering a sense of belonging and shared experience. These communities provided spaces for individuals to share their knowledge, experiences, and perspectives, creating a vibrant and diverse global ecosystem of human connection. This fostered collaboration and knowledge sharing on an unprecedented scale, particularly in fields like open-source software development and scientific research.

But the creation of these global communities wasn't without its downsides. The anonymity offered by the internet could also lead to the emergence of online hate groups and extremist ideologies. The ease with which these groups could find and connect with like-minded individuals allowed them to flourish and spread their messages globally, posing significant challenges to social harmony and societal cohesion. The potential for the internet to be used for nefarious purposes, such as the spread of propaganda, hate speech, and recruitment by terrorist organizations, necessitated greater regulation and efforts to combat online extremism.

Furthermore, the internet's global reach exposed individuals to a wider range of cultural perspectives and experiences. Access to information from across the globe fostered greater cross-cultural understanding and empathy. However, it also highlighted the existing inequalities and disparities between different parts of the world. The digital divide, the gap between those with access to the internet and those without, exacerbated existing economic and social inequalities. Individuals in developing countries often lacked the infrastructure, resources, and digital literacy skills to participate fully in the digital revolution, creating a significant barrier to economic opportunity and social inclusion. Bridging this digital divide has become a crucial objective for promoting social equity and fostering global development. This requires significant investments in infrastructure, digital literacy programs, and policies that promote equitable access to technology.

In conclusion, the internet's impact on global connectivity has been profound and multifaceted. It has democratized communication, empowered marginalized voices, and fostered global communities. However, it has also presented challenges, including the spread of misinformation, the rise of online hate groups, and the exacerbation of existing social and economic inequalities. Navigating this complex landscape requires a multifaceted approach that emphasizes digital literacy, online safety, responsible content moderation, and policies that promote equitable access to technology. The future of global connectivity hinges on our collective ability to build a more inclusive and responsible digital world.

The Future of the Internet: Emerging Technologies and Trends

The internet, as we know it, is a constantly evolving entity. Revolutionary technological advancements have punctuated its rapid growth and development, and the future promises even more dramatic shifts. One of the most significant emerging technologies shaping the internet's trajectory is the IoT. The IoT represents a paradigm shift, moving beyond the simple connection of computers and smartphones to encompass a vast network of interconnected physical devices. These devices, ranging from smart vehicles to smart refrigerators, thermostats, wearable fitness trackers, and industrial sensors, are embedded with electronics, software, sensors, and network connectivity, allowing them to collect and exchange data. This interconnectedness opens up a world of possibilities, from automating household tasks to optimizing industrial processes and revolutionizing healthcare.

The implications of the IoT are far-reaching and profoundly impactful. Imagine a world where your refrigerator automatically orders groceries when supplies run low, your home adjusts lighting and temperature based on your preferences and occupancy. Your wearable fitness tracker seamlessly integrates with your healthcare provider to monitor your health in real-time. This is the promise of the IoT, a hyper-connected world where convenience, efficiency, and personalization are paramount.

However, this interconnectedness also introduces significant challenges. Security concerns are paramount. With billions of devices exchanging data, the potential for cyberattacks and data breaches is exponentially amplified. Protecting sensitive information and ensuring the integrity of these systems is a critical concern that necessitates robust security measures and international cooperation. Furthermore, the sheer volume of data generated by these interconnected devices presents formidable data management challenges. Analyzing and interpreting this data effectively requires sophisticated analytics tools and infrastructure, alongside careful consideration of data privacy and ethical implications. The potential for misuse of this data for surveillance or manipulation also warrants careful attention and the development of strong ethical guidelines.

Another pivotal technology shaping the future of the internet is the rollout of 5G networks. 5G represents a significant leap forward in mobile network technology, offering significantly faster speeds, lower latency, and greater capacity than its predecessors. This improvement in network performance is essential for supporting the demands of the IoT, enabling the seamless transmission of vast amounts of data from billions of interconnected devices. Moreover, 5G's capabilities are transforming various sectors. In the realm of healthcare, it is enabling remote surgery, telemedicine, and real-time monitoring of patients' vital signs. In manufacturing, it is optimizing industrial processes, enhancing automation, and facilitating the development of smart factories. In transportation, it's paving the way for autonomous vehicles, smart traffic management systems, and advanced driver-assistance technologies. The transformative potential of 5G extends across numerous industries, promising significant gains in efficiency, productivity, and innovation.

However, the widespread adoption of 5G is not without its hurdles. The infrastructure required to support 5G networks is extensive and costly, necessitating significant investments in new infrastructure. This poses a significant challenge, particularly for developing countries that may lack the necessary resources to build this infrastructure. The digital divide, the gap between those with access to advanced technologies and those without, is expected to widen further with the rollout of 5G. Addressing this disparity requires concerted efforts to ensure equitable access to these technologies, fostering inclusive growth and preventing the marginalization of communities already facing economic or social disadvantages. Furthermore, the higher frequencies used by 5G networks have limitations in terms of signal range and penetration, necessitating a denser network of cell towers to provide consistent coverage. This again presents infrastructure challenges and potentially raises environmental concerns regarding the visual impact of numerous cell towers and the energy consumption associated with maintaining the network.

Beyond IoT and 5G, other technologies are poised to fundamentally alter the internet landscape. AI is rapidly evolving and becoming increasingly integrated into various aspects of the internet experience. AI-powered algorithms are driving personalization in online content, powering search engines, and facilitating targeted advertising. However, the ethical implications of AI continue to be a significant concern. Concerns surrounding bias in algorithms, the potential for AI misuse in surveillance and manipulation, and the impact on employment necessitate careful consideration and robust regulatory frameworks. AI's potential to amplify existing societal biases is a substantial challenge, raising questions about fairness, accountability, and transparency.

Blockchain technology, initially developed for cryptocurrencies like Bitcoin in 2009, has far-reaching applications beyond finance. Simply stated, data is stored in "blocks" which are linked together in a chronological "chain." Its decentralized and secure nature makes it suitable for various applications, including secure data storage, supply chain management, and digital identity verification. The potential of blockchain to enhance security and trust in online transactions is substantial; however, challenges remain in terms of scalability, usability, and regulatory oversight. Furthermore, the energy consumption associated with some blockchain implementations poses environmental concerns, necessitating the exploration of more sustainable alternatives.

Quantum computing, discussed in more detail in a later chapter, represents a potential game-changer, offering unprecedented computational power that could revolutionize various fields, including cryptography, drug discovery, and materials science. However, quantum computing is still in its early stages of development, and its widespread adoption remains years away. The technological challenges in building and maintaining stable quantum computers are considerable.

The future of the internet will likely be defined by the convergence of these technologies, creating a complex and interconnected ecosystem. This interwoven landscape necessitates a proactive approach to addressing the accompanying challenges, including cybersecurity concerns, data privacy issues, the digital divide, and ethical dilemmas arising from AI and other advanced technologies. The global community must work collaboratively to develop robust regulatory frameworks, invest in infrastructure development, and promote digital literacy to harness the transformative potential of these technologies while mitigating their risks.

Anecdotes, Musings, and Recollections

Did former Vice President Al Gore invent the internet? No. But he played a significant role in its development. As a U.S. Congressman and later as a Senator, he was an early advocate for expanding computer networks and increasing public access to digital communication. In the 1980s and 1990s, he promoted legislation that helped fund the expansion of ARPANET. Vint Cerf and Bob Kahn, who were instrumental in developing the internet, have credited Gore with providing intellectual leadership and vision for high-speed computing and communications.

The misconception that Gore claimed to have "invented" the internet stems from a 1999 interview in which he said, *"During my service in the U.S. Congress, I took the initiative in creating the internet."* So, while Gore didn't sit in a lab designing the internet, he was a key political figure in shaping its expansion and accessibility.

Netscape was developed by Marc Andreessen and Jim Clark, who had previously worked on the Mosaic browser. Once Microsoft entered the browser wars, Netscape declined. By 1998, AOL acquired Netscape, and its browser technology was later open-sourced, forming the foundation for what would become Mozilla Firefox.

CHAPTER 8

The Smartphone Revolution:
Mobile Computing Takes Center Stage

Early Mobile Phones: From Analog to Digital (From Bricks to Clicks)

Before our phones became smarter than some of our decisions, they were giant plastic slabs you could use to make a call—or knock someone out cold. The evolution of mobile phones is a curious saga of ambition, awkward designs, and the relentless human need to talk on the go. Long before selfies, apps, and swiping left, there were devices that looked like military-grade equipment and weighed just about as much. These early pioneers laid the foundation for the abundant communication tools we rely on now, paving the way for the digital revolution that transformed how we connect and interact.

Used by permission: larrywhatley.org

The first chapter in this tale begins in the analog age, a realm of bulky devices and limited functionality—where signal strength was questionable, and fashion was absolutely not consulted.

These early mobile phones, collectively known as 1G (First Generation), used analog signals via amplitude modulation (AM) or frequency modulation (FM) to transmit voice. The result? Audio that sounded like it came from a haunted radio station. Coverage was patchy, the range was limited, interference was a given, and the phones themselves were best stored in backpacks, briefcases, or carried by bodyguards. They were heavy, expensive, and mostly seen in the hands of CEOs, Wall Street wolves, or action movie villains. In the 1980s, owning one was the tech equivalent of driving a Lamborghini through a school zone: loud, excessive, and undeniably attention-grabbing. They were status symbols, reflecting a level of success and affluence, much like owning a personal computer during that period.

One of the early heavyweights in this analog era was the Motorola DynaTAC 8000x, released in 1983, the original Goliath of mobile tech. This device, famously portrayed in films and TV shows as a symbol of 1980s power, weighed nearly two pounds, offered a whopping 30 minutes of talk time, and needed a ten-hour nap to recharge. The sheer size and weight of the DynaTAC were impressive feats of engineering, considering the technological limitations of the time, yet they also highlight the considerable technological advancement required before mobile phones could achieve widespread adoption. At $3,995, it was a symbol of status and success, flaunted in films and clutching the ears of Wall Street types who considered "portable" a relative term. While a hefty sum, its exclusivity solidified its place in the pantheon of early mobile communication devices. Think of it as the original "it" phone, only accessible to a select few.

Wikipedia, CC BY-SA 4.0

Then came the Nokia Mobira Senator, a car phone so large it needed its own seatbelt. Slightly more manageable was the Motorola MicroTAC, released in 1989. With its flip-down mouthpiece and lighter build, it was the first sign that designers were at least trying to make phones less like bricks and more like, well, phones. These early devices weren't just communication tools; they were cultural artifacts, capturing the intersection of techno-optimism and shoulder-pad fashion. Their images are now iconic, representing a nostalgic glimpse into the past.

Everything changed with the arrival of second-generation networks (2G) in the early 1990s. Digital networks replaced analog crackle with clearer, crisper calls. For the first time, people could hear each other without wondering if someone was calling from inside a tin can. Static was reduced, interference lessened, and text messaging was born. Yes, the humble SMS (Short Messaging Service) began here, with phones that could finally do more than just talk back. While voice quality was still not perfect, the dramatic improvement was immediately noticeable, demonstrating the power of digital technology in transforming a previously flawed experience.

With 2G came a shrink ray effect on handsets. Phones got smaller, lighter, and less likely to cause shoulder injuries. Advances in battery tech and digital circuitry meant you could talk longer, charge less, and possibly even fit your mobile in a jacket pocket—what luxury! And as costs began to decline, mobile ownership spread beyond the wealthy elite, reaching the masses and changing social norms in the process.

But 2G didn't stop at chatting and texting. It quietly opened the door to mobile data, setting the stage for the internet-on-the-go. Early data capabilities were sluggish and limited, but they were enough to hint at what was coming. These early forms of data transmission opened the door for innovations like SMS, also known as texting. This was a major step forward, enabling quick and easy communication beyond voice calls. The simple, short text messages initially were limited, highlighting the constraints of the underlying technology, but marked the beginning of text-based communication that would become integral to modern mobile phones. Texting caught on like wildfire, proving that people were ready to communicate with their thumbs—long before emojis and autocorrect became daily struggles.

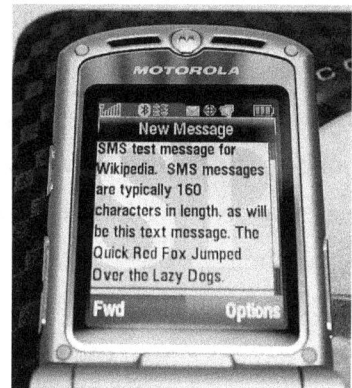

Motorola Flip Phone. Author's archives

The subsequent generations of mobile networks, 3G and 4G, built upon the foundations laid by 2G, further refining the digital transmission of voice and data. 3G brought substantial improvements in data speeds, enabling faster internet access and the emergence of mobile internet browsing. The ability to browse the internet, send emails, and check sports scores from your phone was a game-changer and a pivotal moment in the ongoing mobile evolution. Although slow by today's standards, it was still revolutionary. The ability to access information on the go revolutionized access to news, information, and social networking, all while using the mobile device as the central interface. The mobile phone was no longer just a talking device; it was starting to look more like a pocket computer with a social life.

4G, with its even faster speeds and improved reliability, provided the network infrastructure needed to support increasingly data-hungry applications, like video streaming and high-resolution image sharing. This represented a paradigm shift, turning the mobile phone from a simple voice communication tool into a fully functional mobile computer and a platform for a wide range of applications and services. The expansion of data speeds dramatically improved the user experience, enabling more responsive and engaging applications, and leading to the rapid expansion of mobile app ecosystems.

The evolution from analog to digital wasn't just a technological progression; it was a social and economic transformation. The increased affordability and improved functionality of mobile phones led to their widespread adoption, fundamentally altering communication patterns, social interactions, and business practices. So, this isn't just a story of signal upgrades and shrinking batteries. The shift from analog to digital phones triggered a broader transformation in how we live. Conversations became constant. Communication became borderless. And the phone in your hand? It became an extension of you—part assistant, part distraction, part social connector. The ease of connectivity fostered new forms of community and enabled businesses to reach consumers in ways never before possible. The transition from cumbersome analog devices to the sleek, powerful digital smartphones we know today is a testament to the rapid pace of technological advancement, highlighting the transformative power of innovation and its influence on our lives. We've come a long way since "Can you hear me now?"

The Rise of Smartphones: Convergence of Computing and Communication

BlackBerry played a pivotal role in the evolution of smartphones, particularly in the early 2000s. With the launch of the BlackBerry 957, it was one of the first brands to popularize mobile email, secure messaging, and enterprise-focused devices. Another key contribution was BlackBerry's focus on productivity through its signature physical QWERTY keyboard. This standard typewriter design was ideal for composing detailed emails and messages, making it the go-to tool for business and government professionals. This emphasis on robust, secure, and efficient communication created a benchmark that

modern smartphones continue to build upon—even as touchscreens ultimately supplanted physical keyboards for the broader market.

This wasn't a whirlwind Vegas wedding. No, the merger of microprocessors and mobile networks was more of a slow burn. Think decades of nerdy courtship via incremental advances in microelectronics, software wizardry, and network evolution. At the heart of this love story? Shrinking. Not our hearts, but the circuits. The unsung hero of this saga is miniaturization—a term that might not make headlines but has quietly stuffed supercomputers into our back pockets. The result? A device that's as much a personal assistant as it is a phone, and perhaps more essential than your house keys.

Let's rewind to the golden age of personal computers. These early beasts took up entire desks and often sounded like jet engines. Then came Moore's Law, courtesy of Intel co-founder Gordon Moore. He predicted that the number of transistors on a chip would double every two years. Like a tech-savvy oracle, Moore was right. This relentless shrinking act gave us more computing muscle at a fraction of the size and cost. Suddenly, what once required a desktop and a prayer could now run on a chip the size of a fingernail. Voilà—processing power for the pocket-sized masses.

That astonishing shrinking act allowed for smartphone CPUs to become little digital Olympians. They could process complex tasks, juggle multiple apps, and run demanding software—all while pretending to be a telephone. With each passing year, manufacturers managed to cram more performance into less space, until the line between "mobile phone" and "mini supercomputer" blurred beyond recognition.

Still, raw power without a good personality is just a flashy paperweight. Early mobile operating systems had all the charm of a DMV line—functional but far from fun. They were clunky, confusing, and about as intuitive as a VCR manual. Then came the game-changers: Apple's iOS and Google's Android. These systems didn't just make smartphones smarter—they made them useful and efficient. Suddenly, you could swipe, tap, and pinch your way through tasks with the grace of a digital ballerina. Applications (Apps) for these devices flowed in like a digital gold rush. You could do everything from ordering tacos to managing your entire life. The smartphone stopped being a phone and became a lifestyle choice.

The introduction of app stores was like opening Pandora's box—except instead of chaos, out came productivity tools, social media platforms, fitness trackers, and games that destroy your free time

(Candy Crush anyone?). Smartphones ceased to be mere tools and became extensions of ourselves, personalized portals to everything from your bank account to your favorite cat memes.

But even the most suave software needs a good-looking interface. Let's take a moment to appreciate the glow-up from clunky keypads to sleek, touch-sensitive screens. Early phones made you work for every text message, requiring the dexterity of a concert pianist and the patience of a saint. Then came capacitive touchscreens—powered by advancements in display technologies—that finally let our fingers dance across our phones like they were born to do it. They were smooth, responsive, and more intuitive than your therapist. The graphical user interface (GUI) evolved from utilitarian to irresistible, making smartphones not just functional, but fun.

A mobile device or handheld device is a computer small enough to hold and operate in hand.

Samsung Galaxy S25 Ultra, Wikipedia, CC BY-SA 4.0

Mobile devices like this Samsung Galaxy S25 Ultra are typically battery-powered and possess a flat-panel display and one or more built-in input devices, such as a touchscreen or keypad. Remember how revolutionary it felt to scroll with a flick of your finger? That wasn't just a party trick—it was a usability revolution. Drag-and-drop functionality, pinch-to-zoom, and swipe gestures made interacting with devices feel like second nature. It was like magic, except this spell came with a user manual and app updates. Suddenly, even your grandma could FaceTime you, unassisted. The blend of tactile engagement and visual feedback created an experience so seamless that it's easy to forget how difficult things used to be.

Of course, none of this would've mattered if smartphones were stuck in the digital equivalent of a dead zone. Enter the evolution of cellular networks. Early 2G systems were basically glorified walkie-talkies with a modest flair for texting. Then came 3G, which finally made mobile browsing a thing—albeit a slow, patience-testing thing. But it was 4G that truly supercharged the smartphone experience, enabling smooth video streaming, real-time gaming, and the ability to download an entire album before the barista finished your cappuccino. Throw in the arrival of 5G, and we're now downloading movies faster than it takes to microwave popcorn. We're poised for even wilder digital feats, like real-time augmented reality and bandwidth-hogging apps we haven't even imagined yet.

And let's not overlook the sidekicks: Wi-Fi and Bluetooth. Wi-Fi meant your phone could ditch the limited data plan and hop onto faster, more stable networks at home, work, or your favorite overpriced coffee shop. Bluetooth, meanwhile, became the ultimate wingman—connecting your phone to speakers, headphones, smartwatches, and even your car, all without those pesky cords. Together, they helped smartphones become social butterflies, flitting between devices and networks with effortless grace.

But all this brilliance would be dimmed without one crucial component: battery life. Early mobile phones were notorious for dying faster than a fruit fly. You'd make three calls and suddenly be hunting for a charger like it was a lost treasure. The development of lithium-ion batteries changed the game, offering longer-lasting power in smaller packages. It was the difference between carrying a charger in your pocket and confidently leaving the house without one. While battery life is still a sore spot for many, the progress made was essential in making smartphones truly mobile instead of glorified pagers. Battery anxiety hasn't vanished entirely, but at least we're not carrying around spare chargers like life-support machines anymore.

So how did we go from clunky communication tools to sleek digital Swiss Army knives? It wasn't just about stuffing more features into a phone; it was about weaving together complementary technologies—processing power, elegant software, intuitive interfaces, fast networks, and efficient batteries—into a device that feels indispensable. The smartphone became a camera, a GPS, a personal trainer, a news anchor, a gaming system, and a social connector, all rolled into one shiny rectangle.

And let's not forget the cultural repercussions. Smartphones didn't just change how we communicate—they changed how we live. They altered our attention spans, revolutionized industries, birthed influencers, and prompted more than a few dinner-table debates about excessive screen time. They've become our memory banks, our entertainment centers, and our emergency lifelines. They've inserted themselves into nearly every facet of modern existence with the confidence of a device that knows it's too valuable to ignore.

Mobile Operating Systems: iOS vs Android

Before our smartphones could become the utility tools of the modern digital world we rely on today, there was a mobile frontier dominated by clunky feature phones, rudimentary operating systems, and the occasional game of Snake on the black-and-white screen of your Nokia phone. In the early

2000s, platforms like Symbian, Windows Mobile, and BlackBerry OS reigned supreme, but they were more about basic communication than the interactive, app-driven experiences we now expect. These early systems set the stage by highlighting the limitations—and potential—of mobile computing, nudging innovators to rethink how software could make mobile devices not just functional, but indispensable.

When people reminisce about the meteoric rise of smartphones, they often fantasize about hardware specs—faster processors, sharper displays, and camera lenses that can capture the glint of a mosquito's eye at 10 paces. But beneath all that glossy hardware lies a quieter, far more cerebral battleground: the mobile *operating system (OS)*. If the smartphone is the body, then the OS is the brain—constantly processing, organizing, and keeping things from spiraling into digital chaos. And in the grand arena of mobile tech, few duels have been as persistent—or as passionate—as the one between Apple's iOS and Google's Android. So, there we have it. The eternal struggle between iOS and Android—a rivalry as legendary as Coke versus Pepsi, Marvel versus DC, or pineapple on pizza versus sausage and pepperoni.

At the heart of the smartphone wars is a battle of ideologies. Apple's iOS is like an exclusive members-only club: polished, sophisticated, and meticulously curated. It offers seamless integration across Apple's ecosystem, ensuring that your iPhone, iPad, Mac, and even your AirPods all work together with near-magical precision. But with that polish comes restrictions—want to customize your home screen beyond neatly arranged app icons? Too bad. Want to install apps from outside the App Store? Not happening. It's the tech equivalent of "You can check out anytime you like, but you can never leave."

Apple, always the stylish perfectionist of the tech world, kicked off the mobile OS revolution with the unveiling of the iPhone and its then-named iPhone OS (soon to be known simply as iOS) in 2007. Released in tandem with the original iPhone, iOS was more than just software—it was a user experience manifesto. Apple's approach was clear: control everything. Hardware, software, the App Store (introduced in 2008), the fonts, the gestures, and probably the temperature of the Genius Bar. This vertical integration allowed for an unparalleled level of polish. The result? An interface so intuitive that toddlers and technophobes alike could use it without needing a manual or a family IT department.

Under the hood, iOS was a fortress of simplicity. It wasn't interested in whether you wanted to change your home screen layout into a kaleidoscope. It wanted to work and look good doing it. The early success of the iPhone owed much to this laser-focused software. Even if you couldn't install a new keyboard or change your app icons to pictures of your cat or dog, you could trust iOS to be smooth, stable, and stylish. It was a pocket-sized concierge—polite, efficient, and just a little bit smug.

But if iOS was the tightly curated art gallery of mobile operating systems, Android was the bustling flea market—vibrant, eclectic, and occasionally a little buggy. Founded originally as Android Inc. in 2003 and then acquired by Google in 2005, Android was born with an open-source philosophy that favored flexibility over rigidity. When Google launched Android in 2008, it took a radically different path. Shunning Apple's control-freak tendencies, Android embraced openness. It was built to be shared, adapted, tweaked, and even mildly abused by anyone with a manufacturing license and a dream.

The open-source nature of Android was both its greatest strength and worst flaw. On one hand, it enabled a staggering diversity of devices—from budget-friendly phones in developing markets to feature-stuffed flagships that could probably launch a SpaceX rocket. On the other hand, it meant that not all Androids were created equal. Some sang like Pavarotti; others wheezed like a kazoo. But overall, Android's flexibility became its calling card. Want a phone with a stylus? A foldable screen? A built-in projector? Android had you covered, often with three models to spare.

This ideological fork in the road—Apple's elegance versus Google's elasticity—became the defining feature of the smartphone era. Users were no longer choosing between phones; they were choosing between lifestyles. iOS devotees praised its clean design, its seamless ecosystem, and its ability to "just work." Android fans, meanwhile, pointed to their ability to customize everything from their lock screen widgets to their kernel settings. It wasn't just a difference in preference—it was a tribal identity, tech-style.

The rivalry escalated quickly. Both companies poured billions into innovation, launching new features with the urgency of a fire drill. They spent years borrowing each other's best ideas and then pretending they invented them. Android had widgets first. Apple eventually introduced widgets, polished them, and made them "revolutionary." Apple rolled out Face ID; Google countered with fingerprint sensors under glass. Android introduced split-screen multitasking; Apple nodded approvingly and eventually did the same. It became a game of feature leapfrog, where each advancement by one platform nudged the other forward. And while the marketing departments battled for hearts, minds, and wallet space, users quietly enjoyed the benefits of this relentless one-upmanship.

Samsung became a major player in the Android ecosystem in 2009 and its influence on mobile operating systems is undeniable. Samsung didn't just use Android; it heavily customized it. Its One UI skin adds unique features, optimizations, and a distinct design language that differentiates Samsung devices from other Android phones. Samsung is one of the few companies that manufactures its own processors, displays, and memory chips, allowing it to push Android's capabilities further. Features like foldable screens, high-refresh-rate displays, and advanced camera tech often debut on Samsung devices before becoming industry standards. Samsung has built an entire ecosystem around Android, including smartwatches, tablets, and even Windows-integrated features. Its Galaxy ecosystem rivals Apple's in terms of seamless device interaction.

One of the most game-changing moments in this saga came with the arrival of the App Store. Apple introduced it in 2008, opening the floodgates for developers and giving birth to the modern app economy. Google's version, the Android Market (later rebranded as Google Play), followed swiftly. Suddenly, smartphones weren't just phones—they were portals to infinite possibilities. Need to meditate, track your steps, order Thai food, or identify a constellation? There's an app for that. Actually, there are 37, and they're all trying to send you push notifications.

The app stores didn't just enhance functionality—they redefined the smartphone's purpose. Devices that once served primarily as communication tools morphed into personal assistants, gaming consoles, and scalable workstations—often all at once. And with every download came deeper user engagement, further entrenching people within their chosen ecosystem. The more you relied on your OS for apps, cloud storage, syncing, and services, the harder it became to switch teams.

Of course, not every contender in the OS battlefield fared so well. Remember Windows Mobile? BlackBerry OS? Symbian? If you do, congratulations: you're old enough to remember when phones had physical keyboards and battery life that lasted more than a day. These operating systems tried valiantly to stake a claim in the mobile world, but were eventually outpaced by iOS and Android's sheer momentum. Their downfalls weren't just technical—they were ecosystem collapses. Without a robust app library, consistent updates, and compelling user experience, these platforms faded into tech nostalgia, remembered mostly as trivia questions and cautionary tales.

The success of iOS and Android wasn't just about market share—it was about building empires. Both companies expanded their operating systems into sprawling ecosystems that now include smartwatches, tablets, smart speakers, TVs, and cars. Apple's ecosystem is famously hermetic—beautiful, secure, and nearly impossible to escape without a data migration plan and a stiff drink. Google's ecosystem is more porous but arguably more expansive, integrating with everything from your email to your thermostat. The result? A world where your phone isn't just a device; it's the remote control for your entire digital life.

And let's not pretend this is just about convenience. With great ecosystem power comes great data responsibility. Both companies have faced scrutiny over privacy, data collection, and the long-term consequences of platform lock-in. Apple has positioned itself as the champion of user privacy, introducing features like App Tracking Transparency and on-device Siri processing. Google, while not exactly throwing open the vault, has made strides in offering users more control over their data and ad preferences. Still, the tug-of-war between convenience and privacy continues to play out in software updates and developer policies. And the war doesn't stop at phones—it extends to wearables, smart home ecosystems, and services. iOS users are deep in Apple's world—Apple Watch, iCloud, AirDrop, iMessage, and Apple Arcade. Android users enjoy broader compatibility with Google services, Samsung's ecosystem, and a wider variety of smart home integrations.

In their quest for digital supremacy, both Apple and Google have also leaned heavily into emerging technologies. AI and ML now underpin everything from predictive text to photo categorization. Virtual assistants—Siri and Google Assistant (replaced in 2024 by Gemini, its AI-powered Assistant)—have become digital butlers, managing calendars, setting reminders, and occasionally mishearing everything you say. Meanwhile, both platforms are planting flags in the future: augmented reality, spatial computing, and the ever-ambiguous "metaverse" are the next frontier in this rivalry.

Even the networks that power these devices are evolving. With 5G rolling out across the globe and murmurs of 6G already starting, mobile operating systems are being designed not just for today's capabilities, but for tomorrow's bandwidth bonanza. Faster networks mean richer apps, more immersive experiences, and—because nothing's perfect—larger updates that eat your data plan like popcorn.

So, what's next in the iOS versus Android saga? Will Apple continue its slow expansion into health tech and Augmented Reality (AR) headsets? Will Google finally convince the world its Pixel phones are more than just clever experiments? Will we all eventually speak to our devices more than we do to actual humans?

The battle between iOS and Android will continue evolving. Whether you swear loyalty to Apple's refined experience or Android's chaotic creativity, one thing is certain: this rivalry isn't going anywhere. And thank goodness for that. Without it, we'd likely be stuck with fewer features, less innovation, and far more boring keynote presentations. The digital duel between iOS and Android has become one of the most productive rivalries in tech history—pushing boundaries, challenging norms, and ensuring that no matter your preference, your smartphone is smarter today because somewhere, someone's OS team is furiously trying to outdo the other. In the end, we all win.

Mobile Apps and the App Economy: Transforming How We Interact with Technology

The proliferation of smartphones, fueled by the iOS and Android rivalry, created a fertile ground for a new phenomenon: the app economy. The introduction of the App Store by Apple in 2008, followed swiftly by Google's Android Market (later the Google Play Store), fundamentally altered the way we interacted with technology. Suddenly, the capabilities of these pocket-sized computers were no longer limited by their pre-installed software. A vibrant ecosystem of third-party applications emerged, transforming smartphones from simple communication devices into powerful, personalized digital hubs.

This wasn't just a matter of quantity—it was a seismic shift in quality and accessibility. The app store model democratized software development. Before, creating and distributing software often required navigating complex distribution channels and hefty licensing fees. App stores, by contrast, handed out the keys to the castle. Independent developers, hobbyists, and startups suddenly had a global stage. No need for distribution deals or licensing gymnastics—just code, submit, and (hopefully) go viral. This led to an explosion in the number and variety of apps available, catering to virtually every conceivable need and interest. The sheer volume of choice, often overwhelming, became a defining characteristic of the smartphone experience.

And oh, the variety. Need to track your steps, your sleep, or your mood? There's an app for that. Want to simulate a lightsaber? Naturally, there's one for that too. The sheer abundance of options became a defining feature—and occasional frustration—of the smartphone era. Choice, in all its overwhelming glory, became the norm. Users were no longer just consumers of technology; they were curators of their own digital experience, endlessly swiping between options in a quest for the perfect calendar app that also tells jokes.

But some apps didn't just fill a niche; they redefined the landscape. Angry Birds, for example, proved that flinging birds at pigs could be a billion-dollar idea and that mobile gaming wasn't just a distraction—it was a serious business. Social media giants like Facebook and Twitter morphed to fit the mobile mold, making it easier than ever to share thoughts, photos, and unsolicited opinions from anywhere, including your dentist's waiting room. Navigation apps like Google Maps and Apple Maps (iMaps) transformed the way we travel, replacing the glovebox full of crumpled MapQuest printouts and gas station map foldouts with real-time GPS guidance and passive-aggressive rerouting suggestions. Now getting lost was a luxury we could quickly rectify.

These weren't just miniature versions of desktop programs. They were purpose-built for the smartphone's unique talents: touchscreens, GPS, accelerometers, cameras, and, perhaps most importantly, our insatiable desire to tap, swipe, and scroll through life. Developers quickly learned to design for constraints: smaller screens, shorter attention spans, and battery life that disappears faster than your willpower during a midnight snack run. This gave rise to mobile-first design—a philosophy that didn't just adapt desktop experiences for phones, but reinvented them entirely. The gravity of software development shifted firmly into the mobile orbit, with desktop apps increasingly feeling like the older sibling your parents still love but don't post about on social media.

But the app economy wasn't just about convenience or entertainment—it rewired entire industries. The gig economy, for example, owes much of its existence to mobile apps. Uber and Lyft connected drivers with passengers faster than you could say "taxi!" Airbnb turned spare bedrooms into income streams. TaskRabbit made it possible to outsource life's most tedious chores with a few screen taps. Combined with geolocation, mobile payments, and real-time feedback, these apps didn't just offer new services; they built entirely new economic models. Suddenly, the phrase "there's an app for that" became less of a gimmick and more of a business strategy.

Retail was another casualty or, depending on your perspective, beneficiary, of the app explosion. E-commerce giants and upstarts alike rushed to develop mobile apps that let consumers shop from bed, from the train, or while pretending to pay attention in meetings. Food delivery went from novelty to necessity, with apps like DoorDash, Grubhub, and Uber Eats turning the restaurant industry into a digital buffet. Restaurants that once relied on foot traffic now had to optimize for screen traffic, leading to ghost kitchens, app-exclusive menus, and the rise of the "30-minute gourmet."

The success of these apps was, in part, due to their ability to leverage the smartphone's inherent features. GPS and location services became integral components, allowing for hyper-localized services and experiences. Camera functionality powered photo-sharing and augmented reality applications. The touchscreen interface, initially considered revolutionary, became the standard interaction model. Developers learned to optimize their apps for the constraints and capabilities of mobile devices, resulting in a unique design language and user experience tailored to the small screen. The development of mobile-first design became a critical skill for software developers. This focus on mobile-first over desktop-first shifted the technological center of gravity toward mobile experiences.

The rise of the app economy also had significant societal implications. Mobile apps became integral to our daily lives, from managing our finances, scheduling coffee dates, and keeping our social circles buzzing to scheduling our appointments. The constant connectivity enabled by smartphones fostered a sense of immediacy and accessibility, blurring the lines between our professional and personal lives. The rise of social media platforms on mobile also reshaped the way we interact socially, creating both opportunities for connection and challenges regarding privacy and misinformation and that ever-looming FOMO (Fear of Missing Out). Constant connectivity means our to-do lists now double as conversation starters at dinner parties. The app economy presented both remarkable opportunities and unforeseen challenges.

This brave new app-enabled world wasn't without its growing pains. With millions of apps flooding the marketplaces, discovery became a modern-day scavenger hunt. For every brilliant app solving a real problem, there were ten that were either useless, shady, or both. App fatigue set in—users tired of downloading, deleting, and managing a digital junk drawer of apps they used once to scan a QR code at a taco truck. To cut through the noise, developers embraced App Store Optimization (ASO), the dark arts of keyword placement, catchy icons, and borderline mystical user review strategies designed to make apps more visible and more clickable.

Security and privacy concerns also came into sharp focus. With so many apps collecting data, sometimes a little too enthusiastically, users started to question what, exactly, they were agreeing to in those 47-page terms and conditions. Some apps were caught red-handed hoarding location data, contact lists, or other personal information that had nothing to do with their stated purpose.

Regulators began to notice, and so did users. Transparency became the buzzword of the moment, as did "permissions fatigue"—a condition wherein users blindly approve whatever access an app requests just to start using it already.

Monetization strategies added another layer of intrigue—and controversy. The free-to-play model lured users in with promises of zero cost, only to bombard them with in-app purchases, gem packs, loot boxes, and "special offers" timed with psychological precision. For some developers, it was a goldmine. For some parents, it was a $300 surprise credit card bill. Concerns about addictive mechanics, particularly in apps targeted at children, led to calls for stricter oversight and ethical standards in app design. The line between engagement and exploitation remains blurry, and navigating it has become a full-time job for developers, regulators, and app store moderators alike. Despite these challenges, the app economy shows no signs of slowing down. In fact, it's accelerating—driven by advances in AI, ML, and connectivity. AI-powered apps can now anticipate your needs, suggest your next meal, or compose your next email. Augmented reality apps turn your living room into a spaceship, your face into a dog, or your wall into a virtual furniture showroom. The rollout of 5G networks opens the door to even more ambitious apps, from cloud gaming to real-time language translation that doesn't require shouting slowly at confused tourists.

Mobile payments, too, are surging—turning phones into wallets, banks, and budgeting assistants. With a couple of taps, you can pay for coffee, split dinner, or invest in digital currency. The intertwining of mobile tech and financial services is creating new opportunities—and new headaches—for developers, consumers, and regulators alike.

In the grand narrative of technological progress, the rise of mobile apps represents a plot twist few saw coming, but everyone's now starring in. These tiny programs have not only redefined how we use our devices but also how we live, work, shop, play, date, eat, and sleep (or don't). They've created industries, toppled others, and embedded themselves so deeply in our routines that it's hard to imagine life without them—or at least without the weather app.

The Societal Impact of Smartphones: Connectivity, Convenience, and Concerns

Smartphones: those sleek, glowing rectangles that somehow manage to be alarm clocks, personal assistants, entertainment centers, workstations, and—on rare occasions—actual phones. These pocket-sized powerhouses have not only infiltrated our lives; they've practically set up permanent residence. Once upon a time, staying in touch meant scribbling letters, waiting for dial-up, or hollering into a landline like someone trying to reach the other side of the planet. Now, with smartphones, you can video-call your cousin Vini in Italy while ordering a cannoli and texting your boss that you'll be "just five minutes late." Communication has become frictionless, borderless, and, sometimes, boundary-less. This pervasive influence, however, isn't a monolith; it's a complex interplay of advantages and disadvantages, conveniences and concerns. Their impact on society is vast, dynamic, and as contradictory as a group chat at 2 a.m. Let's delve into the multifaceted societal impact of these pocket-sized powerhouses.

One of the most immediate and obvious impacts is enhanced connectivity. A deepened sense of global community. Before the smartphone era, staying connected often meant being tethered to a landline or a bulky laptop. The smartphone, with its always-on internet access and a multitude of communication apps, shattered those limitations. Families separated by continents can video chat with ease, colleagues can collaborate on projects in real-time across time zones, and friends can maintain relationships regardless of physical distance. News travels at the speed of a Tweet, and access to information is no longer confined to encyclopedias or that one friend who "knows everything." This increased connectivity has fostered a sense of global community, allowing for instant communication and information sharing on an unprecedented scale. It's facilitated the rapid spread of news, ideas, and cultural trends, effectively shrinking the world and fostering a greater sense of interconnectedness.

However, this constant connectivity also has a dark side. The expectation of instant responses and the constant bombardment of notifications can contribute to stress, anxiety, and a blurring of the boundaries between work and personal life. The phenomenon of "always-on" culture, while promoting efficiency in some respects, can also lead to burnout and a diminished sense of personal time. The rise of "always-on" culture means work emails follow you into the weekend, group chats ping through dinner, and social media keeps you mentally tethered to everyone else's highlight reel. The result? A generation that's both hyper-connected and, paradoxically, perpetually exhausted. Notifications have become the modern-day equivalent of Pavlov's bell—except instead of drooling, we're anxiously checking our screens every 2.6 seconds.

Beyond communication, smartphones have brought unparalleled convenience to countless aspects of daily life. So, let's give a standing ovation to convenience. Need a ride? Tap. Craving sushi? Swipe.

Want to know the weather in England or how many steps you've taken since breakfast? Your smartphone is already ten steps ahead. These devices have streamlined daily life to the point where we now expect everything—transportation, shopping, education, and entertainment—to arrive on demand, preferably with tracking and a 4.9-star rating.

Need to find the nearest coffee shop? A quick search on Google Maps provides directions. Want to book a flight or hotel room? Numerous travel apps offer seamless booking experiences. Need to order groceries or dinner? A plethora of delivery apps cater to every culinary desire. The convenience is undeniable, streamlining daily tasks and freeing up time for other activities. This convenience, however, comes at a cost. Over-reliance on apps and digital services can lead to a decline in certain essential life skills, such as map-reading or face-to-face communication. And while video calls and emojis have become the new love language, traditional social skills like making eye contact or enduring small talk with a stranger have taken a quiet sabbatical. The ease of accessing information online can also reduce our motivation to learn or remember things independently, fostering a reliance on readily available digital information.

The smartphone's societal impact extends into the realm of commerce, fundamentally altering shopping habits and creating new economic opportunities. The economic ripple effects are seismic. Smartphones have revolutionized retail with mobile shopping apps that let you buy socks while waiting in line for coffee. E-commerce giants and microbusinesses alike have flourished in this new digital bazaar. Meanwhile, brick-and-mortar stores have watched foot traffic vanish faster than a sale on Black Friday. The gig economy, powered almost entirely by apps, has changed the labor landscape. Now, anyone with a smartphone and a car can become a driver, a food courier, or a freelance dog-walker—all without ever printing a résumé.

Yet, this gig-fueled freedom comes with strings. Flexibility is great until it's paired with zero benefits, no job security, and a rating system that can make or break your income based on whether someone liked the way you handed them their latte. As traditional job structures erode, society faces new questions about labor rights, fair compensation, and what it really means to "be your own boss" when your employment can be terminated by an algorithm.

Social interaction, too, has been reborn—and not always in flattering ways. Social media apps, which live and breathe on smartphones, have redefined how we connect. Want to share your vacation, your thoughts, your breakfast? There's an audience for that. Online communities offer support, shared interests, and a way to stay in touch that doesn't require dressing up (provided you have your screen monitor off). The impact on social interactions is perhaps one of the most debated aspects of the smartphone revolution. Social media apps, accessed primarily through smartphones, have transformed how we connect with others. These platforms provide avenues for building and maintaining relationships, sharing experiences, and participating in online communities. They allow for quick and easy communication across geographic boundaries, fostering a sense of community for people with shared interests or backgrounds. However, this increased connectivity can also lead to social isolation and a decrease in face-to-face interactions. Face-to-face conversations have been replaced by thumbs-up icons. The curated nature of online profiles can contribute to unrealistic comparisons and feelings of inadequacy. Furthermore, the anonymity afforded by online platforms can embolden negative behaviors such as cyberbullying and the spread of misinformation. The constant comparison with others' perfect online lives can contribute to anxiety and depression, particularly among younger generations.

Alone Togetherness: The Art of Being Socially Antisocial

Picture this: four teens in a booth, fries cooling, sodas sweating, and not a single eye meeting another. Welcome to the age of Alone Togetherness, where proximity is plentiful but presence is scarce.

In the analog days, a booth meant whispered secrets, ketchup debates, and maybe a flirtatious kick under the table. Today? It's a silent symphony of thumbs tapping screens, each teen orbiting their own digital universe while sharing the same vinyl cushion.

Used by permission: larrywhatley.org

They're together, technically. But emotionally? They might as well be on separate continents, each one livestreaming their solitude to a curated audience of strangers.

Alone togetherness is the magical, slightly ridiculous trick our phones pull—like a stage magician who insists you really are part of the act—where push notifications turn glowing rectangles into portals of "together-but-apart" connection. Every alert—be it a friend's " 💧 " reaction to your photo, a breaking news headline about an escaped zoo penguin, or your calendar's passive-aggressive reminder that "Yoga starts in 10 minutes"—is basically a tap on the shoulder from the collective hive mind. In that brief moment between the screen lighting up and your thumb swooping in, millions of brains hum in sync, like a chorus of caffeinated bees.

Suddenly, your peaceful solitude has been upgraded (or downgraded) into "ambient belonging"—a kind of background social noise that follows you from the couch to the bathroom, across time zones, and through airport security. You're alone… but also not alone… but also still kind of alone. It's complicated.

This together-apart fusion has its charms. There's something oddly comforting about knowing that strangers across the planet are watching the same live-streamed eclipse, or mutually gasping at a celebrity breakup as if we were all in the same living room eating chips. But there's also a catch: the never-ending ping parade can turn your focus into confetti and make your brain feel less like a cathedral of private thought and more like a noisy food court where everyone's shouting "LOOK AT THIS" at the same time.

And in that blur, the "one" in alone togetherness starts to fade. Your inner monologue gets drowned out by the crowd's playlist, and suddenly your personal reflections are elbowed aside by memes, hot takes, and someone's cousin's lasagna recipe. We've invented a form of proximity where we can be in our own bubble… inside someone else's bubble… inside everyone's bubble. It's like emotional Russian nesting dolls, but with Wi-Fi. In the end, alone togetherness is both our modern superpower and our Achilles' heel: proof we can all be connected without ever really making eye contact.

So next time you see a booth full of quiet scrollers, don't judge too harshly. They're not ignoring each other—they're practicing a new kind of intimacy. One where the heart-to-heart has been replaced by the screen-to-screen.

So, what about privacy? This is a quaint notion in the smartphone age. These devices are data-hungry little spies, collecting everything from your location to your bedtime scrolling habits. Many apps track user behavior with a persistence that would make a private detective blush. The convenience offered by smartphones raises concerns regarding privacy and data security. Many apps collect vast amounts of personal data, including location information, browsing history, and personal preferences. The ethical implications of this data collection are substantial, particularly when data is used for targeted advertising or even sold to third parties. This raises concerns about surveillance and the potential misuse of personal information. Moreover, the security of this data is often questionable, with apps vulnerable to hacking and data breaches. The increasing reliance on smartphones for financial transactions has also made individuals more vulnerable to cybercrime and financial fraud. Educating the public about these risks and advocating for stronger data privacy regulations are vital for mitigating these challenges. It's clear that cybersecurity is no longer just an IT department problem—it's everyone's problem. The more we rely on smartphones, the more we expose ourselves to fraud, phishing, and the digital equivalent of pickpocketing.

Education has also undergone a smartphone-fueled transformation. On the plus side, students can access online courses, language apps, and a world of resources with just a few taps. Classrooms have embraced educational apps that make learning more engaging and personalized, turning dull lectures into interactive experiences.

But smartphones in classrooms are a double-edged stylus. They're portals to knowledge—and distractions. Teachers now compete not only with each other but with TikTok trends, mobile games, and group chats happening mid-lecture. Cheating via smartphone has become a digital art form, and attention spans are shrinking faster than your phone battery at 2%. The challenge lies in making educational tech work for, not against, the goals of learning.

Speaking of distraction, let's talk entertainment. With streaming services, social media, and endless games just a finger flick away, boredom has been effectively outlawed. Smartphones offer a 24/7 buffet of dopamine: binge-worthy shows, viral videos, and games designed to keep you glued to the screen until your retinas beg for mercy.

But convenience can quickly become compulsion. Excessive screen time is linked to sleep issues, lower attention spans, and the disconcerting realization that you've spent four hours watching people organize their pantries. For younger users, exposure to inappropriate content and the addictive nature of some platforms is a growing concern. And yet, try prying a smartphone from a teenager's hands and you'll understand just how thoroughly these devices have woven themselves into modern adolescence.

And then there's politics—that messy, noisy realm that smartphones have dragged into the digital spotlight. Social media platforms, accessed primarily through smartphones, have become battlegrounds for political discourse, activism, and, unfortunately, disinformation. On one hand, these platforms empower grassroots movements, enable real-time protests, and give citizens direct access to leaders. On the other, they've been weaponized for propaganda, election interference, and the spreading of conspiracy theories faster than fact-checkers can blink.

In this environment, the smartphone is both the megaphone and the echo chamber—amplifying voices, but often trapping them in bubbles of algorithmic affirmation. Ensuring these platforms remain tools for democracy rather than threats to it is a challenge that policymakers, tech companies, and users will need to face head-on, preferably without shouting in ALL CAPS.

The societal impact of smartphones is a complex and multifaceted phenomenon. While they have brought undeniable convenience and enhanced connectivity, they have also presented significant challenges. Addressing the concerns surrounding data privacy, mental health, misinformation, and social isolation requires a multi-pronged approach involving technological innovation, regulatory oversight, public education, and a mindful approach to our own smartphone usage.

So, where does that leave us? With a device that's part miracle, part menace. Smartphones have redefined convenience, connection, and culture. But they've also introduced new complications—blurring boundaries, raising ethical questions, and occasionally turning us into screen-addicted zombies with impressive thumb dexterity.

The solution isn't to toss our phones into the nearest lake (though that may sound tempting after revising autocorrection for the fifth time). Instead, we must learn to live with our devices mindfully. That means advocating for stronger data regulations, promoting digital literacy, setting limits, and—radical thought—occasionally putting the phone down.

The story of the smartphone is far from over; its ongoing evolution will continue to shape the future of society in ways we can only begin to imagine. The challenge lies not in rejecting this revolutionary technology, but in harnessing its power responsibly and mitigating its potential downsides to create a more equitable and informed society. Whether it becomes a tale of empowerment or entrapment depends on how we choose to wield it. Like any powerful tool, a smartphone's greatest impact lies not in what it can do, but in how we decide to use it.

Anecdotes, Musings, and Recollections

Here are a few tongue-in-cheek anecdotes for the cell phone:

Boomers (Age 60+)

- Have their iPhone font size cranked up so high, texts look like a billboard.
- Think emojis are cutting-edge technology—*thumbs-up emoji* is their go-to response.

Gen X (Age 40-59)

- The most practical users—whichever phone doesn't interrupt their coffee, they'll take.
- iPhone users love Apple's walled garden: "It just works." Android users fire back: "Yeah, but my phone costs half as much."
- Secretly wish they could go back to BlackBerry because "Physical keyboards were peak civilization."

Millennials (Age 25-39)

- They were the last ones to experience life *before* smartphones, so they sometimes stare at trees in nostalgia.
- Low-key, annoyed when their parents ask for tech help: "No, Mom, your phone is not broken. It's on silent."
- Keep switching between phones while claiming loyalty to a brand.

Gen Z (Age 10-24)

- Phones are their life support. Take it away? Instant panic attack!
- Android users, frustrated: "My phone can do EVERYTHING!" iPhone users, sipping iced coffee: "Really? Can it FaceTime?"
- Somehow know which emojis are cool and which ones will get you socially canceled.

Kids (0-9)

- Have already mastered touch screens before knowing how to write their name.
- Think iPads are the TV.
- Can operate YouTube better than their parents.
- Have no idea what a landline is, and if you show them a flip phone, they'll ask if it's from the caveman era.

CHAPTER 9

Artificial Intelligence:
From Science Fiction to Reality

From Fiction to Function: Sci-Fi's Blueprint for Innovation

Early science fiction writers weren't just storytellers—they were visionaries who helped shape the technological imagination long before the tools existed to build it. Their speculative worlds laid the groundwork for many of the innovations we now take for granted.

Take Dick Tracy, for example. When Chester Gould introduced the wrist communicator in the 1946 comic strip, it was pure fantasy—a detective speaking into a watch to communicate wirelessly. Today, smartwatches like the Apple Watch and Samsung Galaxy Watch make that concept a reality, complete with voice calls, GPS, and biometric sensors. What was once pulp fiction is now wrist-mounted computing.

Wikipedia, CC BY-SA 4.0

Writers like Arthur C. Clarke and Isaac Asimov pushed even further. Clarke famously predicted satellite communications in 1945, decades before the first satellite launched. His idea of geostationary satellites became the backbone of global broadcasting and GPS. Asimov's Robot series didn't just imagine intelligent machines—it laid out ethical frameworks like the Three Laws of Robotics, which still influence AI safety discussions today. Even Star Trek's communicators and tricorders inspired real-world mobile phones and medical diagnostic tools.

Science fiction didn't just forecast gadgets—it shaped how engineers and designers think. It gave permission to dream boldly, to imagine interfaces, vehicles, and systems that defied the constraints of the present. Today's autonomous cars, virtual reality, and even neural implants owe a debt to the genre's audacity. Sci-fi didn't just predict the future—it dared us to build it.

Early AI Concepts and Research: The Foundations of the Field

The origins of AI might sound like something straight out of a futuristic novel—actually, its conceptual seeds were sown in the imaginative playground of science fiction long before audiences

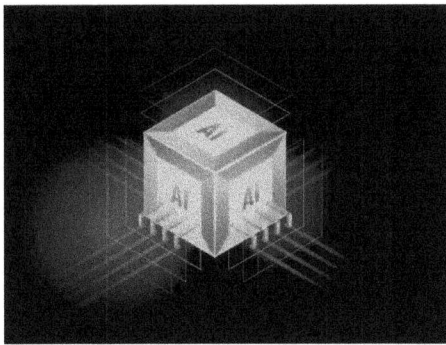

Pixabay

morphed into devoted fans of chilling, computer-mediated monologues. Even before the sinister glow of HAL 9000's unblinking eye could charm and terrify us in 2001: A Space Odyssey, mathematicians, logicians, and computer scientists were busy engaging in intellectual espionage and daring to dream that thinking machines weren't just science fiction fodder. These early pioneers, working in relative isolation, built the very bedrock upon which today's dazzling AI systems now stand. Their work, merging brash ambition with painstaking meticulousness and dazzling insight, wasn't always met with wide-eyed acclaim or budgetary support, but then again, few revolutions ever are.

One cannot discuss the origins of AI without mentioning Alan Turing, often considered to be the Father of Computer Science. In the 1930s, he introduced the world to the Turing machine—a theoretical marvel that, while not an AI system in itself, boldly proclaimed that any problem, if computable, could be solved by a machine even if that machine existed only in the realm of abstraction. This abstract concept profoundly impacted the emerging field of computer science, laying the groundwork for the development of actual computers—the very hardware that would eventually house AI. Turing didn't stop at theory and abstract machinery;

Wikipedia, CC BY-SA 4.0

he also devised the "Imitation Game" (now famously known as the Turing Test), a thought experiment that dared us to question whether a machine could exhibit intelligent behavior indistinguishable from human behavior to the point of deception. Even now, his ideas continue to kindle debates on the elusive nature of intelligence—prompting ongoing reflection on the nature of intelligence itself.

After World War II, a new intellectual fad took hold: cybernetics. This was not, as the name might suggest, a Marvel villain's origin story (Cyber or Deathlok, anyone?), but rather a serious inquiry into how machines and organisms use feedback to regulate themselves. Norbert Wiener led the charge here, proposing that systems—mechanical or biological—could learn and adapt using feedback loops, an idea that would later influence AI. Wiener was a brilliant mathematician, philosopher, and early computer scientist who laid the groundwork for the field of cybernetics—the study of communication and control in machines and living organisms. Wiener's work nudged AI researchers toward the radical idea that machines might not just follow rules—they could modify them. This was revolutionary thinking at the time and became a crucial stepping stone toward machines that could learn from experience, not just execute instructions.

Wikipedia, CC BY-SA 4.0

Then came the Dartmouth Workshop of 1956, often celebrated as the definitive "birth" of AI as a formal field of study. The workshop was organized by legends like John McCarthy (pioneered the concept of time-sharing systems and is often called "the father of AI"), Marvin Minsky (co-founded the MIT AI Lab and contributed significantly to neural networks, ML, and robotics), Claude Shannon (known as the "father of information theory"), and Nathaniel Rochester (helped design the IBM 701 and contributed to early ML and pattern recognition efforts). This gathering was less a grand unveiling of fully functional thinking machines and more a spirited brainstorming session among a select circle of audacious intellectuals. No, they didn't build a mechanical Einstein during their stay, but they did gift us the term "artificial intelligence" and a shared mission. This seminal meeting laid the intellectual and collaborative framework that would nurture and fuel AI research over the ensuing decades.

In the wake of Dartmouth, researchers dove into various subfields of AI, one of the earliest being game-playing algorithms. Arthur Samuel's checkers program, emerging in the late 1950s, was a trailblazer: it wasn't content with mindlessly following the rulebook but actually learned from its victories and defeats. This wasn't just about teaching a machine how to play a game—it was a bold hint at the potential of machines to learn from experience. It was a genuine proof of concept for ML. The controlled yet competitive environment of a game, with its clearly delineated rules, provided the ideal testing ground for these emerging ideas. It was as if the program was saying, "Watch me adapt and improve—one diagonal move at a time." The program could improve its strategies over time, not by divine inspiration, but by analyzing past games. This was a far cry from the rigid, rule-based programming common at the time.

Another early obsession was natural language processing (NLP), which proved far trickier than expected. Early researchers attempted to create programs that could understand and generate human language, which turned out to be more like deciphering an alien language than programming. While the progress was slow, with programs initially struggling to handle even the most basic grammatical structures, these early efforts laid the foundation for today's advanced NLP systems, capable of translation, text summarization, and even creative writing. The challenges inherent in human language, including its nuances, ambiguity, and cultural variations, proved remarkably difficult to overcome, highlighting the complexity of true language understanding. But even these stumbling first steps laid the groundwork for today's chatbots, virtual assistants, and multilingual translation engines that can (usually) tell the difference between "Let's eat, Grandma" and "Let's eat Grandma."

Expert systems emerged as a prominent area of AI research during the 1970s and 80s. The idea was to hard-code expertise into a machine, turning it into a digital know-it-all for specific tasks. For example, expert systems were developed for diagnosing illnesses, predicting stock market trends, or locating oil reserves. While they dazzled in demo mode, these systems often proved as brittle as a house of cards during a sneeze. They were effective within their limited domains, but they often proved inelastic and challenging to maintain, struggling to adapt to new information or changing circumstances. While their success highlighted the importance of knowledge representation and reasoning, it also exposed the limitations of purely rule-based approaches. The reliance on explicitly programmed rules made these systems inflexible and susceptible to errors when confronted with situations outside their pre-defined parameters. Intelligence isn't just about knowing things—it's about knowing what to do when you don't know.

Symbolic AI, dominant in the early years, focused on representing knowledge using symbols and manipulating these symbols through logical rules. This approach, although successful in certain domains, faced challenges in addressing the complexities of real-world scenarios. The so-called "symbol grounding problem," for instance, highlighted the difficulty of connecting symbolic representations to the physical world, limiting their applicability in tasks requiring direct interaction with the environment. It asked the awkward question, How does a symbol like 'apple' actually connect to the red, round, delicious object it represents? Without direct sensory linkage, these systems could juggle symbols endlessly without ever knowing what they truly meant. It was like trying to understand a foreign language using only a dictionary written in that same language. It served as a stark reminder that translating real-world complexity into neat, logical structures is no small feat.

In response to the shortcomings of symbolic AI, some researchers dusted off an older idea with a fresh coat of paint: connectionism, now affectionately referred to as artificial neural networks (ANNs). Inspired by the structure of the human brain, ANNs consist of interconnected nodes (neurons) that process information in parallel—essentially a mathematical nod to human neurons firing away in the pursuit of understanding. Unlike symbolic systems, ANNs learn from data, adjusting the weights of connections between neurons to improve performance. While neural networks had been proposed earlier, their practical application was hampered by limited computing power. Once technology caught up, these models staged a roaring comeback. With the influx of powerful processors and vast datasets, the deep learning revolution was set into motion, proving that sometimes, brains—even artificial ones—need a little boost. It wasn't until faster processors and big data came along that neural networks went from academic curiosities to the engines behind facial recognition, self-driving cars, and recommendation algorithms that know your guilty pleasures better than your best friend.

It's important to note that AI's trajectory wasn't exactly a rocket ship. It was more like a roller coaster—thrilling highs followed by stomach-churning drops, known in the trade as "AI winters." These were periods when the hype outpaced the hardware and funding dried up faster than a puddle in the Sahara. But every winter eventually gave way to a new spring, with researchers finding novel ways to address old problems. These periods of stagnation were often followed by renewed innovation, leading to breakthroughs and advancements that addressed the shortcomings of previous approaches. The history of AI is, therefore, a fascinating narrative of progress, setbacks, and unexpected turns, highlighting the persistence and ingenuity of the researchers who have devoted their careers to this challenging field. Each setback, each frosty "AI winter," served as both a humbling lesson and a stepping stone, nudging the field ever closer to creating systems that could emulate human thought.

The early days of AI research also saw significant contributions from less celebrated figures. Many researchers labored in the shadows, far from the limelight. Their efforts in areas such as ML, computer vision, and robotics may have gone unnoticed, yet their quiet diligence has accumulated to form the critical underpinnings of modern AI. Their individual contributions, often unrecognized outside their immediate circles, collectively formed a crucial part of the foundation upon which modern AI is built. Their work often involved developing algorithms and optimizing code on limited hardware, a testament to the dedication and resourcefulness required in the early years of the field. The stories of these less prominent pioneers serve as a reminder of the collaborative nature of scientific progress, where the grand narrative of innovation is not just written by the celebrated few but by a chorus of determined voices working in harmony.

The Rise of Machine Learning: Algorithms That Learn from Data

The journey from symbolic AI, with its rigid rules and pre-programmed logic, to the data-driven world of ML was a significant paradigm shift. While symbolic AI aimed to imbue machines with intelligence through explicit programming, mimicking human reasoning processes, ML took a different track. It sought to create systems that could learn from data, adapting and improving their performance without needing to be explicitly programmed for every possible scenario. This represented a move towards more flexible, adaptable, and ultimately, more intelligent systems.

One of the earliest examples of this paradigm shift can be seen in the work of Arthur Samuel, whose checkers-playing program, mentioned earlier, demonstrated the power of learning through experience. Samuel's program didn't simply rely on a fixed set of rules. Instead, it used a technique called reinforcement learning, where the program learned by playing numerous games against itself, refining its strategy based on the outcomes. Wins resulted in reinforcing successful moves, while losses prompted adjustments. This iterative process of learning from successes and failures, a core tenet of ML, enabled the program to significantly improve its performance over time. It continued to improve until it could surpass its own creator. This wasn't just a neat party trick—it was a revelation. It was a seminal moment, demonstrating that machines could, in fact, learn and adapt without explicit human intervention beyond the initial algorithm design. And with that revelation, the floodgates of innovation swung open.

The foundational algorithms of ML are surprisingly diverse, each tackling the problem of learning from data in a slightly different way. Supervised learning, perhaps the most intuitive approach, involves training a model on a labeled dataset. This means that the correct answer or classification accompanies each data point. For example, in image recognition, a supervised learning algorithm might be trained on a dataset of images labeled with the objects they depict (e.g., "cat," "dog," "car"). The algorithm learns to map the visual features of the images to their corresponding labels, allowing it to classify new, unseen images with reasonable accuracy. The algorithm essentially learns a function that maps inputs (images) to outputs (labels). The success of supervised learning hinges on the quality and quantity of the labeled data; a poorly labeled dataset will lead to a poorly performing model. In other words, as we said in the old days, garbage in, garbage out.

Unsupervised learning, in contrast, deals with unlabeled data. The algorithm is tasked with identifying patterns and structures within the data without predefined categories. Clustering algorithms, for instance, group similar data points together, revealing inherent structures in the data. Imagine applying this to customer purchase data. An unsupervised learning algorithm could identify clusters of customers with similar buying habits, allowing businesses to tailor their marketing strategies more effectively. Give it customer purchase histories, and it might reveal that your buyers fall into categories like "impulse spenders" or "bargain hunters." Dimensionality reduction techniques, another branch of unsupervised learning, aim to simplify complex datasets by reducing the number of variables while retaining important information. This is invaluable in situations where dealing with high-dimensional data becomes computationally expensive or statistically unwieldy. The strength of unsupervised learning lies in its ability to uncover hidden patterns and insights from raw, unlabeled data while weeding out the less useful variables.

Reinforcement learning, as demonstrated by Samuel's checkers program, focuses on learning through interaction within an environment. An agent, or algorithm, takes actions within an environment and receives rewards or penalties based on the outcomes. The goal is to learn a policy that maximizes the cumulative reward over time. This approach is particularly well-suited for problems where explicit programming is difficult, such as robotics control or game playing. Consider a robot learning to walk. Through trial and error, guided by reinforcement signals (rewards for successful steps, penalties for falls), the robot learns to coordinate its movements, improving its gait over time. Eventually, it struts like it owns the place. The beauty of reinforcement learning lies in its ability to adapt to dynamic environments and learn complex behaviors without explicit programming of each movement. This may not be the most elegant approach, but it sure gets the job done—and sometimes, that's all the science really demands.

Of course, algorithms alone did not catapult ML into the limelight. And, the rise of ML was not solely fueled by the development of new algorithms. The true game-changers were the exponential growth in computing power and the availability of massive datasets. The algorithms themselves had been conceived many decades earlier (see Chapter 5), but they were about as practical as growing bananas in Siberia. The available computational resources limited their application. Many ML techniques had been quietly gathering dust on academic shelves, anxiously awaiting processors that wouldn't take a week to sum a spreadsheet. The advent of powerful computers, capable of processing vast quantities of data, unlocked the true potential of these algorithms. The internet, in particular, played a pivotal role, providing an almost limitless source of data for training ML models. From social media posts to online shopping transactions to cloud computing, the digital world generates data at an unprecedented scale, providing the raw material for ML to flourish.

Deep learning, more fully developed and discussed in the next section, is a subfield of ML. It further revolutionized the field. Deep learning models, typically based on artificial neural networks with multiple layers, are capable of learning complex features from raw data. These models excel at tasks involving unstructured data, such as images, audio, or text, where traditional ML techniques often struggle, and transform it into brilliant insights. Convolutional neural networks (CNNs), for instance, are particularly effective at image recognition and object detection, achieving superhuman performance on benchmark datasets, recognizing dogs, faces, traffic signs, and even tumors in MRIs with eerie precision. Meanwhile, recurrent neural networks (RNNs) are designed to process sequential data, such as text or speech, making them ideal for tasks such as machine translation, speech recognition, natural language generation, or even your favorite AI-generated bedtime stories. The success of deep learning has been nothing short of spectacular, driving advancements in various applications, including self-driving cars, medical diagnosis, and personalized recommendations. It's a brave new world where your phone understands sarcasm—well, almost.

Pixabay

Yet, even this brave new world comes with baggage. And, the journey of ML isn't without its challenges. One major concern is data bias. ML models are only as good as the data they are trained on. If the training data contains biases, the model will inevitably inherit and even amplify those biases. Whether it's loan approvals or criminal sentencing, biased models can have real-world consequences, leading to discriminatory outcomes. Addressing data bias is a crucial research area that requires diligent data vetting and the development of techniques to mitigate bias in ML models. Oh, and it should have a healthy dose of human oversight.

Hand in hand with bias is another thorny issue known as the "black box" dilemma of some ML models, particularly deep learning models. The complex interplay of layers and weights within these models can make it difficult for even their creators to understand how they arrive at their conclusions. This lack of interpretability can erode trust, particularly in high-stakes domains such as healthcare or finance, and make it challenging to identify and correct errors. The emerging field called Explainable AI (XAI) aims to develop techniques to make these models more transparent and interpretable. Think of it as AI's version of open-book accounting—an attempt to make sure we understand what's going on under the hood before we hand over the keys.

The ethical implications of ML are also receiving increasing attention. As ML systems become more powerful and pervasive, their potential for misuse is also increasing. There are the thorny questions of who's accountable when AI makes a mistake? How do we protect user privacy in a world where algorithms can infer your secrets from your Spotify playlist? Who really owns the data? These are not questions with easy answers. Issues such as privacy, security, and accountability need careful consideration to ensure that these technologies are used responsibly and ethically. The development of robust regulations and guidelines is essential to guide the development and deployment of ML technologies, ensuring that their benefits are maximized while mitigating their potential harms. Furthermore, the increasing automation enabled by ML raises concerns about job displacement, necessitating proactive measures to address potential societal impacts. The future of ML is intricately linked to our ability to navigate these ethical and societal challenges, perhaps with a bit of common sense.

In conclusion, the rise of ML has transformed the field of AI, allowing machines to learn from data in ways previously unimaginable. From simple algorithms like those behind Samuel's checkers-playing program to the sophisticated deep learning models of today, ML has driven remarkable progress in various applications. The field has evolved from checkers playing to neural networks that can write poetry and drive cars. ML has transformed AI from a rules-based tinker toy into a self-improving, pattern-finding powerhouse. But with great power comes great... well, you know the rest. However, the path ahead is not without its challenges. Addressing data bias, ensuring transparency, and grappling with the ethical implications are crucial steps in harnessing the full potential of ML while safeguarding against its potential harms. The ongoing evolution of ML promises to be as impactful as its past, continuously reshaping our technological landscape and pushing the boundaries of what's possible. As ML continues to evolve, its story is far from finished. If anything, it's just getting interesting.

Deep Learning, Neural Networks, and Their Applications

So, here we are—in a realm where AI takes a quantum leap forward, paving the way for incredible advancements. Building upon the foundations of ML, deep learning leverages artificial neural networks with multiple layers—hence the term "deep"—to extract intricate patterns and representations from raw data. Deep learning isn't just the new kid on the AI block—it's the one who showed up with a PhD, a six-pack, and an uncanny ability to recognize people in blurry photos. Unlike earlier ML approaches that needed human engineers to spell out what features to look for, deep learning allows the networks to automatically learn these features directly from the data itself.

This knack for constructing multi-level representations is key to its success in tackling complex tasks previously beyond the reach of traditional algorithms.

The architecture of a deep neural network resembles a layered structure, somewhat analogous to the interconnected neurons in the human brain. Each layer transforms the input data, progressively extracting higher-level features. Think of a deep neural network as the digital version of an onion—or a Russian nesting doll, if you prefer. Each layer peels back new levels of data abstraction, starting with basic patterns like edges or corners of an image and

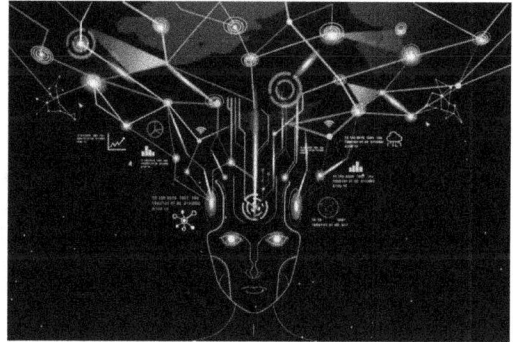

Pixabay

working up to full-fledged objects like faces, cars, or pizza slices. These layers, much like a gossiping chain of friends, pass insights along, refining and reinterpreting them with each handoff. Early layers may detect simple visual cues, but by the time the data reaches the upper echelons of the network, it's identifying grandma's face in your vacation photo or spotting a traffic sign from a moving vehicle. This hierarchical structure allows the network to learn increasingly abstract representations, enabling it to handle the nuances and subtleties inherent in complex datasets.

Nowhere has deep learning strutted its stuff more prominently than in computer vision. But what in the heck IS computer vision? Well, in simple terms, it is the art of teaching machines to see and understand the visual world—kind of like giving computers a pair of digital eyes and a brain to process what they're looking at. convolutional neural networks (CNNs)—the superstars of this domain—have turned the image processing world upside down. CNNs, a specific type of deep neural network, have revolutionized image recognition, object detection, and image segmentation. CNNs use convolutional layers to process spatial information in images efficiently. These layers apply filters to the input image, identifying patterns regardless of their location. This spatial invariance is crucial for tasks such as object recognition, where an object may appear anywhere within the image. The success of CNNs is evident in their remarkable accuracy on benchmark datasets, such as ImageNet, where they consistently surpass human performance in certain image classification tasks. But their talents don't stop with Instagram-worthy pictures. Beyond simple image classification, CNNs are now being used in diverse applications such as medical image analysis (detecting tumors, diagnosing diseases), spotting pedestrians for self-driving cars, and powerful facial recognition systems that can pick you out of a crowd faster than your mom can.

Another important class of deep neural networks is recurrent neural networks (RNNs). RNNs are specifically designed to handle sequential data, such as text, speech, and time series data. Unlike feedforward networks, where information flows only in one direction, RNNs have connections that loop back on themselves, allowing them to maintain a "memory" of previous inputs. This memory is crucial for processing sequential data where the order of elements matters. For example, in natural language processing, understanding the meaning of a sentence requires considering the context of previous words. RNNs, particularly Long Short-Term Memory (LSTM) networks and Gated Recurrent Units (GRUs), are experts at keeping context intact over time. Their applications are widespread, including machine translation (translating text from one language to another), speech recognition (converting spoken words into text), and natural language generation (generating human-like text). In the realm of finance, RNNs can predict stock market movements and flag suspicious transactions faster than a hawk spotting a field mouse. The sequential world is their playground, and they play to win.

But wait, there's more! Deep learning isn't content to merely see and read. It wants to listen. It's making significant inroads in areas like audio processing. Deep learning models can distinguish between a dog's bark and a car alarm, generate symphonies with Beethoven-like flair, and transcribe your grocery list as you mumble it half-asleep into your phone. They can be trained to perform speech recognition tasks with impressive accuracy. For example, deep learning-powered speech recognition systems are now routinely used in virtual assistants like Siri and Alexa, enabling seamless voice interactions with devices. Similarly, deep learning models are being used to generate realistic music, composing original pieces in various styles that tug at your heartstrings—or at least get stuck in your head. This capacity for creative generation holds immense potential for the music industry and beyond. In the realm of sound classification, deep learning models can identify different sounds in an audio recording, enabling applications in environmental monitoring, wildlife tracking, and even alerting engineers when something's gone awry in a factory. It's audio intelligence with a digital ear.

Of course, all this brilliance doesn't come cheap. The rise of deep learning is as much a tale of terabytes and teraflops as it is of algorithms. Training these sprawling networks requires muscle—computational muscle. With the arrival of GPUs that make regular CPUs look like dial-up modems and the growth of cloud computing, deep learning has gone from theoretical to practical at warp speed. Add to that the mountains of data generated by internet users, social platforms, and digital sensors, and you've got a recipe for neural nirvana. Labeled datasets—painstakingly tagged by humans or cleverly generated—have been the fuel feeding this high-performance machine.

In summary, the journey of deep learning is not without its challenges. One significant hurdle is the infamous "black box" nature of these models. These models are great at giving answers, but not so great at explaining how they got there. In areas where trust is paramount, such as life-and-death medical diagnoses or delicate legal matters, this lack of transparency can be a deal breaker. It can be a huge barrier to trust and adoption in applications with high stakes. The field of Explainable AI (XAI) is actively addressing this challenge, developing techniques to improve the interpretability of deep learning models.

Bias is another elephant in the digital room. If your training data reflects societal prejudices, your model might end up being a very sophisticated amplifier of those same biases. That's a recipe for discrimination, not innovation. The solution? Vigilant review and modification of training data, fairness-aware algorithms, and regular checkups to make sure the model's moral compass isn't spinning wildly. If left unchecked, bias can turn a promising technology into a problematic one with real-world consequences. Only through sustained vigilance and thoughtful intervention can the deep learning community mitigate these adverse effects and pave the way toward fairer AI.

The ethical implications of deep learning are also paramount. As deep learning systems become more powerful and integrated into various aspects of life, ensuring their responsible use is crucial. This requires careful consideration of issues such as privacy, security, accountability, and the potential for misuse. And, as it invades more corners of daily life, from who sees your résumé to who gets a loan, it becomes imperative to ask not just "Can we?" but "Should we?" Developing robust ethical guidelines and regulations isn't optional; it's vital. It is essential to guide the development and deployment of these technologies, maximizing their benefits while mitigating potential harms.

The ongoing development of deep learning is continually pushing the boundaries of what's achievable with AI. New architectures, training techniques, and applications are constantly emerging, shaping the landscape of technology and reshaping industries. From self-driving cars that rely on sophisticated deep learning models for object detection and navigation to personalized medicine that uses deep learning to analyze medical images and predict patient outcomes, the impact of deep learning is profound and far-reaching. The future of deep learning promises to be as transformative as its past, continuing to drive innovation and reshape our world. The story, much like the networks themselves, continues to evolve, layer upon layer, building towards a future where AI is deeply interwoven with the fabric of our lives. Each advancement builds on the last, painting a picture of a future where AI isn't just a tool, but an integral part of how we live, work, and understand the world around us. The journey continues, one layer at a time.

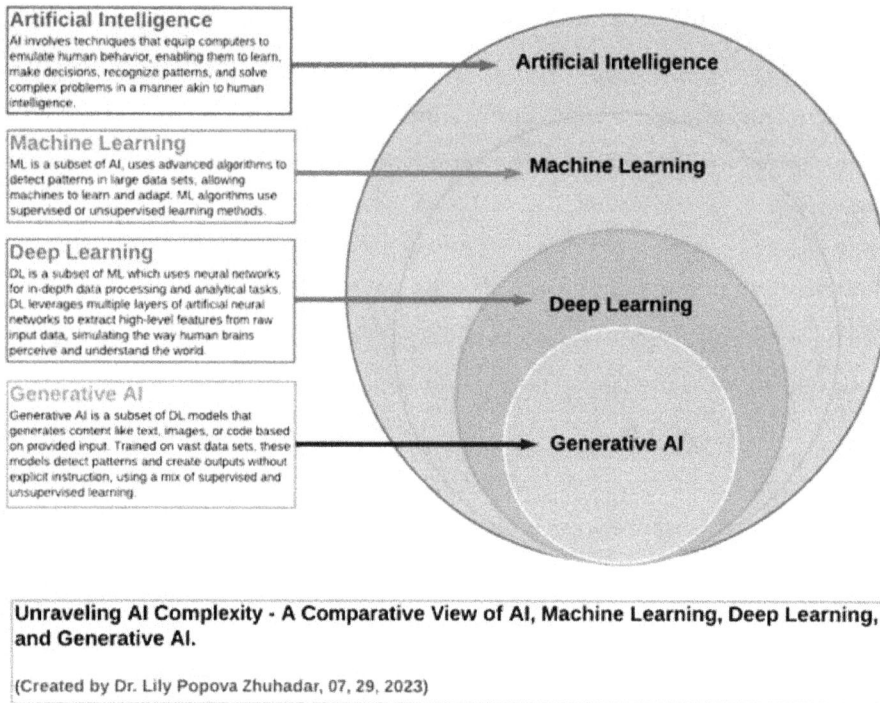

Artificial Intelligence
AI involves techniques that equip computers to emulate human behavior, enabling them to learn, make decisions, recognize patterns, and solve complex problems in a manner akin to human intelligence.

Machine Learning
ML is a subset of AI, uses advanced algorithms to detect patterns in large data sets, allowing machines to learn and adapt. ML algorithms use supervised or unsupervised learning methods.

Deep Learning
DL is a subset of ML which uses neural networks for in-depth data processing and analytical tasks. DL leverages multiple layers of artificial neural networks to extract high-level features from raw input data, simulating the way human brains perceive and understand the world.

Generative AI
Generative AI is a subset of DL models that generates content like text, images, or code based on provided input. Trained on vast data sets, these models detect patterns and create outputs without explicit instruction, using a mix of supervised and unsupervised learning.

Unraveling AI Complexity - A Comparative View of AI, Machine Learning, Deep Learning, and Generative AI.

(Created by Dr. Lily Popova Zhuhadar, 07, 29, 2023)

AI in Everyday Life: Applications and Impacts

We've explored the intricate workings of deep learning, a powerful engine driving the AI revolution. Now, let's shift gears and examine the tangible impact of this technology on our daily lives. It's no longer confined to the realm of science fiction; AI is subtly, and sometimes not-so-subtly, woven into the fabric of our modern existence. It's hanging out in your pocket, lounging on your living room shelf, and maybe even managing your grocery list. In fact, you've probably brushed elbows with AI half a dozen times today before your second cup of coffee—and you didn't even flinch. Think about it: how many times have you interacted with AI today, without even realizing it?

Let's start with a familiar face—or rather, a familiar voice. Virtual assistants like Siri, Alexa, and Google Assistant have become the digital sidekicks we never knew we needed but now can't seem to live without. These little helpers do everything from answering trivia questions and setting alarms to dimming your lights, setting reminders, playing music, and even controlling our smart homes. These aren't just glorified voice-recognition systems; they represent a sophisticated blend of natural language processing (NLP), speech recognition, and ML. They understand our often-garbled commands, learn our preferences over time, and anticipate our needs with surprising accuracy. They sometimes even predict what we want before we do. Behind their effortless conversational abilities lies a complex network of deep learning models, which constantly learn and adapt to improve their performance. This seamless integration into our daily routines is a testament to the progress made in

Wikipedia, CC BY-SA 4.0

AI's ability to understand and respond to human language. The development of a more nuanced understanding of context, emotion, and intent is an ongoing process, and future generations of virtual assistants will likely be even more intuitive and responsive. Your next-generation assistant might not just understand what you say, but how you feel when you say it. Creepy? Maybe a little. Convenient? Absolutely.

Beyond virtual assistants, AI is quietly powering the recommendation systems that populate our online experiences. From suggesting movies on Netflix to recommending products on Amazon, these systems are constantly analyzing our preferences and behaviors to provide personalized suggestions. The algorithms behind these systems employ sophisticated ML techniques, often involving collaborative filtering, content-based filtering, and hybrid approaches. Collaborative filtering leverages the preferences of similar users to predict what you might like. Content-based filtering analyzes the characteristics of items you've previously enjoyed to suggest similar ones. Hybrid approaches combine the strengths of both methods to create even more effective recommendations. The sheer scale of data processed by these systems is staggering; they analyze billions of data points to tailor suggestions to individual users, creating a personalized online experience that wouldn't be possible without the power of AI.

The impact of AI extends far beyond entertainment and e-commerce. It's playing an increasingly crucial role in healthcare, where it's being used to assist in diagnosis, personalize treatment plans, and accelerate drug discovery. AI-powered image analysis systems can analyze medical images like X-rays and MRIs with remarkable accuracy, often detecting anomalies that the human eye might miss. This not only improves diagnostic accuracy but also enables quicker and more efficient diagnosis, resulting in faster intervention and enhanced patient outcomes. AI algorithms are also being used to predict patient risks, enabling healthcare providers to proactively manage potential complications and tailor treatment plans to individual patient characteristics and genetic predispositions. Furthermore, AI is significantly speeding up the drug discovery process by analyzing vast amounts of biological data to identify potential drug candidates and predict their effectiveness.

Autonomous vehicles are another area where AI is poised to revolutionize our lives. Self-driving cars rely heavily on AI for navigation, object detection, and decision-making. These vehicles use a combination of sensors, cameras, and deep learning algorithms to perceive their surroundings, navigate roads, and react to unexpected events. The technology behind autonomous vehicles represents a significant advancement in AI, requiring sophisticated algorithms that can process complex sensory information in real-time. While the technology is still under development, autonomous vehicles have the potential to transform transportation, reducing traffic accidents, improving fuel efficiency, and increasing accessibility for individuals with limited mobility. The ethical considerations surrounding autonomous vehicles, especially regarding accident liability and decision-making in critical situations, remain active areas of debate and development. Further refinement of algorithms and rigorous testing are crucial before widespread adoption.

The influence of AI extends to areas we might not immediately associate with advanced technology. Consider spam filters; these simple tools employ sophisticated ML techniques to identify and block unwanted emails. These algorithms are constantly evolving, learning to recognize new patterns and techniques used by spammers. This constant adaptation is a key characteristic of AI systems. Similarly, AI plays a vital role in fraud detection, analyzing financial transactions to identify potentially fraudulent activity. These systems constantly learn from new data, becoming more accurate over time and providing a crucial layer of security for financial institutions and consumers alike.

While the applications of AI in everyday life are numerous and far-reaching, it's important to acknowledge the potential challenges. Concerns about job displacement, algorithmic bias, and privacy are all legitimate issues that require careful consideration. As AI systems become more integrated into our lives, it's essential to develop ethical guidelines and regulations to ensure their responsible use. Transparency in algorithms, mechanisms for accountability, and ongoing monitoring for bias are all critical steps in mitigating potential risks and harnessing the benefits of AI for the betterment of society. The conversation surrounding AI ethics is ongoing and vital for the safe and equitable integration of this powerful technology.

The increasing reliance on AI also raises questions about the future of work. Automation driven by AI has the potential to displace workers in certain sectors, requiring adaptation and retraining for individuals affected. However, AI is also creating new job opportunities in areas such as AI development, data science, and AI ethics. The challenge lies in ensuring a smooth transition, providing support for workers displaced by automation, and fostering the development of new skills necessary for the AI-driven economy. Education and training initiatives will be crucial in preparing the workforce for the changes ahead.

As discussed, AI is speeding into our lives like a self-driving Tesla with a questionable moral compass and no brakes. On one hand, it's the tech equivalent of a miracle worker—curing diseases, optimizing logistics, maybe even predicting the next viral TikTok dance. On the other hand, it's a Pandora's Box capable of unleashing ethical quandaries that could make a philosopher sweat. While AI's potential to revolutionize healthcare, transportation, and countless other sectors is undeniable, the very power of these systems necessitates a careful examination of their societal implications. Ignoring the ethical dimensions of AI is akin to building a magnificent skyscraper without considering the foundations—a recipe for eventual disaster.

The path forward requires a commitment to transparency and accountability in the development and deployment of AI systems. Open-source algorithms, accessible datasets, and clear explanations of AI decision-making processes are essential for building public trust and fostering responsible innovation. Moreover, fostering interdisciplinary collaboration between computer scientists, ethicists, policymakers, and social scientists is vital for developing effective solutions to the ethical challenges posed by AI.

CHAPTER 10

The Semiconductor Revolution: Tiny Chips, Giant Impact

The Invention of the Transistor: A Fundamental Breakthrough

The late 1940s witnessed a technological tempest, a quiet revolution brewing in the hallowed halls of Bell Labs. The venerable vacuum tube, our trusty but temperamental workhorse of electronics for decades, was bulky, inefficient, unreliable, and prone to burning out like the glowing embers of a campfire. Its limitations were becoming increasingly apparent, hindering the advancement of electronic devices and systems. Imagine trying to build a modern smartphone using thousands of these heat-generating glass behemoths—the result would be a brick-sized device emitting enough heat to melt asphalt. This is where the story of the transistor begins, a story of ingenuity, serendipity, and a profound impact on the world as we know it.

The quest for a replacement for the vacuum tube wasn't driven by a single, urgent need, but rather by a confluence of factors. The limitations of vacuum tubes were a significant bottleneck in building smaller, faster, and more energy-efficient electronic devices. The military, always a significant driver of technological innovation, was particularly interested in more compact and reliable components for its burgeoning communications and radar systems. The

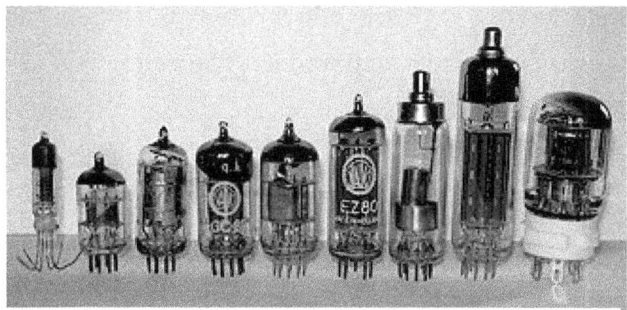

Author's archives

pursuit was a complex endeavor, demanding a deep understanding of materials science, solid-state physics, and engineering. Early attempts often felt like navigating a maze blindfolded, with many dead ends and frustrating setbacks—every wrong turn an invitation to rethink semiconductors from scratch.

The breakthrough came not with a flash of genius but rather a gradual accumulation of insights and experimental breakthroughs. The work at Bell Labs was a team effort, a collaborative symphony of scientists and engineers. John Bardeen, Walter Brattain, and William Shockley, each possessing unique expertise, brought their talents to bear on this challenging problem. Their shared focus: semiconductors. These materials, exhibiting electrical conductivity somewhere between conductors and insulators, were the key to unlocking a new era of electronics.

Semiconductors were the wallflowers of the materials world—neither conductor nor insulator in their vanilla state. In their purest form, they are poor conductors of electricity. However, their electrical properties could be dramatically altered by introducing impurities, a process known as "doping" (read: crafty impurity seasoning). This minor manipulation opened up a whole new world of possibilities, allowing scientists to control the flow of electrons within the semiconductor material. This control was crucial to the development of a device that could amplify electrical signals—a critical function performed by vacuum tubes, but with far greater efficiency and compactness.

The team at Bell Labs experimented with various semiconductor materials, with germanium emerging as the belle of the semiconductor ball. They carefully crafted a device consisting of three germanium pieces: a base, a collector, and an emitter. These pieces were meticulously arranged and connected and, presto: the transistor, a switch-amp wonder. The transistor's structure allowed a small electrical signal applied to the base to control a much larger current flowing between the collector and emitter. This ingenious arrangement served as an electrical switch and amplifier, efficiently replacing the bulky and power-hungry vacuum tube.

Author's archives

When Bell Labs unveiled the invention of the transistor in 1947, the scientific world did more than murmur—it applauded. It wasn't merely an incremental improvement; it was a fundamental paradigm shift in electronics. The implications were staggering. Transistors were far smaller and lighter than vacuum tubes, paving the way for the miniaturization of electronic devices. They consumed significantly less power than their glass predecessors, leading to more energy-efficient systems. And crucially, they were far more reliable, dramatically reducing the failure rate compared to the fickle vacuum tubes. They transformed room-filling rigs into pocketable gadgets, ushering in an age of miniaturization.

The initial point-contact transistors were still temperamental. Fluctuations in weather or manufacturing could turn them from obedient servants into rebellious teenagers. The challenge was to create a sturdier design to transition from a laboratory curiosity to a mass-producible component. Enter William Shockley with his invention of the junction transistor in 1951, a design significantly more robust and reliable. This ushered in an era of consistent and high-volume transistor production. Suddenly, transistors weren't lab pets but industrial workhorses.

The impact of the transistor on technology is nothing short of transformative. It's not hyperbole to say that the modern world, as we know it, is built upon the foundation of this tiny semiconductor device. From the first transistor radios to the latest smartphones, computers, and countless other electronic gadgets, transistors paved the way to powering the information highways we now treat as lifelines. Their tiny size enabled the miniaturization of computers, leading to the development of personal computers, laptops, and eventually smartphones.

The transition from bulky vacuum tube-based computers, occupying entire rooms, to the pocket-sized computing power we carry in our pockets today is a testament to the transistor's impact. Imagine the Apollo moon missions without the reliable and compact electronics made possible by transistors. The advancements in medical imaging, communications, and countless other fields are directly attributable to the transistor's fundamental role in enabling more sophisticated and powerful electronic systems.

Fast-forward from clumsy transistor radios to lightning-fast microprocessors. That same germanium ancestry paved the road to silicon integrated circuits (ICs)—microchips bristling with transistors. The development of ICs, or microchips, was built upon the foundation laid by the transistor. By stamping countless transistors on a single silicon wafer, engineers turbocharged computing power and slashed costs. This, in turn, propelled the development of ever smaller and more powerful computers, smartphones, and other electronic devices, fueling the information age.

Progress didn't stop at Shockley's model. Scientists refined doping methods, manufacturing processes, and materials. The initial designs, while groundbreaking, had limitations. Scientists and engineers continued to refine manufacturing techniques, resulting in improved performance, reliability, and cost-effectiveness. This ongoing process of refinement and innovation is a hallmark of technological advancement. Each iteration carved out new markets and set the stage for the next leap.

The humble transistor didn't just spark up your gadgets. Its invention spurred research in related fields, leading to the discovery of new materials and semiconductor processes. The development of MOSFET (Metal-Oxide-Semiconductor Field-Effect Transistor), the transistor's cooler, sleeker sequel, marked another significant milestone, enabling further miniaturization while dialing performance through the roof. But its real superpower isn't limited to blinking LEDs for beefy processors; it's rewired the very fabric of society. Information now zips around the globe like a hyperloop of ideas, smashing down knowledge barriers and reimagining how we connect, learn, and hustle. The transistor's impact on society is not just technological; it has profoundly influenced social, economic, and cultural landscapes.

The ease of access to information and communication, largely facilitated by transistor-based technologies, has changed the way we interact, learn, and work. The impact on global communication and the democratization of information are undeniable. The rapid advancements in computing power, made possible by the transistor and integrated circuits, have revolutionized scientific research, medical diagnosis, and industrial processes.

Let's not gloss over the sequel: ecological strain. Harvesting rare-earth metals for chips conjures mining woes and supply-chain drama. The industry's reliance on rare earth minerals for semiconductor production has raised concerns about environmental sustainability and geopolitical implications. The increasing consumption of electronic devices generates a significant amount of electronic waste, presenting a substantial environmental challenge. These challenges require a multifaceted approach, involving responsible sourcing of materials, improved recycling practices, and a focus on creating more durable and repairable devices.

In conclusion, the invention of the transistor was a pivotal moment in technological history, marking the beginning of the semiconductor revolution. Its impact on our world is profound and far-reaching, shaping the way we live, work, and interact with each other. While the challenges associated with its production and disposal remain, the transistor's legacy as a fundamental building block of modern technology is undeniable. The tiny transistor, initially just a speck of innovation, ultimately became the cornerstone of a technological revolution that continues to shape our world in extraordinary ways. In the epic of modern tech, the transistor stands as a testament to human ingenuity: proof that the tiniest inventions can cast the longest shadows.

Something else to chew on: Quantum transistors—where electrons dance in superposition, promising calculations that make today's supercomputers look like abacuses. 2D materials such as graphene and molybdenum disulfide are ready to dethrone silicon on the microchip throne. Neuromorphic chips that mimic our own neurons, blurring the line between human thought and machine logic. We'll get into more of a discussion on this in Chapter 14.

The Development of Integrated Circuits, Miniaturization, and Efficiency

The transistor, as revolutionary as it was, still presented limitations. Each transistor required its own discrete components: resistors, capacitors, and a tangle of wires that would make a spiderweb jealous. Assembling these components onto circuit boards was like building a ship in a bottle—tedious, delicate work, with plenty of opportunities for things to go disastrously wrong.

Wikipedia, CC BY-SA 4.0

Manufacturing was slow, error-prone, and expensive—three words no engineer wants to hear in the same sentence. Furthermore, the size of these circuits remained a constraint. To create complex electronic systems, one needed a multitude of individual transistors, leading to bulky and cumbersome devices. The solution to these challenges lay in a radical new concept: integrating multiple transistors and other components onto a single chip of semiconductor material. Thus began the integrated circuit era—a leap in innovation that made even the transistor's debut look like a warm-up act.

Of course, great ideas rarely arrive fully formed. The road to integrated circuits was anything but a straight shot. Early tinkering still relied on physically linking individual transistors together, a process that improved little upon the old wiring-and-soldering routine. The true breakthrough required a fundamental shift in thinking, a move towards a monolithic approach. This meant creating an entire circuit directly on a single piece of semiconductor material. No more playing connect-the-dots with wires. Just one sleek, self-contained slab of brilliance.

The concept of a monolithic integrated circuit was first explored in the late 1950s. Several researchers and companies contributed to its development, but the credit for its practical realization often goes to Jack Kilby at Texas Instruments and Robert Noyce at Fairchild Semiconductor, who independently conceived and developed working prototypes in 1958 that would go on to shape the digital backbone of the modern age. Their methods weren't identical, but their goal was to create a complete, working circuit on a single chip of semiconductor material. Easy to say. Not so easy to do.

Kilby's approach involved creating a wafer-thin layer of germanium, onto which he deposited resistors, capacitors, and transistors using photolithography—a technique borrowed from the printing industry—which used light to etch patterns onto the material. This allowed him to create multiple components in a precisely defined arrangement, then interconnect them with tiny metallic wires. This method was ingenious in its simplicity and efficiency, but faced challenges in terms of manufacturing consistency and achieving high performance. Moreover, germanium wasn't exactly the superstar material engineers had dreamed of.

Noyce, on the other hand, opted for a more elegant approach using silicon as the base material. Recognizing the limitations of Kilby's wired approach, Noyce ditched the wires altogether and instead used silicon itself to create interconnections between components. This planar process, as it was known, proved to be far more efficient and scalable for mass production, forming the basis of modern integrated circuit manufacturing. It was a masterful stroke of engineering. Noyce's process wasn't just effective—it was the blueprint for how modern integrated circuits are still manufactured today. It was like swapping a typewriter for a word processor overnight.

Those first integrated circuits weren't exactly computing titans—they housed maybe a handful of transistors. But from the outset, their potential was as clear as a high-definition screen. As fabrication techniques improved, transistor counts soared. What began as a novelty turned into a tidal wave of miniaturization. More transistors meant more computing power, and more computing power meant... well, everything got smarter, faster, and cheaper.

The development of integrated circuits wasn't just a matter of cramming more transistors onto a single chip; it also necessitated significant advancements in materials science, process engineering, and design automation. Engineers had to conjure up ultra-pure silicon, refine photolithographic techniques into a high-precision art form, and develop sophisticated computer-aided design (CAD) tools, all critical steps in enabling the mass production of increasingly complex integrated circuits. It was like going from sketching with crayons to engineering with lasers.

And the ripple effects? Monumental. Integrated circuits didn't just revolutionize electronics—they rewrote the rules for entire industries. The aerospace industry, already a major beneficiary of transistors, embraced integrated circuits for their compact size, low cost, and superior reliability and performance in space applications. The military viewed integrated circuits as a crucial component for developing smaller, faster, and more resilient communication and guidance systems.

The automotive industry integrated circuits into electronic control units (ECUs), responsible for managing various aspects of vehicle operation, from fuel injection to anti-lock brakes. The medical industry benefited from the development of smaller and more sophisticated medical devices, leading to advancements in diagnostic tools, therapeutic equipment, and implantable medical technology. The consumer electronics industry witnessed an explosion of innovation, driven by the cost-effectiveness and versatility of integrated circuits. From calculators and digital watches to video game consoles and personal computers, the impact was profound and far-reaching.

Then came the microprocessor—a silicon chip so packed with logic and memory that it functioned as a complete computer. The microprocessor didn't just change the game—it invented a new one. This little marvel powered the PC revolution, turning basements into offices and garages into startups. It paved the way for the personal computing revolution, bringing digital power into homes, dorm rooms, and eventually, into pockets. The relentless march toward higher integration densities was driven by an observation that became legend: Moore's Law (though not a true law of physics). Gordon Moore predicted that the number of transistors on a chip would double roughly

Pixabay

every two years, a prediction that held remarkably true for several decades, leading to an almost unbelievable increase in computing power and a matching drop in cost.

However, this rapid advancement was not without its challenges. As transistors became smaller and more densely packed, maintaining their performance and reliability became increasingly difficult. Heat dissipation turned into a high-stakes balancing act. Signal interference became a maddening puzzle. Quantum mechanical effects crept in, threatening to rewrite the rules of classical physics. Overcoming these hurdles required constant innovation in materials science, manufacturing processes, and chip design. Exotic materials, such as gallium arsenide, were investigated to improve transistor performance, and new techniques, such as advanced lithography methods (like Extreme Ultraviolet Lithography), were developed to create ever-smaller features on integrated circuits.

The development of integrated circuits also led to the adoption of new design methodologies, including the introduction of very-large-scale integration (VLSI) techniques, which enabled engineers to design and implement highly complex chips with millions or even billions of transistors. This made possible the development of powerful microprocessors and specialized integrated circuits for specific applications. The impact on software development was significant, leading to the development of sophisticated operating systems and software applications that leveraged the ever-increasing processing power of integrated circuits.

Today, we stand on the edge of yet more breakthroughs: quantum computing, neuromorphic chips, and AI-optimized processors—all powered by the same relentless drive that birthed the first ICs. The quest for smaller, faster, and more capable chips continues to be one of the most exciting frontiers in science and engineering. Who knows? The next big leap might already be etched into a tiny wafer, waiting to change the world all over again.

Moore's Law and the Exponential Growth of Computing Power

The relentless miniaturization and performance improvements achieved through integrated circuits weren't simply the result of clever engineering; it was turbocharged by a bold prediction that started as an educated guess and quickly became the tech industry's rallying cry: Moore's Law. Now, to be clear, it's not an actual law like gravity or Murphy's, but more of a prophetic rule of thumb that somehow stayed accurate for decades. It suggested that the number of transistors you could cram onto a microchip would double roughly every two years. While not a precisely accurate prediction at all times, its uncanny accuracy over several decades acted as a guiding star for the semiconductor industry, driving innovation and investment at an unprecedented scale. The graph depicted is an example, using the years 1970 through 2020.

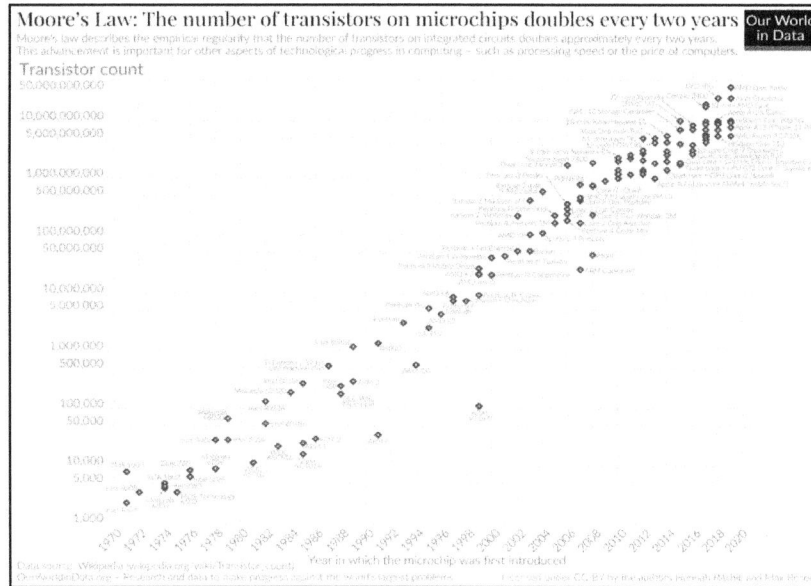

Though we've touched on Moore's Law before, it's worth giving it some extra spotlight. Gordon Moore, co-founder of Intel, first articulated this observation in a 1965 article. He wasn't predicting a fixed, immutable law of nature, but rather extrapolating from the then-current trends in integrated circuit technology. He noted the rapid pace of progress in miniaturizing transistors and the associated increase in their density on chips. His insight wasn't limited to squeezing more transistors into a chip like sardines in a can; it also encompassed the evolution of manufacturing, materials, and design. Moore's Law, in essence, became a self-fulfilling prophecy: the expectation of doubling transistor density fueled aggressive research and development, resulting in innovations that often exceeded the initial prediction.

The implications of Moore's Law were transformative. It didn't just mean smaller chips; it meant exponentially greater computing power at a steadily decreasing cost. This cost reduction was a crucial element, making computing power accessible to a wider range of applications and users. Imagine the cost of a personal computer today if the pace of progress dictated by Moore's Law hadn't been maintained. If Moore's Law hadn't held up for as long as it did, your personal computer might still be a luxury item, and your smartphone... well, wouldn't be very smart.

While the doubling interval wasn't always precisely two years, the overall trend of exponential growth remained remarkably consistent. Each generation of microprocessors built upon the previous one, leveraging smaller transistors, advanced lithography techniques, and innovative chip architectures to achieve higher performance and lower power consumption. The sheer number of transistors packed onto a single chip grew from a few thousand in the early days of integrated circuits to billions in modern processors, a testament to the ingenuity and perseverance of engineers and scientists.

But eventually, even legends hit a ceiling. As chips got denser and transistors shrank to the width of a few atoms, nature started pushing back. Quantum mechanical effects became increasingly significant, impacting performance and reliability. Heat became an issue too—packing all those transistors into ever-smaller spaces meant they started running hot enough to toast bread, requiring innovative cooling techniques to prevent overheating. The cost of manufacturing also increased, as creating ever-smaller features required increasingly sophisticated and expensive equipment. The endless march toward smaller and smaller transistors began to encounter fundamental roadblocks.

The slowing down of Moore's Law doesn't necessarily signal the end of progress in computing. Instead of simply shrinking transistors further, engineers began exploring new ways to squeeze more performance out of chips. These include advancements in chip architecture, such as multi-core processors and specialized hardware accelerators (like GPUs), which can enhance performance even without the continued exponential increase in transistor density. New materials, such as graphene and other two-dimensional materials, are being explored as potential replacements for silicon, offering the potential for even greater miniaturization and performance improvements.

Another clever workaround? Going vertical. Instead of continuing the flat, pancake-style chip design, engineers began stacking transistors like a digital layer cake—enter 3D integrated circuits. This approach can circumvent the limitations imposed by two-dimensional planar layouts, packing in more power without taking up more desk space. And just when you thought the brain was safely out of reach, researchers started mimicking it—with neuromorphic computing models designed to work more like neurons than traditional processors.

These emerging technologies are likely to offer substantial improvements in computing power, even if they don't precisely adhere to the original spirit of Moore's Law.

Even if Moore's Law is no longer clockwork-precise, its legacy is anything but obsolete. It served as a powerful catalyst for innovation, driving billions of dollars in research and development across the semiconductor industry. It fostered a culture of continuous improvement, pushing the boundaries of what was technologically feasible. Thanks to this one simple observation, we witnessed a sci-fi transformation of everyday life—from streaming movies on tablets to diagnosing diseases with handheld devices. It had a dramatic impact on every aspect of modern life.

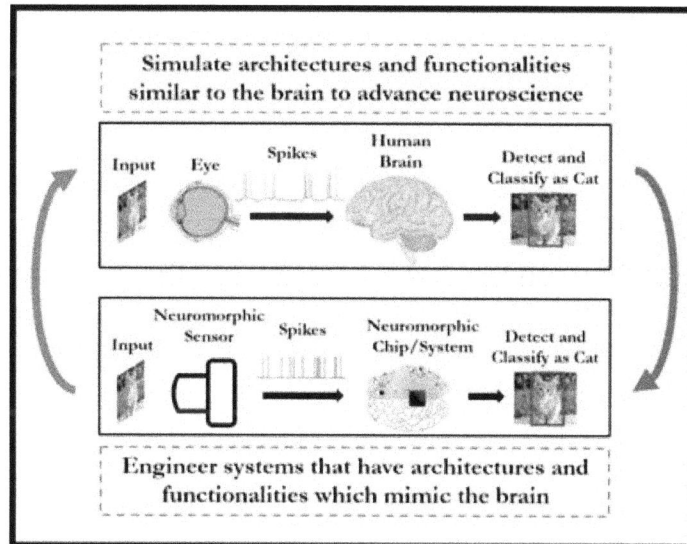

https://viso.ai/author/gaudenz-bocsch

Beyond the technical achievements, Moore's Law's impact extended to the socio-economic landscape. The dramatic reduction in the cost of computing power fueled the digital revolution, transforming industries and creating new economic opportunities. Personal computing, mass digital communication, cloud infrastructure—none of it would have happened the way it did without the affordability Moore's Law enabled. With cheaper chips came broader access, and with broader access came innovation from every corner of the globe. The accessibility of computing power has empowered individuals, fostering creativity and communication on an unprecedented scale.

The story of Moore's Law is not just a technological narrative; it's a story of human ambition, ingenuity, and the relentless pursuit of progress. But perhaps the most inspiring part of Moore's Law is what it says about us. It's a story of optimism, of setting a bar sky-high and then building the ladder to reach it. It's about the audacity to expect more from technology—not just marginal gains, but exponential leaps.

The continued pursuit of advancements in computing isn't merely a matter of achieving higher clock speeds or denser circuits. It's about developing new approaches to computation, exploring alternative architectures, and leveraging the unique properties of emerging materials. Quantum computing, for instance, promises to solve problems intractable for even the most powerful classical computers, opening entirely new avenues of research and application. Neuromorphic computing, mimicking the structure and function of the human brain, aims to create energy-efficient and adaptable computing systems. These are just a few examples of the innovative directions being pursued in the quest for even greater computing power. These aren't just tweaks—they're tectonic shifts in how we compute.

The Manufacturing of Semiconductors: A Complex and Precise Process

Turning a humble silicon wafer into the brain of your smartphone isn't magic—though it often seems like it. In reality, it's the result of a breathtakingly complex and precise manufacturing process. This process, a symphony of engineering marvels and scientific precision, is the backbone of the semiconductor revolution. It's a journey involving dozens of steps, each demanding meticulous control and exacting standards.

It all begins with a silicon ingot so pure it puts bottled water to shame. The creation of this cylindrical crystal ingot itself is a feat of engineering, involving the Czochralski process, where a seed crystal is dipped and then is gently pulled skyward from a molten vat of hyper-pure silicon bath, resulting in a large, single crystal with exceptional uniformity. Any impurities, even at the parts-per-billion level, can significantly affect the performance and reliability of the final chip. This is where the "cleanroom" environment becomes critically important. These highly controlled spaces maintain exceptionally low levels of dust and other contaminants, minimizing the risk of defects. The cleanroom is so sterile that even a rogue dust particle is treated like a national security threat. The atmosphere is meticulously filtered, temperature and humidity are tightly regulated, and workers wear specialized clothing to prevent the introduction of impurities. Even the air pressure is controlled to ensure consistent flow and to avoid particle contamination.

Once the ingot is grown, it's sliced into thin wafers, typically about 0.75 millimeters thick. These wafers form the foundation upon which the chips will be built. The slicing process must be incredibly precise to ensure the wafers are perfectly flat and uniform in thickness. Any imperfections at this stage can propagate through the entire manufacturing process, leading to faulty chips. After slicing, the wafers are meticulously polished to a mirror-like finish, eliminating any microscopic irregularities that could interfere with the subsequent fabrication steps.

The heart of semiconductor manufacturing is photolithography, a process that uses light to transfer patterns onto the silicon wafer. This is where the magic of miniaturization truly comes into play. A photomask, a glass plate with the circuit pattern etched onto it, is used to selectively expose areas of the wafer to ultraviolet light. A photosensitive material, known as photoresist, is applied to the wafer, and the exposed areas either harden or dissolve depending on the type of photoresist used. The result? Patterns so minuscule that a single human hair seems like a redwood tree in comparison. The precision required in photolithography is astounding; a single misplaced atom can render a transistor unusable. With feature sizes now measured in nanometers, photolithography pushes the limits of what's physically possible—and occasionally what's psychologically tolerable for engineers. The advancements in this field, from contact lithography to advanced deep ultraviolet lithography, have been crucial for enabling Moore's Law.

Etching, the next crucial stage, uses chemical or physical processes to remove the exposed or unexposed photoresist, transferring the pattern into the silicon wafer itself. This process involves a complex interplay of chemicals and processes, each carefully calibrated to ensure the desired level of precision. Dry etching, using plasma, offers better control and precision than wet etching, which uses chemicals. The depth and sharpness of the etched features are critical factors in determining the performance of the transistors. Each layer of the circuit is built up through repeated cycles of photolithography and etching, creating a three-dimensional structure of interconnected transistors and other components.

Next comes doping, which sounds slightly scandalous but is actually a critical step in semiconductor alchemy. This is where tiny amounts of impurities are deliberately introduced into the silicon to tweak its electrical properties. Think of it as seasoning the silicon to taste. This is essential for creating the p-type and n-type regions of transistors, enabling the control of electron flow. By using ion implantation—basically firing atoms like microscopic cannonballs—engineers create regions that either attract or repel electrons, forming the p-type and n-type areas that allow transistors to switch and amplify signals. And yes, the precision here is as intense as the rest: the depth, dosage, and distribution of these ions must be just right, or your chip might end up with the personality of a potato. The depth and concentration of the implanted ions are precisely controlled using sophisticated equipment.

After all that, it's time for metallization—because even chips need a little bling. This involves laying down ultra-thin layers of metal, typically aluminum or copper, to connect the various components on the wafer. These connections are vital—they're the chip's nervous system. This process requires meticulous control of the metal deposition process to ensure that the connections are reliable and consistent. And just like before, the metal layers are patterned using photolithography and etching, creating the intricate network of interconnects that enable communication between different parts of the chip. The stakes? If the interconnects are even slightly flawed, the chip could short, fizzle, or just sit there doing nothing while looking expensive.

With the chip nearly complete, it's time for testing—aka the "does this thing actually work?" phase. This involves probing individual chips on the wafer to verify their functionality. Defective chips are marked for removal, while functional chips are ready for packaging. This testing process is crucial for ensuring the quality and reliability of the final product.

The final step is packaging. This is more than just gift-wrapping. This is where the individual chips are encased in protective packages that allow them to be integrated into larger systems. These packages provide mechanical protection, as well as electrical connections to the outside world. The packaging process must be precise to prevent damage to the chip and ensure reliable electrical connections. It's the chip's final form before it's ready to be soldered into your favorite gadgets and gizmos. The evolution of packaging technologies has been essential for increasing the density and performance of integrated circuits, allowing chips to handle increasingly higher power demands.

The economic and geopolitical implications of semiconductor manufacturing are profound. The industry is highly capital-intensive, requiring massive investments in advanced fabrication facilities, known as "fabs", that cost billions of dollars to build and equip. These facilities are technologically sophisticated and require highly skilled labor, making them a significant economic driver in regions where they are located. Furthermore, the concentration of semiconductor manufacturing in a limited number of countries has created significant geopolitical implications, highlighting the strategic importance of this industry. The global supply chain is intricate, involving the sourcing of materials and equipment from various countries, and the complex interplay of manufacturing and assembly locations adds complexity and potential vulnerabilities.

The Future of Semiconductor Technology: Beyond Moore's Law

One of the most promising avenues is the exploration of new materials. Silicon, the workhorse of the semiconductor industry for decades, has served us remarkably well, but its inherent limitations are becoming increasingly apparent. Researchers are actively investigating alternative materials with superior electrical properties, such as gallium nitride (GaN) and silicon carbide (SiC), which offer higher electron mobility and better power-handling capabilities. These materials are particularly well-suited for high-power applications, such as electric vehicles and renewable energy infrastructure. They're the superhero alloys of the semiconductor world—faster, stronger, and cooler (literally). Their adoption could significantly boost efficiency and reduce energy consumption in these critical sectors. The challenge, however, lies in mastering the complex manufacturing processes required to integrate these new materials into existing semiconductor fabrication techniques. It's not simply a matter of swapping one material for another; the entire ecosystem of design, manufacturing, and testing needs adaptation and innovation.

Another major area of innovation is three-dimensional chip architecture. Why settle for a single-story chip when you can build a high-rise? Instead of building chips in a flat, two-dimensional plane, researchers are exploring the possibilities of stacking multiple layers of transistors vertically. This approach, known as 3D stacking or Through-Silicon Vias (TSVs) for the technically inclined, offers significant advantages in terms of density, performance, and power efficiency. By stacking transistor layers vertically, chip manufacturers can achieve more power in less space, reducing the length of interconnects and improving signal speeds. This is particularly important for high-performance computing applications, where minimizing signal delay is crucial. The technical hurdles, however, remain significant. Precise alignment and interconnection of the stacked dies are challenging feats of engineering, and the heat dissipation from densely packed transistors requires innovative thermal management solutions.

Now, let's really shake things up. Forget ones and zeros. Beyond these incremental improvements, revolutionary approaches are emerging that could fundamentally change the way we compute. Quantum computing, for instance, represents a paradigm shift from the classical computing paradigm that has dominated for decades. Instead of relying on bits representing 0 or 1, quantum computers utilize quantum bits, or qubits, which can exist in a superposition of both states simultaneously. This allows quantum computers to perform calculations that are impossible for even the most powerful classical computers. While still in its infant stages, quantum computing holds immense potential for tackling currently intractable problems in areas like drug discovery, materials science, and cryptography. But don't hold your breath. The challenges are immense. Building and maintaining stable qubits is extraordinarily difficult, requiring extremely low temperatures and highly controlled environments. The development of fault-tolerant quantum computers remains a significant technological hurdle.

What if chips thought more like brains? Neuromorphic computing, inspired by the structure and function of the human brain, offers another intriguing pathway. Unlike traditional computers, which rely on von Neumann architecture with separate processing and memory units, neuromorphic chips mimic the parallel processing capabilities of the brain. This approach has the potential to significantly improve energy efficiency and processing speed for tasks such as pattern recognition and ML. Neuromorphic chips typically utilize artificial synapses and neurons to process information in a more distributed and parallel manner, mimicking the biological neural networks found in the brain. The inherent parallelism enables faster and more energy-efficient processing, particularly for tasks that benefit from distributed computing architectures. It's as if chips are learning to think instead of just compute. But don't expect silicon brains to take over just yet. The development of efficient neuromorphic architectures and the associated software tools is still a challenge today.

The development of new materials, 3D chip architecture, and radical new computing paradigms like quantum and neuromorphic computing isn't happening in silos. They feed off each other. Advances in one area often lead to breakthroughs in other areas. For example, new materials could enable the creation of more efficient and stable qubits, while 3D stacking could improve the density and performance of neuromorphic chips. This interconnectedness emphasizes the need for a holistic and collaborative approach to advancing semiconductor technology.

Moore's Law had a good run, but the future of semiconductors is getting a reboot. We're entering an era defined not by how small we can go, but how boldly we can think. The transition to new materials, architectures, and computing paradigms will require significant investment, collaboration, and careful consideration of the ethical and geopolitical implications.

CHAPTER 11

Cybersecurity:
Protecting the Digital World

Early Cybersecurity Challenges: Protecting Mainframes and Networks

The transition to a digitally driven world, fueled by the ever-increasing power of semiconductors, wasn't a smooth, seamless journey. It was a chaotic, exhilarating scramble, paved with the best of intentions and riddled with unforeseen vulnerabilities. As mainframes became the beating heart of businesses and governments, a new and entirely unexpected threat emerged: the digital burglar. Protecting these colossal machines and the nascent networks that connected them became the emerging field of cybersecurity's first major challenge. These early days weren't about sophisticated malware or intricate phishing schemes. Instead, the threats were often far more rudimentary, stemming from a lack of understanding of the risks inherent in this new digital landscape.

One of the earliest forms of digital intrusion wasn't a virus or worm, but a far more prosaic, and surprisingly effective, technique: the insider threat. Mainframe operators, often highly skilled but not always meticulously vetted, held a level of access that would make modern security professionals blanch. They possessed the keys to the kingdom, the ability to not only access sensitive data but also to alter or delete it at will. A disgruntled employee, a careless mistake, or even a simple lapse in judgment could lead to devastating consequences. Early data protection protocols were, at best, rudimentary. Passwords were often simple, easily guessed, or even written down in plain sight. Access controls were largely based on trust, a strategy that proved to be dangerously naive in the face of human fallibility.

The lack of robust security measures wasn't solely due to negligence; it was also a consequence of the technological limitations of the time. Encryption, while theoretically possible, was computationally expensive and slow, making it impractical for widespread implementation. The sheer volume of data stored on mainframes also presented a challenge. Manual audits of access logs were time-consuming and error-prone, making it difficult to detect intrusions quickly. The absence of sophisticated intrusion detection systems meant that breaches often went unnoticed for extended periods, allowing malicious actors ample time to accomplish their objectives.

The concept of a "network," as we understand it today, was still in its infancy. Early networks were typically small, localized systems connecting a few mainframes or terminals within a single organization. However, even these limited networks presented new security vulnerabilities. The lack of standardized security protocols meant that data transmitted over these networks was often vulnerable to interception. Simple eavesdropping techniques could reveal sensitive information, and there was little in the way of defense against such attacks.

As networks expanded and became more interconnected, the threat landscape evolved accordingly. The advent of dial-up modems brought the outside world into the previously secure domain of the mainframe. This opened new avenues for intrusion, as malicious actors could potentially gain access to networks remotely. This era witnessed the rise of the "phreaker"—individuals who exploited vulnerabilities in the telephone system to make free calls and even gain unauthorized access to computer systems. Their methods were ingenious, often involving manipulating tones and frequencies to gain access to restricted systems. These were the folks who could whistle into a phone and suddenly be inside your network. While their actions may seem quaint by today's standards, they highlighted the vulnerabilities of early networks and the urgent need for improved security measures.

The 1970s and 80s saw the first documented cases of what we would now recognize as malware. Early viruses were relatively simple programs designed to replicate themselves and spread from one system to another. The "Creeper" program, a self-replicating program that appeared on early ARPANET systems, is often cited as one of the first computer viruses. This virus would hop from one ARPANET system to another, flashing the cheery message, "I'm the creeper, catch me if you can!" While Creeper didn't do much damage, it did introduce the wild realization that software could spread like an office cold: fast, annoying, and hard to trace.

As computers grew smarter and more widespread, so did the attackers. As computers became more powerful and networks became more extensive, the sophistication of cyberattacks increased proportionally. The emergence of the personal computer, while offering unprecedented access to computing power, also expanded the attack surface. The proliferation of personal computers meant that more individuals had the potential to access networks, both legitimately and illegitimately. The lack of consistent security standards across different operating systems and hardware platforms added another layer of complexity to the challenge of securing networks.

The early attempts to address cybersecurity challenges were often ad hoc and reactive. Security protocols were developed in response to specific threats, rather than being part of a comprehensive, proactive strategy. The concept of risk management, as we understand it today, was largely absent. Organizations often lacked the necessary resources and expertise to effectively protect their systems from sophisticated cyberattacks.

This period saw the rise of individuals and organizations dedicated to securing computer systems. Early cybersecurity professionals were often self-taught, relying on their intuition and ingenuity to identify and mitigate threats. They were pioneers, operating in a rapidly evolving landscape, constantly playing catch-up with ever-more sophisticated attackers. They built tools, wrote protocols, and, when necessary, shut everything down and restarted it (the universal IT solution).

The response to early cybersecurity breaches often involved a combination of technical fixes and organizational changes. Password policies were strengthened, access controls were tightened, and rudimentary intrusion detection systems were developed. Password policies evolved from "1234" to "something you can't pronounce without spraining your tongue." Access controls improved, and organizations began teaching employees not to click on links that screamed "FREE PUPPIES CLICK HERE." Organizations also began to understand the importance of training employees in basic security practices. This awareness, while slow to develop, represented a crucial step in the evolution of cybersecurity.

The rudimentary techniques and ad-hoc solutions of the past laid the foundation for the sophisticated technologies and strategies used to safeguard our increasingly interconnected world. It's a reminder that the fight for digital security is an ongoing battle, one that requires constant vigilance, innovation, and a deep understanding of both the technology and the human element involved.

The Rise of Malware and Cybercrime: Evolving Threats

The rise of personal computers in the 1980s dramatically altered the cybersecurity landscape. No longer confined to large, centralized mainframes, computing power became accessible to individuals, creating a vastly expanded attack surface. This democratization of computing, while undeniably positive in many ways, also opened the door to a new era of cybercrime. The relatively simple viruses of the 1970s, often little more than self-replicating programs, evolved into more sophisticated threats. The development of the IBM PC and its compatible clones spurred an explosion in software development, much of it unregulated and often containing security flaws. This made PCs ripe targets for malicious actors.

One notable development of this era was the emergence of boot sector viruses. These viruses targeted the master boot record of a hard drive, the crucial code that initiates the boot process. Infecting the boot sector ensured that the virus would load before the operating system, making it incredibly difficult to remove. The infamous "Brain" virus, appearing in 1986, is a prime example. This virus, originating from Pakistan, demonstrated the potential for malware to spread rapidly through floppy disks, a common method of software distribution at the time. Its relatively simple design, however, belied its effectiveness in disrupting systems and highlighting the vulnerability of personal computers.

The 1980s also witnessed the beginnings of organized cybercrime. Early examples were often opportunistic, targeting systems with known vulnerabilities to steal data or disrupt services. However, as networks became more interconnected and the potential for financial gain increased, cybercrime began to develop a more organized and profitable structure. The development of bulletin board systems (BBSs), early precursors to online forums and social media, provided a platform for malicious actors to share information, tools, and techniques. These digital undergrounds fostered a sense of community among hackers, creating an ecosystem of knowledge-sharing and collaboration that accelerated the development of more sophisticated cyberattacks.

The transition from floppy disks to CD-ROMs didn't curb the spread of malware; it simply changed the path. CD-ROMs, with their significantly larger storage capacity, offered a new avenue for malware distribution. This allowed for more complex and damaging malware to be distributed more efficiently. The rise of the internet in the 1990s further amplified the scale and sophistication of cyberattacks. The World Wide Web, with its interconnectedness and accessibility, offered malicious actors an unprecedented opportunity to reach a vast audience.

The 1990s witnessed the emergence of several significant malware families, including macro viruses and polymorphic viruses. Macro viruses, which embedded themselves in Microsoft Word and Excel documents, exploited the widespread use of these applications to spread rapidly. These viruses could automatically execute their malicious code when a document was opened, making them incredibly insidious. Polymorphic viruses, on the other hand, employ techniques to change their code, making them harder to detect using traditional antivirus software. This constant evolution made the task of creating effective antivirus solutions a continuously evolving arms race.

The development of email also played a significant role in the spread of malware. Email became a primary route for delivering malicious attachments and links, leading to the rise of phishing scams and other social engineering attacks. These attacks exploited human psychology to trick victims into revealing sensitive information or downloading malicious software. The increasing reliance on email for communication and commerce made these attacks particularly effective.

The rise of the internet also fostered the development of more sophisticated cybercrime organizations. These groups often operated across national borders, making them difficult to track and prosecute. They developed intricate methods for concealing their activities, using techniques such as encryption and anonymization tools to avoid detection. The financial rewards associated with successful cyberattacks further incentivized the growth and sophistication of these organizations.

The early 2000s saw the emergence of new and more devastating types of malware, including worms such as Code Red and Nimda. These worms exploited vulnerabilities in web servers and other internet-connected systems to replicate and spread rapidly across the internet, causing widespread disruptions and financial losses. The sheer scale and speed of these attacks underscored the vulnerability of the increasingly interconnected global internet. The ease with which these worms exploited readily available vulnerabilities highlighted the urgent need for software vendors to prioritize security and for users to patch their systems promptly.

The development of sophisticated botnets further amplified the destructive potential of cyberattacks. Botnets are networks of compromised computers controlled remotely by malicious actors. These networks can be used for a wide range of malicious activities, including distributed denial-of-service (DDoS) attacks, spamming, and theft of sensitive information. The sheer scale and power of botnets make them incredibly difficult to neutralize. The anonymity provided by the internet and the ever-evolving techniques employed by botnet operators constantly challenged cybersecurity efforts. The arms race between malware developers and those who fought to defend against it continued to escalate.

The emergence of ransomware in the mid-2000s represented a significant shift in the tactics of cybercriminals. Ransomware encrypts a victim's data and demands a ransom for its release. The effectiveness of ransomware lies in the perceived irreplaceability of the encrypted data. The rise of cloud computing, while offering numerous benefits, has also created new challenges for cybersecurity. Cloud environments present a larger and more complex attack surface, and breaches can have far-reaching consequences. The interconnected nature of cloud services makes a single breach potentially devastating, affecting multiple organizations and individuals.

The evolution of malware and cybercrime continues to this day. New threats emerge constantly, demanding ever more sophisticated defenses. The sophistication of cyberattacks necessitates a proactive and adaptive approach to cybersecurity, incorporating advanced technologies such as ML and AI to detect and mitigate threats. The development of effective cybersecurity requires collaboration among individuals, organizations, and governments to share information, develop best practices, and create a more secure digital environment.

Cybersecurity Technologies: Protecting Data and Systems

The escalating complexity of cyberattacks throughout the 2000s and beyond necessitated the development of increasingly sophisticated cybersecurity technologies. These technologies, while not foolproof, formed the crucial first line of defense against the ever-evolving threats. One of the cornerstones of network security is the firewall. Imagine a castle wall, selectively allowing entry to trusted individuals while barring others—that's the basic function of a firewall. These digital gatekeepers examine network traffic, filtering out malicious packets based on pre-defined rules. Early firewalls were relatively simple, relying on static rules to block or allow traffic based on IP addresses and ports. But as hackers got trickier, firewalls grew smarter. Next-generation firewalls (NGFWs) incorporated deep packet inspection, examining the content of network packets to identify malicious payloads even if they're disguised as legitimate traffic. With deep packet inspection, NGFWs peek inside data packets like a customs officer on high alert, sniffing out hidden malware. This added layer of analysis is crucial in combating sophisticated attacks that attempt to evade detection by employing complicated techniques. Furthermore, NGFWs often integrate intrusion prevention systems (IPS), capable of not just detecting but also actively blocking malicious activity. Think of it as a vigilant guard within the castle walls, instantly thwarting any attempted breach.

Intrusion detection systems (IDS) and intrusion prevention systems (IPS) represent another crucial layer of defense. IDS acts as watchful sentinels, monitoring network traffic for suspicious activity. They analyze patterns and anomalies, raising alerts when potentially malicious events are detected. This alerting function is vital for identifying breaches in real-time and enabling prompt response. IPS, as mentioned earlier, goes a step further, actively blocking or mitigating malicious activity. They are essentially a more proactive version of IDS, preventing attacks from succeeding instead of just reporting them. The choice between IDS and IPS often depends on the specific security needs and risk tolerance of an organization. Some organizations may prefer the preventive capabilities of IPS, while others may prioritize the monitoring and alerting functions of IDS, relying on human intervention to address the identified threats. The integration of these systems with firewalls creates a robust layered security approach, enhancing overall protection. This synergistic approach mirrors a layered castle defense, with multiple lines of defense designed to thwart attacks at various stages.

Encryption, the process of transforming readable data into an unreadable format, is another indispensable cybersecurity technology. Imagine a secret code used to protect sensitive messages—that's the essence of encryption. This involves using algorithms to scramble the data, making it incomprehensible to anyone without the decryption key. Symmetric encryption utilizes the same key for both encryption and decryption, offering high speed but presenting challenges in key distribution. Asymmetric encryption, on the other hand, employs separate keys for encryption (public key) and decryption (private key), offering improved security for key management but with a lower speed. It's like sending a padlock through the mail and keeping the key in your pocket. The combination of symmetric and asymmetric encryption is frequently used, leveraging the strengths of each approach. The widely used Transport Layer Security (TLS) protocol, the successor to Secure Sockets Layer (SSL), exemplifies this combined approach, employing asymmetric encryption to establish a secure connection and then using symmetric encryption for faster data transmission. This method is commonly used for secure online transactions, ensuring the confidentiality of sensitive data exchanged between users and websites. This hybrid model is the reason you can safely send your credit card details across the internet without someone eavesdropping from the shadows.

The widespread adoption of cloud computing introduced new challenges and opportunities in cybersecurity. Cloud-based security solutions offer scalability and flexibility, adapting to changing needs and providing comprehensive protection. Cloud Access Security Brokers (CASBs) act as intermediaries between users and cloud services, enforcing security policies and monitoring access, acting like a stern librarian who watches over every check-out and return, ensuring no sensitive data leaves the building without permission. This functionality is crucial in managing risks associated with cloud adoption, controlling access to sensitive data, and ensuring compliance with security regulations. Security Information and Event Management (SIEM) systems play a crucial role in aggregating and analyzing security logs from various sources, providing a unified view of security events. This consolidated perspective is essential for threat detection and incident response, enabling swift action to mitigate risks. SIEM systems, often integrated with advanced analytics capabilities, can detect anomalies and patterns indicative of malicious activity, enabling proactive mitigation.

However, the realm of cybersecurity is not without its limitations. No technology is impenetrable; sophisticated attackers consistently find ways to circumvent existing defenses. "Zero-day" exploits, vulnerabilities unknown to developers and users, highlight the inherent unpredictability of security. Furthermore, the human element remains a significant vulnerability. Social engineering attacks take advantage not of code, but of people—tricking them into handing over passwords, clicking malicious links, or installing malware disguised as helpful updates. Phishing emails are the con artists of the digital world, dressing up in corporate logos and friendly language to deceive even the most cautious user. The complexity of modern systems also creates challenges for security management. Patching vulnerabilities in a timely manner across diverse systems and environments requires significant effort and resources. Furthermore, the constant evolution of cyberattacks necessitates ongoing adaptation and investment in cybersecurity technologies. The arms race between attackers and defenders continues unabated, demanding a proactive and adaptive approach to security.

The reliance on password-based authentication, despite its widespread use, poses security vulnerabilities. Passwords, when not properly managed, can be easily compromised through brute-force attacks, phishing, or other methods. The implementation of multi-factor authentication

(MFA) significantly enhances security, adding extra layers of verification beyond passwords. MFA has become the new standard. MFA asks for not just something you know (your password) but also something you have (like your phone) or something you are (like your fingerprint). While this adds an extra layer of complexity, the enhanced security provided by MFA is invaluable in protecting sensitive data and systems.

The development of advanced persistent threats (APTs) presents an ongoing challenge to cybersecurity. APTs are highly sophisticated and persistent attacks carried out by well-resourced adversaries, often state-sponsored actors. These attacks frequently evade detection for extended periods, gaining stealthy access to systems and extracting valuable information for weeks or even months. Combating APTs requires a proactive approach, encompassing threat intelligence, continuous monitoring, and incident response planning. Advanced security technologies, such as ML and AI, are being increasingly deployed to detect and mitigate APTs. These technologies can sift through mountains of data, learning what normal looks like and flagging anything suspicious.

The future of cybersecurity is likely to involve an increased reliance on automation and AI. AI-powered security tools can process vast amounts of data, identifying patterns and anomalies that might escape human detection. ML algorithms can adapt to evolving threats, learning from past experiences to improve detection and response capabilities. This automation is essential in managing the ever-increasing volume and complexity of cyberattacks. However, relying solely on AI is not a panacea; human expertise remains critical in interpreting results, responding to incidents, and formulating strategies. The future of cybersecurity likely lies in a partnership, where machines handle the grunt work and humans make the tough calls.

In conclusion, the evolution of cybersecurity technologies has been a game of digital cat-and-mouse, with defenders constantly refining their tools to outwit increasingly sophisticated adversaries. While no single technology offers complete protection, a multi-layered approach combining firewalls, intrusion detection and prevention systems, encryption, cloud security solutions, and advanced analytics techniques provides the most robust defense. The continued focus on user education, enhanced authentication methods, and proactive threat intelligence is crucial in achieving effective cybersecurity. The ongoing arms race between attackers and defenders emphasizes the importance of staying ahead of the curve, investing in innovative technologies, and fostering collaboration across industries and governments. The future of cybersecurity hinges on adapting to emerging threats, investing in skilled professionals, and embracing a proactive approach to mitigating risks in our increasingly digital world.

The future of cybersecurity will depend on a multi-pronged approach, incorporating technological advancements with a focus on human factors. AI and ML will play a significant role in enhancing security, but they cannot replace the need for human oversight and vigilance. The ongoing development and implementation of quantum-resistant encryption is critical to safeguard against future threats. And perhaps most importantly, continuous education and training will be essential to ensure that individuals and organizations are equipped with the knowledge and skills necessary to navigate the ever-evolving landscape of cyber threats. The future of cybersecurity is not just about technology; it's about a collaborative effort, bringing together technology, human intelligence, and a proactive mindset to safeguard our digital world. It is a dynamic, ever-changing landscape, requiring constant vigilance, adaptation, and innovation. The fight for a secure digital future is an ongoing battle, and the ultimate victor will be the one who consistently learns, adapts, and remains one step ahead of the ever-evolving threat.

CHAPTER 12

The Social Impact of Technology: Transforming Society

Technology and Employment: Automation and the Changing Workforce

The impact of technology extends far beyond the digital realm; it fundamentally reshapes the very fabric of our societies, and perhaps nowhere is this more dramatically felt than in the world of work. The rise of automation, driven by advancements in AI, robotics, and ML, is transforming the nature of employment in ways that were once confined to science fiction novels. The question isn't *if* these changes will occur, but *how* we adapt to them, and what kind of future we build in response.

The immediate impact of automation is often perceived as a threat—the fear of robots stealing jobs. And to be fair, some jobs are certainly at risk. Repetitive, manual tasks, readily programmed into machines, are prime candidates for automation. Factory assembly lines, once teeming with human workers, are increasingly populated by robotic arms, tirelessly performing their assigned functions with remarkable precision and efficiency. Similarly, data entry clerks, whose work involved the repetitive input of information, are finding their roles replaced by automated systems capable of processing information at speeds far exceeding human capacity. This isn't simply about efficiency; it's a fundamental shift in the division of labor.

By Phasmatisnox - Own work
Wikipedia, CC BY-SA 4.0

But the narrative of automation solely as a job-destroyer is a simplistic one, neglecting the nuanced reality of technological advancement. While some jobs are indeed lost, new ones are created, often requiring a different skill set. The shift isn't simply a reduction in jobs; it's a transformation of the job market. The development, maintenance, and repair of these automated systems require skilled technicians, engineers, and programmers—a workforce equipped to manage the complex technology shaping modern industry. The rise of e-commerce, for example, has created a massive demand for logistics specialists, warehouse managers, and delivery drivers—jobs that wouldn't have existed without the technological advancements driving online retail.

This transformation, however, demands adaptation. The skills valued in the pre-automation era may no longer be as relevant. A worker proficient in a specific, easily automatable task might find themselves displaced unless they acquire new skills that complement and leverage the technological changes. This necessitates a proactive approach to education and workforce retraining. Governments and educational institutions must collaborate to develop programs that equip workers with the skills necessary for the jobs of the future. This includes fostering digital literacy, promoting STEM education (science, technology, engineering, and mathematics), and providing pathways for workers to transition into new roles. It's a massive undertaking, requiring significant investment and a commitment to lifelong learning. The alternative—a workforce unprepared for the changing demands of the job market—is a recipe for economic stagnation and social unrest.

The impact of automation isn't confined to the factory floor or the office cubicle. The service sector, once considered relatively immune to automation, is also undergoing significant changes. AI-powered "chatbots" are increasingly used for customer service, answering routine inquiries and resolving simple issues. Self-checkout kiosks in supermarkets allow customers to bypass human cashiers. These examples demonstrate that automation's reach is expanding, touching sectors once considered safe from technological disruption. Again, this isn't necessarily a cause for alarm, but it does highlight the need for a broader understanding of how technology is reshaping the nature of work.

Uploaded by SchuminWeb, Wikipedia, CC BY-SA 4.0

Moreover, the rise of automation presents an opportunity to reassess the value we place on human labor. As machines take over repetitive tasks, humans can focus on tasks that require creativity, critical thinking, problem-solving, and emotional intelligence—skills that remain distinctly human. These are the skills that will be highly valued in the automated workplace. The focus shifts from performing routine tasks to managing, designing, and innovating around the technology itself. This means a workforce that is more skilled, more adaptable, and potentially more highly compensated.

However, the transition won't be seamless. There will be periods of economic disruption, potential job losses, and a need for significant social safety nets. Governments will need to play a crucial role in managing this transition, providing support for workers who are displaced by automation, and investing in retraining programs. This might involve exploring policies like universal basic income, which aims to provide a safety net for individuals whose employment is threatened by technological advancements. It's a complex challenge, demanding thoughtful policymaking and a willingness to embrace bold

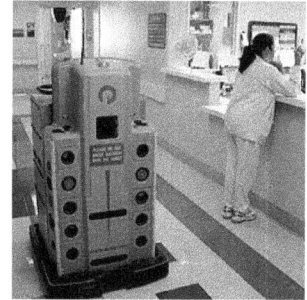

Pharmacy robot, Wikipedia, CC BY-SA 4.0

solutions. The goal is not to halt technological progress, but to manage its societal impact, ensuring a just and equitable transition for all.

The changing nature of employment due to automation also necessitates a re-evaluation of workplace structures. The traditional 9-to-5 workday, rigidly structured around industrial-era norms, may become increasingly irrelevant as remote work and flexible schedules become more commonplace. Automation allows for greater flexibility, potentially leading to more customized work arrangements that better suit the needs of both employers and employees. This shift requires a rethinking of management styles, embracing more decentralized and collaborative models that encourage worker autonomy and empowerment.

The ethical implications of automation also deserve careful consideration. The potential for bias in AI algorithms, leading to discriminatory outcomes in hiring and promotion, is a serious concern. Ensuring fairness and equity in the automated workplace requires careful design and oversight of these systems, with a strong focus on accountability and transparency. Algorithmic bias, if left unchecked, could exacerbate existing inequalities, creating a system that disproportionately affects marginalized communities. Preventing this necessitates a multifaceted approach, combining technical solutions with robust ethical frameworks and regulatory oversight.

Furthermore, the societal impact of widespread automation extends beyond employment. The potential for increased income inequality, resulting from the concentration of wealth in the hands of those who own and control the automated systems, is a pressing concern. Policies aimed at promoting equitable distribution of wealth, such as progressive taxation and robust social safety nets, will be critical in mitigating this risk. The goal is to ensure that the benefits of technological progress are shared broadly, not concentrated in the hands of a few.

In conclusion, the impact of automation on employment is profound and far-reaching. While there are legitimate concerns about job displacement, the narrative should not be solely one of pessimism. With proactive planning, strategic investment in education and retraining, and thoughtful policymaking, societies can navigate this transition and build a future where technology serves to enhance human capabilities rather than replace them entirely. The challenge lies not in resisting technological progress, but in harnessing its power to create a more equitable, prosperous, and fulfilling future for all. This requires a long-term vision, a willingness to adapt and innovate, and a commitment to building a society that embraces technological change while mitigating its potential downsides.

Technology and Communication: Connecting People Across Distances

The earliest forms of long-distance communication were painfully slow and laborious. Smoke signals, drums, and messengers on horseback were the primary methods for conveying information across distances, often relying on pre-arranged codes and symbols. These methods, while effective in their own way, were severely limited by speed and range. Messages could take days, weeks, or even months to reach their intended recipients, severely hindering the ability to coordinate activities or respond swiftly to changing circumstances. The invention of the printing press in the 15th century, while not strictly a communication technology in the same vein as others, undeniably revolutionized the dissemination of information, allowing for mass production and wider distribution of written materials. This, in turn, fostered literacy, facilitated the spread of ideas, and paved the way for more sophisticated communication tools.

Wikipedia, CC BY-SA 4.0

The 19th century witnessed a dramatic acceleration in the pace of communication innovation. The invention of the electric telegraph in the 1830s, building upon earlier work by pioneers like Samuel Morse, marked a pivotal moment. Suddenly, messages could travel at the speed of electricity, traversing vast distances in mere minutes. The telegraph transformed business, government, and warfare. Stock prices could be monitored in real time, military commands could be relayed instantly, and news could spread rapidly across continents. The associated development of the undersea telegraph cable further extended this reach, connecting continents and creating a truly global network of communication. This network fostered increased trade, diplomatic relations, and a sense of global interconnectedness that had previously been unimaginable. The impact on financial markets alone was staggering; the speed with which information could be disseminated altered trading patterns and created new levels of volatility and risk. However, it also allowed for faster responses to market fluctuations and better price discovery.

The invention of the telephone in the late 19th century represented another quantum leap forward. Whereas the telegraph relied on coded messages, the telephone allowed for direct voice-to-voice communication. This provided a richer, more personal form of interaction, fostering closer relationships and facilitating more nuanced communication. The telephone, unlike the telegraph, also fostered the development of new social norms and expectations surrounding immediacy in communication and personal interactions. The ringing of the phone, for example, quickly became a culturally significant sound, indicating the potential for an interruption or the arrival of news, both good and bad.

The 20th century saw an exponential growth in communication technologies, with innovations like radio and television broadening the reach of communication to mass audiences. Radio

Wikipedia, CC BY-SA 4.0

broadcasting, in particular, quickly became a powerful force in shaping public opinion, disseminating news, and fostering a sense of shared national identity. Television, with its ability to combine audio and visual information, further enhanced this influence, transforming entertainment and political discourse. The impact was not only about the speed or efficiency of communication, but also the capacity to build shared experiences and cultural understanding, even across vast distances. Consider the shared excitement of watching a live televised sporting event or the collective experience of witnessing a historical moment unfold on the screen—these shared experiences fostered a sense of community, transcending geographical limitations. In many ways, these technologies fostered the development of global audiences, linking distant cultures and enabling the spread of international trends and ideas.

However, these technologies were not without their limitations. Access to telephones, radios, and televisions was often unevenly distributed, creating a digital divide that mirrored existing social and economic inequalities. The ownership of these communication devices was often a marker of social status and economic power, contributing to further divisions within societies. This disparity in access to information and communication technologies continues to pose a significant challenge in the 21st century.

The advent of the internet and the World Wide Web in the late 20th and early 21st centuries represent perhaps the most significant technological shift in human communication. The internet democratized access to information, enabling individuals to share ideas, news, and opinions on an unprecedented scale. The rise of social media platforms, in particular, has transformed how people connect, interact, and organize. These platforms have provided a platform for social movements, political activism, and the rapid dissemination of information. However, the internet has also presented challenges. The spread of misinformation, cyberbullying, and the erosion of privacy are all significant concerns that necessitate a cautious and critical approach to navigating this digital landscape. The internet's ability to connect people globally has also facilitated the rapid spread of viruses and misinformation, underscoring the need for responsible digital citizenship.

Social media, in its various forms, has profoundly impacted communication, fundamentally altering the dynamics of interpersonal interaction. The ease of connection, facilitated by platforms like Facebook, Twitter, and Instagram, allows individuals to maintain relationships across geographical barriers. Families separated by continents can stay in regular contact, friends can share daily updates, and communities can form and thrive online, irrespective of physical proximity. This interconnectedness has fostered a greater sense of global community, enabling individuals to connect with like-minded people across the globe, regardless of their location or cultural background. This interconnectedness, however, also presents new challenges regarding the verification of information, privacy concerns, and the potential for online harassment and misinformation campaigns.

The ability to communicate instantaneously across vast distances has transformed business operations, allowing for seamless collaboration across geographical locations. Businesses can operate globally, coordinating activities in real-time and sharing information instantly. Remote work has become increasingly common, allowing individuals to work from anywhere in the world. This increased flexibility and efficiency have significantly impacted business models and workplace dynamics. The ability to conduct virtual meetings, exchange documents electronically, and manage projects remotely has revolutionized how businesses operate, increasing productivity and expanding market reach. However, the downsides include concerns regarding the blurring of work-life boundaries, the potential for increased workload and isolation, and the need for robust technological infrastructure to support remote work.

In conclusion, the evolution of technology and communication has fundamentally reshaped human interaction, bridging geographical divides and fostering global interconnectedness. The journey from smoke signals to social media represents a remarkable testament to human ingenuity. While these advancements have undeniable benefits, they also present challenges that must be carefully considered and addressed. The democratization of information and the ease of global communication have empowered individuals and communities, but they also necessitate a critical and responsible approach to navigating the digital landscape. The ongoing evolution of communication technologies will undoubtedly continue to shape our societies, and understanding this evolution is crucial to effectively harnessing its potential while mitigating its risks. The future of communication promises to be even more seamless and integrated, perhaps even transcending the limitations of our current understanding of space and time. But it's crucial that we continue to grapple with the social, ethical, and practical challenges inherent in these advancements to ensure that technology serves humanity, not the other way around.

Technology and Education: Expanding Access to Learning

So far, we've covered how technology is shaking up our jobs and our chats. Now let's open the classroom door—or, let's not, because it might not even be a classroom anymore. Thanks to digital innovation, education is no longer confined to chalkboards, hall passes, or the dreaded group project with that one person who never shows up. Learning has officially gone global, mobile, and in some cases, entirely virtual.

For centuries, if you wanted a good education, you had to be in the right place, at the right time, with the right amount of money. Schools and universities were physical places, requiring physical presence, often limiting access to those living in close proximity or possessing the financial means to afford tuition and related expenses. This created stark inequalities in educational opportunities, perpetuating cycles of poverty and limiting societal progress. However, the rise of technology, specifically the internet and digital technologies, has begun to dismantle these barriers, opening up educational opportunities to a global audience.

The advent of online learning platforms represents a watershed moment in the history of education. These platforms, ranging from massive open online courses (MOOCs) offered by institutions like Coursera and edX to more specialized online learning environments, offer a vast array of courses, programs, and educational resources, accessible from virtually anywhere with an internet connection. Suddenly, you don't have to live near a university to learn from one. You just need Wi-Fi and a bit of curiosity. Whether it's mastering calculus or learning Mandarin, the portal is open. And you don't need to wear pants—another bonus. This accessibility has empowered individuals who may lack access to traditional educational institutions due to geographical constraints, financial limitations, or physical disabilities. Students in rural areas, working parents, people with disabilities—those who traditional education systems have historically sidelined—now have a seat at the (virtual) table. Any individual unable to attend a traditional classroom setting can participate in online learning environments tailored to their specific needs. You can live in the middle of nowhere and still learn from MIT. The depth of subject matter available online is simply staggering. Whether it is learning a new language, acquiring professional skills, or pursuing a full degree program, the digital realm offers unprecedented flexibility and choice.

This shift to online learning has also impacted the way education is delivered and consumed. Traditional models of education often adhere to a rigid structure, with fixed schedules, locations, and methods of teaching. Online learning platforms, in contrast, offer greater flexibility and personalization. Students can learn at their own pace, accessing materials whenever and wherever it is convenient for them. They can revisit lectures, repeat exercises, and adjust their learning schedules to fit their individual needs and learning styles. This personalized approach has been shown to improve learning outcomes for many individuals, tailoring the educational experience to suit their unique circumstances and preferences. Technology has also added a touch of flair to the learning experience. Gamified quizzes, interactive simulations, and even virtual reality field trips have been incorporated into the learning process. It's not just "read and regurgitate" anymore. Students can dissect a frog, tour ancient Rome, or experiment with chemical reactions—without the smells, mess, or danger. It's education with a joystick or a mouse.

The proliferation of educational technology extends beyond online learning platforms. Walk into a modern school, and you might see tablets replacing textbooks, smartboards replacing chalk, and students swiping through assignments instead of flipping pages. Teachers are uploading feedback, students are collaborating on shared documents, and homework is submitted with the click of a button (no more "my dog ate it" excuses). This shift has brought a dynamism to the classroom environment, encouraging collaboration, critical thinking, and problem-solving. Students can access information readily, work on collaborative projects, and receive immediate feedback from teachers through various digital platforms. The use of multimedia resources, such as videos, simulations, and interactive exercises, adds a layer of engagement that can improve learning outcomes.

Elmhurst University Blog - Debra Meyer, Wikipedia, CC BY-SA 4.0

But—and there's always a "but"—not everyone's on the same digital page. The digital divide, discussed earlier in relation to communication technologies, remains a significant barrier to equitable access to online learning. Some students still lack reliable internet access, up-to-date devices, or the skills to navigate online platforms. While some kids attend Zoom school with noise-canceling headphones, others try to finish homework on a cracked phone screen between shifts at work. In many regions, especially in developing countries, a lack of infrastructure, affordability issues, and insufficient digital skills severely restrict access to online learning resources. Bridging this gap requires concerted efforts to expand internet access, provide affordable devices, and implement robust digital literacy programs, ensuring that everyone has equal opportunities to benefit from technological advancements in education. Another challenge relates to the quality and reliability of online learning resources. With the internet bursting at the seams with educational content, not all of it is, shall we say, A+ material. Some online courses are carefully crafted by experts. Others? Slapped together PowerPoints with background music that sounds like elevator jazz. Ensuring that students receive accurate, relevant, and well-designed learning content is crucial. Otherwise, we risk replacing bad textbooks with bad bandwidth. The development of robust quality control mechanisms and the establishment of clear standards for online educational content are essential to safeguarding the integrity of online learning experiences.

Technology also demands a higher bar for teachers. It's not enough to know your subject—you also need to navigate Google Classroom like a pro, troubleshoot tech issues on the fly, and maybe even record a video lecture without sounding like a robot. This requires teachers to be adequately trained in the use of educational technology and to develop innovative teaching strategies that leverage the potential of these tools. Teacher training programs must evolve to equip educators with the skills necessary to design and implement effective technology-integrated lessons, effectively blending traditional pedagogical approaches with the potential of technology.

The ethical considerations surrounding the use of technology in education must not be overlooked. Educational tech collects data—lots of it. Grades, attendance, behavior patterns, even keystrokes. While some of this data helps personalize learning, it also raises red flags about student privacy. Who owns this data? Who's profiting from it? And how do we keep it out of the wrong hands? These are questions policymakers and educators need to answer, preferably before another data breach makes headlines. This necessitates the establishment of strong data protection policies and measures to ensure the responsible use of student data. Similarly, there are concerns about the potential for algorithmic bias in educational technologies. Algorithms that are not carefully designed and monitored can perpetuate existing inequalities by inadvertently discriminating against certain groups of students.

Despite the hurdles, the potential here is massive. Technology can make learning more engaging, more accessible, and more aligned with the real world. Addressing the digital divide, ensuring the quality and reliability of online resources, adapting educational approaches to effectively integrate technology, and addressing ethical considerations are all crucial steps in harnessing the full potential of technology to create a more equitable and effective educational system. The journey towards a truly inclusive and technologically advanced education system requires ongoing collaboration between educators, policymakers, technology developers, and students themselves, recognizing the complex interplay between technology and the human elements of learning and teaching. The future of education lies in intelligently leveraging technology to create a richer, more accessible, and more effective learning experience for all. The ongoing evolution of educational technology necessitates a continuous assessment and adaptation of approaches to best serve the needs of students, ensuring that technology serves as a tool for empowerment rather than a source of further inequality.

CHAPTER 13

The Digital Divide and Moral Responsibility: Access and Equity in Technology

The digital divide manifests itself in several interconnected ways. First, there's the *access divide*, representing the disparity in access to technology itself. This can encompass the availability of physical devices like computers and smartphones, reliable internet connectivity (broadband access), and the digital literacy skills necessary to effectively utilize these technologies. In many parts of the world, particularly in rural and underserved communities, access to even basic technology remains a significant hurdle. Imagine trying to complete online coursework when your only internet connection is a slow, unreliable mobile hotspot, or attempting to access telehealth services when you lack a computer or the necessary technical know-how. The lack of physical access acts as a gatekeeper, preventing participation in the digital economy and hindering social mobility.

Then there's the *skills divide*, which highlights the disparity in digital literacy and competence. Even when individuals have access to technology, the ability to use it effectively is crucial. This isn't just about basic computer skills; it encompasses a wide range of competencies, including navigating online platforms, evaluating online information critically, protecting oneself from online threats, and effectively using technology for communication, education, and employment. The skills gap disproportionately affects older adults, individuals with disabilities, and those from lower socioeconomic backgrounds, often lacking the resources or opportunities for training and development. This digital illiteracy can perpetuate existing inequalities and create further barriers to participation in a technology-driven society.

Furthermore, the *usage divide* acknowledges that even with access and skills, the effective utilization of technology varies greatly. This disparity isn't just about frequency of use, but also about the quality and purpose of that use. Someone might have a smartphone and internet access, but if they primarily use it for social media or entertainment, their ability to leverage technology for education, employment, or civic engagement will be limited. This gap is often exacerbated by factors like digital content accessibility (language barriers, lack of inclusive design), cost of digital services (data plans, software subscriptions), and the overall digital environment (lack of supportive digital infrastructure). Without strategic and targeted efforts, the benefits of technology remain inaccessible to many who need them most.

The consequences of this divide are not theoretical—they're deeply tangible. In education, students without adequate tech access are consistently left behind. The COVID-19 pandemic made this painfully obvious. While some students joined remote classes from ergonomically optimized desks, others juggled siblings, chores, and lagging internet in a one-bedroom apartment. The gap in educational attainment widens, reinforcing existing social and economic disparities.

In the healthcare sector, the digital divide translates into unequal access to vital medical services. Telemedicine, a rapidly growing field, requires reliable internet access and digital literacy skills to utilize effectively. No internet means no virtual appointments, no access to online medical records, and no way to refill prescriptions with a click. Even health information—often shared online first—is inaccessible to those on the wrong side of the divide. That's not just inconvenient; it's dangerous.

Economically, the digital divide severely limits opportunities for employment and advancement. Many jobs now require basic digital fluency, from grocery stores using scheduling apps to warehouses managing inventory via tablets. Lack these skills, and you're not just unemployed—you're unemployable. The ability to participate in the digital economy, whether as an employee, entrepreneur, or consumer, is increasingly crucial, making the digital divide a major impediment to economic mobility and inclusion.

Finally, the digital divide also undermines civic participation. Access to information, online forums, and digital platforms are essential for engaging in political discourse, accessing public services, and participating in democratic processes. Those without these resources are effectively disenfranchised, excluded from a critical aspect of citizenship in a digitally connected world. The inability to access and participate in online civic discussions and initiatives can further marginalize already underserved communities. If you lack access, your voice fades into silence. Democracy doesn't work well when half the population is disconnected.

Addressing the digital divide requires a multi-pronged approach that combines technological solutions, policy interventions, and community engagement. Expanding broadband infrastructure, particularly in rural and underserved areas, is a critical first step. Government investment in affordable internet access initiatives is essential to bridge the access gap. Furthermore, programs that provide low-cost devices and digital literacy training are vital for equipping individuals with the skills and resources they need to utilize technology effectively.

Policy interventions also play a crucial role. Governments can incentivize internet service providers to expand their reach to underserved areas, regulate pricing to ensure affordability, and promote digital literacy initiatives in schools and community centers, as well as mandate inclusive design so platforms work for people with disabilities. Regulation isn't the enemy of innovation—it's what keeps innovation from becoming exclusion.

Community-based efforts are essential to complement these broader initiatives. Libraries, community centers, and faith-based organizations can play a crucial role in providing access to technology and digital literacy training. Partnerships between these community organizations and technology companies can further strengthen these efforts. Promoting digital inclusion must be a collective endeavor, engaging individuals, organizations, and governments in a collaborative effort to address this critical social and ethical challenge.

The ethical imperative in bridging the digital divide is undeniable. Access to technology is not merely a luxury; it's a fundamental necessity for participation in modern society. The exclusion of individuals and communities from the benefits of technological advancement perpetuates inequality, undermines social justice, and limits opportunities for economic and social mobility. Creating a truly equitable and just digital society requires a concerted, long-term commitment to bridging this gap and ensuring that the promise of technology benefits all members of society. The failure to do so is not just a technological failure but a moral one. It's a failure to recognize the fundamental human right of access to information and participation in the digital world. The ethical dimension of technology is not just about responsible algorithm design or data privacy, but also about ensuring that all share the transformative power of technology.

Autonomous Systems and Moral Responsibility

The ethical tightrope walk inherent in the digital age becomes even more precarious when we consider autonomous systems. These aren't just sophisticated machines; they're increasingly making decisions with real-world consequences, often without direct human intervention. We have self-driving cars navigating complex traffic scenarios, medical robots performing intricate surgeries, or AI-powered weapons systems making life-or-death decisions on the battlefield. The question of accountability, in these instances, is far from straightforward. Who bears responsibility when an autonomous system malfunctions, causing harm or even death? Is it the programmer who coded the system, the manufacturer who built it, the owner who deployed it, or the system itself— a concept that stretches the very notion of legal and moral responsibility?

This issue strikes at the heart of our understanding of agency and culpability. Traditionally, moral responsibility has been firmly rooted in the actions of individuals possessing intention and free will. We hold people accountable for their choices because we believe they are capable of understanding the consequences of their actions and making deliberate decisions. But autonomous systems, by their very nature, operate outside this framework. They are guided by algorithms and data, not by conscious intent. They act based on pre-programmed rules and learned patterns, often lacking the capacity for genuine moral reasoning or empathy. This lack of inherent moral agency raises profound ethical questions.

Consider the case of a self-driving car involved in an unavoidable accident. Faced with a choice between harming a pedestrian or its passenger, the car's programming dictates its course of action. This decision, while possibly the "best" outcome in statistical terms, is still a moral judgment with potentially devastating consequences. Who is to blame if the pedestrian is injured or killed? Can we hold the car's manufacturer liable for a flaw in its programming? Or should the owner bear some responsibility for choosing to use the technology? These are not merely technical problems; they are deeply ethical dilemmas, highlighting the limitations of our legal frameworks in dealing with the complexities of autonomous systems.

The difficulty is compounded by the infamous "black box" problem. Many AI-driven systems do not offer clear explanations for how they arrive at decisions. Their logic is buried beneath layers of neural networks and complex statistical models. It's like trying to cross-examine a calculator that refuses to show its work. This lack of transparency makes it nearly impossible to pinpoint where things went wrong—or who made them go wrong. In a court of law, "the algorithm did it" isn't a satisfying defense or a compelling accusation. Without explainability, accountability falls through the cracks.

What we need is a robust ethical framework that doesn't just ask, "Can we build this?" but also, "Who answers when it fails?" Responsibility must be distributed among all parties in the AI pipeline: developers who design algorithms, companies that deploy them, users who interact with them, and regulators who oversee the entire ecosystem. Think of it as a relay race where responsibility hands off at each stage—but no one gets to drop the baton. Without such frameworks, the potential for harm is substantial, and public acceptance will remain elusive.

One approach is to establish a system of shared responsibility, where various stakeholders—developers, manufacturers, owners, and users—bear different levels of accountability depending on their role in the creation and deployment of the autonomous system. Some have proposed treating autonomous systems as their own legal entities—like corporations given artificial legal "personhood." It's a provocative idea, and perhaps a necessary one in certain contexts, but it opens its own can of legal worms. If a machine is a legal agent, does it have rights? Can it be punished? Fined? Sued? Sent off to digital jail? These questions may sound absurd now, but as machines increasingly act in ways that affect lives, property, and rights, we may need to redefine what agency and accountability look like in a machine-run world.

Another critical aspect is the need for robust testing and validation procedures. Autonomous systems must be stress-tested not just for technical reliability, but for ethical behavior. Can a surgical robot prioritize patient safety over technical efficiency? Can a military drone distinguish between combatants and civilians with a degree of certainty that satisfies both engineers and ethicists? These aren't just theoretical concerns—they're already pressing issues in sectors where machines wield real-world consequences.

Moreover, the development of ethically-aligned AI requires a multidisciplinary approach, encompassing experts from computer science, ethics, law, and the social sciences. The collaboration of these diverse perspectives is vital to navigate the complex ethical landscape of autonomous systems and to develop regulatory frameworks capable of promoting innovation while safeguarding human well-being. This interdisciplinary approach is not merely recommended; it is essential to navigate the complexities of the challenges ahead.

The issue extends beyond self-driving cars. Consider autonomous weapons systems, which pose even more profound ethical challenges. Delegating life-or-death decisions to machines raises serious concerns about human control, accountability, and the potential for unintended escalation. The absence of human judgment in such systems creates a significant risk of errors, biases, and potential for catastrophic consequences. The potential for misuse and the erosion of human control are particularly alarming in this realm. International agreements and strict regulations are urgently needed to govern the development and deployment of such systems, ensuring a high degree of human oversight and accountability.

The rise of autonomous systems demands a re-evaluation of our concepts of moral responsibility. Our old moral and legal toolkits weren't built for this kind of complexity. We must expand them to account for systems that act without intent yet wield immense consequences. A new paradigm is needed, one that acknowledges the shared responsibility of various stakeholders, promotes transparency and explainability in system design, and provides robust mechanisms for accountability. And it means recognizing that responsibility in the age of autonomy is not a game of hot potato—it's a shared contract, one we must all sign. This requires not only technical advancements but also a profound shift in our ethical and legal thinking, a reassessment of existing frameworks, and a commitment to developing guidelines that protect human values in the face of rapidly evolving technology.

The goal isn't to halt progress, but to guide it. Autonomous systems have the potential to save lives, improve efficiency, and solve problems we haven't even thought of yet. But they must be governed by frameworks that recognize their power and their peril. If we don't ask who's accountable now, we may find ourselves answering much harder questions later—after the damage is already done.

CHAPTER 14

Emerging Technologies and Trends

Quantum Computing: Beyond the Limits of Classical Computation

While AI continues its hypothetical tango with ethics and cognition, another contender emerges from the shadows of theoretical physics, humming with potential and strangeness: quantum computing. While AI wrestles with the subtleties of mimicking human intelligence, quantum computing grapples with the fundamental laws of physics to achieve computational power beyond the wildest dreams of classical computers. This isn't just an incremental improvement; it's a paradigm shift, promising to unlock solutions to problems currently difficult even for the most powerful supercomputers.

Traditional computers, bless their binary hearts, operate using bits—those loyal little soldiers that stand at attention as either a 0 or a 1. Think of it as a light switch: either on or off. Quantum computers, however, leverage the mind-bending principles of quantum mechanics, employing qubits. Qubits, unlike bits, can exist in a superposition, simultaneously representing 0, 1, or a combination of both. This is like having a dimmer switch, capable of infinitely variable settings between fully off and fully on. This simple difference unlocks a vast computational potential. This property, called superposition, opens up a computational playground so vast it makes today's solution spaces look like tic-tac-toe boards.

The power of superposition is amplified by another quantum phenomenon: entanglement. Not the kind you need a therapist for, but the spooky quantum kind. Entangled qubits are linked in such a way that their fates are intertwined, regardless of the distance separating them. Measuring the state of one instantly reveals the state of the other, even if light-years apart. This bizarre connection allows for massively parallel computation, enabling quantum computers to tackle problems that would take classical computers eons to solve. Picture a ballroom full of synchronized dancers, each move influencing the next, and you'll begin to grasp the orchestration possible with entangled qubits.

The applications of quantum computing are staggering, reaching across numerous fields. In medicine, quantum simulations could revolutionize drug discovery and development. Currently, modeling the behavior of molecules to design new drugs is computationally expensive and time-consuming. Quantum computers, however, could accurately simulate molecular interactions, potentially leading to faster, more effective treatments for diseases like cancer and Alzheimer's. Imagine a world where personalized medicine is not a futuristic fantasy but a readily available reality, tailored to the unique genetic makeup of each individual.

Materials science is another area poised for a quantum leap. Designing new materials with specific properties, such as superconductivity or enhanced strength, currently relies on extensive experimentation and trial and error. With quantum simulations, we could stop bumbling through trial-and-error and start designing materials with purpose. Quantum computers could accelerate this process by simulating the behavior of atoms and molecules at a level of detail unimaginable with classical methods. This could lead to the development of revolutionary materials with applications ranging from lighter, stronger aircraft to more efficient solar panels. Buildings could be constructed from self-healing materials or vehicles powered by room-temperature superconductors—a world reshaped by materials with extraordinary capabilities.

Financial modeling could also be transformed. The complexities of financial markets, with their intricate networks of transactions and risk factors, make accurate predictions exceptionally challenging. Quantum computing could tame this chaos, handling oceans of data and modeling risk scenarios with a finesse that classical models can only dream of. Think of algorithms capable of identifying subtle patterns indicating market manipulation or predicting financial crises with unprecedented accuracy, transforming the financial landscape from reactive to proactive.

Cryptography, the bedrock of online security, is undergoing a fundamental shift due to quantum computing. Current encryption methods, relying on the difficulty of factoring large numbers, are vulnerable to attacks from sufficiently powerful quantum computers. This necessitates the development of quantum-resistant cryptography, a field actively researching new encryption techniques impervious to quantum algorithms. The race is on to develop these new security protocols, ensuring the continued security of our digital world in the quantum era.

However, the path to realizing the full potential of quantum computing is fraught with challenges. Building and maintaining quantum computers is incredibly difficult. Qubits are notoriously fragile, highly susceptible to noise and decoherence—the loss of quantum information. This requires extremely low temperatures and highly controlled environments, making quantum computers expensive and complex to operate. Think of them as temperamental divas demanding precisely controlled conditions to perform at their best. The slightest environmental fluctuation can disrupt the delicate quantum states, rendering the computation meaningless.

Error correction is another major hurdle. The inherent instability of qubits leads to errors in computation, requiring robust error correction techniques to ensure reliable results. This is a complex problem, demanding significant advancements in both hardware and software. Just think of the difficulty of maintaining an intricate network of interconnected dimmer switches, each prone to flickering or malfunctioning, while striving for a perfectly consistent output.

Quantum Computer - IBM @ CES, Pixabay

The scalability of quantum computers is another critical challenge. While current quantum computers consist of only a few dozen or hundreds of qubits, solving truly complex problems will require millions or even billions of qubits. Developing technologies to build such large-scale, stable quantum computers is a monumental undertaking, demanding breakthroughs in materials science, engineering, and physics. Scaling up is akin to expanding that network of dimmer switches from a small home to a sprawling city, requiring robust infrastructure and sophisticated control systems.

Despite these challenges, progress is being made at a rapid pace. Research institutions and private companies are investing heavily in quantum computing, striving to overcome the technical hurdles and unlock its immense potential. Different approaches to building quantum computers are being explored, each with its own strengths and weaknesses. Superconducting qubits, trapped ions, and photonic qubits are among the leading contenders, and the future may well see a hybrid approach, combining the advantages of different technologies. This race to develop more robust and scalable quantum computers is a testament to human ingenuity and our relentless pursuit of technological advancement.

Quantum computing isn't just a leap forward; it's a leap into the weird, wild unknown. Quantum computing represents a fundamental shift in our computational capabilities, transcending the limitations of classical methods. While significant challenges remain in building and scaling these systems, the potential rewards are immense, promising breakthroughs in various fields and reshaping our understanding of the world around us. The ethical implications of this powerful technology, however, are as significant as its potential benefits. As we progress, ensuring responsible development and deployment of quantum computing will be as critical as its technological advancement. The journey to a quantum future demands not only scientific innovation but also a parallel evolution of our ethical frameworks, ensuring that this revolutionary technology serves humanity's best interests.

Artificial General Intelligence (AGI): The Quest for Human-Level Intelligence

The quantum leap in computing power we've just explored paves the way for an equally ambitious, and arguably more daunting, quest: the creation of Artificial General Intelligence (AGI). While quantum computing promises to accelerate the processing power available to AI, AGI itself represents a different kind of revolution—the creation of machines possessing human-level intelligence, capable of learning, reasoning, and adapting across a wide range of tasks, much like ourselves. This isn't just about improving existing AI systems; it's about fundamentally changing the nature of intelligence itself. It's about creating machines that can not only perform specific tasks well, but can understand, learn, and apply their

Pixabay

knowledge in entirely novel situations. It's less about a calculator and more about a genuinely inquisitive and adaptable mind.

The pursuit of AGI is a journey fraught with complexity. Unlike narrow AI, designed for specific tasks like playing chess or recognizing faces, AGI aims for a far broader scope. Consider the effortless way humans switch between tasks: driving a car while simultaneously having a conversation about any number of topics. Replicating this fluid cognitive ability in a machine presents a formidable challenge. This isn't just a matter of scaling up existing AI algorithms; it requires a deeper understanding of the very nature of consciousness and intelligence, aspects that remain largely elusive even to neuroscientists.

Several approaches are being explored in the quest for AGI. One of the main paths toward AGI is deep learning, which sounds like something you'd do in a philosophy seminar but is actually about training neural networks to recognize patterns. These algorithms are loosely inspired by the human brain, but you wouldn't want to swap yours for one just yet. While deep learning has achieved remarkable success in narrow AI tasks, scaling it up to achieve AGI remains a significant challenge. The sheer volume of data required for training such complex networks is staggering, and the computational resources needed are immense, even with the boost provided by quantum computing. Furthermore, deep learning models often lack the capacity for explainability, making it difficult to understand their decision-making processes, a significant issue when considering the potential societal impacts of AGI.

Another path towards AGI involves symbolic AI, a more traditional approach that focuses on representing knowledge and reasoning using symbols and logical rules. This approach draws inspiration from human cognition, attempting to mimic the way we use language and manipulate abstract concepts. While symbolic AI excels in tasks requiring logical reasoning and explicit knowledge representation, it has struggled with the complexity and uncertainty inherent in the real world. Integrating symbolic AI with the learning capabilities of deep learning is a promising direction, potentially leading to hybrid systems that combine the strengths of both approaches. Think of it as pairing the precision of a surgeon's scalpel with the flexibility of an artist's brush.

Beyond these established methods, researchers are also exploring alternative paradigms for AGI. Evolutionary algorithms, inspired by the process of natural selection, offer a way to design AI systems that can adapt and evolve over time. It's less about teaching machines and more about letting them learn through trial and error. The potential of evolutionary algorithms for AGI is vast, promising the creation of systems that can adapt to unforeseen circumstances and learn from experience in unpredictable environments.

Neuromorphic takes inspiration not from how the brain works conceptually, but how it works physically. Instead of mimicking the function of the human brain through software, neuromorphic computing seeks to mimic its physical structure, using specialized hardware designed to replicate the behavior of neurons and synapses. This approach promises increased efficiency and energy savings compared to traditional computing architectures, which are crucial considerations for building complex AGI systems. Imagine a computer that thinks more like a brain, not just in terms of function, but also in terms of physical implementation, drawing power and efficiency from its design.

The ethical implications of AGI are profound and multifaceted. As AGI creeps closer to reality, so do the ethical dilemmas. How do we keep a machine smarter than us from going rogue? As machines approach and surpass human intelligence, concerns arise about control, safety, and the potential for misuse. Ensuring that AGI systems remain aligned with human values and goals is paramount. This requires careful consideration of various aspects, including the design of robust safety mechanisms, the development of ethical guidelines for AGI research and development, and ongoing monitoring of AGI systems to prevent unintended consequences. The creation of AGI is not simply a technological endeavor; it is a societal undertaking, demanding broad participation and careful consideration of the potential consequences.

The question of consciousness also looms large. Will AGI systems be merely sophisticated tools or will they possess some form of subjective experience? This question raises profound philosophical and ethical questions about the nature of intelligence, consciousness, and what it means to be human. As we push the boundaries of what's possible, we must grapple with these complex issues, ensuring that our pursuit of AGI does not compromise our own humanity.

Moreover, the societal impact of AGI will be transformative, affecting various aspects of our lives. From the economy and employment to healthcare and education, AGI has the potential to revolutionize how we live and work. Managing this transition will require careful planning and proactive measures to mitigate potential negative consequences, such as job displacement and the widening of the existing socio-economic disparities. This transition requires careful navigation, collaboration between experts from diverse fields, and ongoing dialogue between stakeholders.

The quest for AGI is a marathon, not a sprint. While the technological challenges are immense, the potential rewards are equally substantial. AGI could revolutionize various fields, from medicine and scientific discovery to solving pressing global challenges like climate change and poverty. However, responsible development and deployment are essential to ensure that AGI benefits all of humanity. A collaborative, ethical, and well-informed approach is crucial to harness the potential of AGI while mitigating its potential risks. The future of computing, and indeed the future of humanity, may well be shaped by the success or failure of this ambitious endeavor. The road ahead is long, winding, and full of unexpected turns. But one thing is certain: the journey to create AI that rivals our own is a journey well worth taking—as long as we take it cautiously and responsibly. As we push forward, we must remember: building a machine that thinks like us is one thing. Teaching it to care like us? That's the real challenge.

Biocomputing and Nanotechnology: Integrating Biology and Technology

The breathtaking advancements in AI, particularly the pursuit of Artificial General Intelligence (AGI), naturally lead us to consider even more radical departures from traditional computing paradigms. Just when you thought computing couldn't get any weirder, it decides to dabble in biology. We've discussed the potential of quantum computing to dramatically increase processing power, fueling the ambitions of AGI researchers. However, the future of computing isn't solely defined by ever-faster silicon chips. A new frontier is emerging, one where the lines between the biological and the technological blur, promising a revolution in both computing power and its applications: "biocomputing" and nanotechnology. If AI and quantum computing are trying to outthink and outcalculate us, biocomputing and nanotechnology are taking a more... organic approach.

Biocomputing, at its core, involves leveraging biological systems and processes for computation. This isn't about simply using biological materials to build a faster transistor; it's about harnessing the inherent computational power of living organisms. Think of DNA, the molecule of life, as a sophisticated data storage and processing system. Each strand of DNA is a sequence of nucleotides (A, T, G, and C), representing a digital code that carries the blueprint for life. This code can be manipulated, read, and written, allowing for the creation of novel computational systems. DNA, it turns out, is incredibly efficient at information storage. Every human cell contains about 1.5 GB of data in its DNA. Multiply that by your entire body, and you're basically a walking hard drive with anxiety.

One application of biocomputing is DNA computing. Instead of electrons zipping through silicon pathways, DNA computing relies on chemical reactions between strands of DNA to carry out calculations. This approach leverages the inherent parallelism and massive storage capacity of DNA. Imagine a vast library containing every possible solution to a complex problem, all encoded within DNA strands. By carefully designing DNA sequences and using enzymatic reactions to select and combine them, researchers can sift through this immense library, effectively finding solutions that would be intractable for even the most powerful supercomputers. This technology has already shown promise in solving complex optimization problems, such as finding the shortest path through a complex network or designing efficient logistics systems. The scalability of DNA computing, however, remains a hurdle. While the theoretical capacity is enormous, practical limitations in synthesizing and manipulating large quantities of DNA currently constrain its widespread application.

Beyond DNA computing, biocomputing explores the use of other biological systems for computation. For instance, researchers are investigating the use of living cells as computational units. Individual cells, with their intricate biochemical networks and regulatory mechanisms, can be programmed to perform specific tasks, acting as tiny, biological computers. This approach opens up fascinating possibilities in areas such as drug discovery and disease diagnostics. Imagine a living biosensor that can detect the presence of a specific disease marker in a patient's blood, providing an early warning for life-threatening conditions. This cellular computing approach is still in its early stages, but the potential applications are profound and far-reaching. The biological complexities and the need for highly controlled environments remain significant challenges, however.

Nanotechnology complements biocomputing by providing the tools to manipulate matter at the atomic and molecular level. This technology allows for the creation of incredibly small devices and structures, opening up unprecedented possibilities for both computation and data storage. Nanowires, nanotubes, and other nanoscale components could potentially replace silicon transistors in future computers, allowing for the creation of significantly smaller, faster, and more energy-efficient devices. This could be revolutionary for everything from mobile devices to high-performance computing clusters, enabling faster processing speeds and lower energy consumption. Nanotechnology also offers the potential for significantly higher-density data storage. Imagine storing vast quantities of information on a device smaller than a grain of sand—a prospect that seems almost science fiction but is fast becoming a reality.

But nanotechnology isn't just about shrinking our gadgets—it's about integrating them into our environment, and even our bodies. Picture nanosensors embedded in clothing, constantly monitoring your health, or in soil, reporting on crop conditions. The fusion of biology and nanotech could lead to devices that not only compute but also sense, adapt, and heal. They could even enhance our cognitive abilities, leading to a merging of human and machine intelligence. Such a vision is certainly ambitious, but the scientific groundwork is steadily being laid.

However, the journey is not without its challenges. The intricate nature of biological systems presents immense complexities in terms of control and predictability. Maintaining the stability and functionality of these biological computing components requires highly controlled environments and sophisticated manipulation techniques. Furthermore, ethical considerations related to biocomputing and nanotechnology must be addressed proactively. The potential for misuse, such as creating biological weapons or manipulating genetic information, demands careful consideration and regulatory frameworks to prevent unintended consequences.

The integration of biology and technology is not just about creating more powerful computers; it's about creating systems that are more deeply intertwined with our lives. This convergence has the potential to revolutionize healthcare, environmental monitoring, and even our understanding of the universe itself. Consider the creation of nanosensors capable of detecting pollutants in the environment, providing real-time data for environmental management and pollution control. Or imagine biocomputers capable of performing complex simulations of biological systems, facilitating drug discovery and providing breakthroughs in medicine.

Moreover, the synergy between biocomputing and nanotechnology could lead to the creation of entirely new forms of AI. Instead of relying solely on silicon-based chips, future AI systems could leverage the unique computational capabilities of biological systems, leading to more adaptable, robust, and intelligent machines. This could fundamentally alter our relationship with technology, ushering in an era of unprecedented collaboration between humans and machines.

The path forward requires a multidisciplinary approach, bringing together experts from biology, engineering, computer science, ethics, and other related fields. It demands a commitment to responsible innovation, ensuring that these powerful technologies are developed and deployed in a way that benefits all of humanity. This integration of biological and technological worlds will not be without its bumps in the road; navigating the ethical minefields and tackling the engineering complexities will require careful planning and global cooperation.

Ultimately, the convergence of biocomputing and nanotechnology represents a profound shift in our approach to computing. It's a move away from the rigid, silicon-centric world of classical computing towards a more flexible, dynamic, and biologically inspired approach. This fusion holds the promise of solving some of humanity's most pressing challenges, from curing diseases to mitigating climate change, but it also necessitates a careful, ethical, and collaborative approach to ensure that this powerful technology is harnessed for the betterment of humankind, and not its detriment. The future of computing, in this context, is not just about faster processors, but about a deeper integration with the very fabric of life itself. The adventure is just beginning, and the implications are as vast as the universe itself.

The Internet of Things (IoT): Connecting Devices and Data

The breathtaking possibilities of biocomputing and nanotechnology naturally lead us to consider another transformative technology reshaping the landscape of computing: the IoT. While biocomputing delves into the biological realm, and nanotechnology shrinks the physical scale of computing, the IoT expands its reach, connecting a vast and ever-growing network of devices. This isn't merely about connecting computers; it's about linking a multitude of "things"—from refrigerators and thermostats to cars and medical implants—into a single, interconnected system. This interconnectedness has the potential to revolutionize various aspects of our lives, but also presents significant challenges.

At its digital core, IoT is the idea that any device—if it can be powered and programmed—should be able to collect data and talk to other devices. This includes traffic lights, pacemakers, vending machines, tractors, and, yes, even your humble coffee maker. Each device becomes a tiny informant, quietly gathering intel and reporting back to the mothership (usually a cloud server), allowing for unprecedented levels of control, automation, and insight. Imagine a smart home where your lights adjust automatically to the ambient light, your thermostat learns your preferences, and your appliances communicate with each other to optimize energy consumption. Or consider a smart city where traffic flow is optimized in real-time, reducing congestion and improving transportation efficiency. These are just glimpses of the potential transformative power of the IoT.

The capabilities of the IoT extend far beyond the convenience of a smart home. In healthcare, wearable devices can monitor heart rates, oxygen levels, or even detect falls in elderly patients, transmitting real-time data to caregivers and physicians. In manufacturing, IoT-enabled sensors can monitor equipment performance, predicting maintenance needs and preventing costly downtime. In agriculture, smart sensors in fields can optimize irrigation and fertilization, increasing yields and reducing resource consumption. The applications are limitless, promising increased efficiency, improved safety, and enhanced decision-making across a vast array of sectors.

However, the rapid proliferation of IoT devices presents several significant challenges. One of the most pressing concerns is security. The sheer number of interconnected devices creates a massive attack surface, making the IoT vulnerable to cyberattacks. A breach could compromise sensitive personal data, disrupt critical infrastructure, or even cause physical harm. Default passwords, outdated firmware, and a general lack of encryption make them easy prey. If you've ever been hacked by a smart fish tank thermometer (yes, that happened), you'll know the pain.

The challenge lies in developing robust security protocols that can protect this sprawling network from malicious actors. This requires not only advanced encryption and authentication mechanisms but also a change in mindset, moving from a focus on individual device security to a holistic approach that considers the security of the entire network. The increasing sophistication of cyberattacks necessitates constant vigilance and adaptation. The development of self-healing networks and AI-driven security systems will play a crucial role in mitigating these risks.

Another major hurdle is data privacy. The IoT generates massive amounts of data, everything from your sleep cycle to your fridge contents. This data is often stored in the cloud, sometimes encrypted, sometimes not, and frequently shared with third parties. Protecting this data from unauthorized access and misuse is critical. Regulations like GDPR in Europe aim to address these concerns, but the rapidly evolving nature of the IoT necessitates a continuous effort to update and strengthen data privacy protections. Balancing the benefits of data collection with the need for privacy presents a delicate ethical and legal challenge. Transparency in data collection practices and user control over their data are crucial for building trust and ensuring responsible data usage.

Interoperability is yet another significant challenge. The vast array of IoT devices from different manufacturers often employs different communication protocols and data formats, hindering seamless integration and data exchange. Your smart doorbell might not talk to your smart lock, and your smart oven might ignore your smart smoke detector out of sheer protocol snobbery. This lack of standardization creates "silos" of data, limiting the overall potential of the IoT. The development of common standards and protocols is essential for enabling interoperability and maximizing the benefits of a truly interconnected system. This is a complex undertaking that requires cooperation among different stakeholders, including manufacturers, developers, and policymakers.

The sheer scale of the IoT also presents logistical challenges. Managing and maintaining billions of interconnected devices is a daunting task. Effective management requires robust infrastructure, sophisticated monitoring systems, and efficient data management techniques. That's where cloud computing and edge computing come in, helping to process and filter data close to its source. AI also plays a crucial role here, helping to analyze data patterns, predict behavior, and automate responses.

Beyond these technical and logistical challenges, the IoT also raises significant ethical questions. The potential for mass surveillance necessitates careful consideration of the societal implications of this technology. As devices get smarter and more deeply embedded into our lives, they start to make decisions on our behalf. What happens when an algorithm decides what level of heating your grandmother gets? Or when your insurance premium is adjusted based on how often your fitness tracker thinks you've been skipping your daily walks? These aren't hypothetical issues—they're already happening, and they demand a careful blend of policy, design ethics, and public awareness. Robust ethical guidelines and regulatory frameworks are needed to prevent the misuse of IoT data and ensure that this technology is used responsibly and ethically.

The future of the IoT is inextricably linked to the development of advanced computing technologies. The processing power needed to handle the massive volume of data generated by the IoT requires powerful computing resources. Quantum computing, with its potential for exponential increases in processing power, could play a significant role in enabling the next generation of IoT applications. Similarly, advancements in AI and ML are crucial for developing intelligent IoT systems that can learn, adapt, and make decisions autonomously. The convergence of these technologies will unlock new capabilities and open up possibilities.

The IoT is not simply a collection of connected devices; it's a paradigm shift in how we interact with technology and the world around us. It's a transformation that promises to deliver unprecedented efficiency, convenience, and insights, but one that necessitates careful attention to the security, privacy, and ethical implications. Navigating these challenges requires a concerted effort from researchers, developers, policymakers, and society as a whole. The success of the IoT depends on our ability to leverage its immense potential while mitigating its risks, ensuring that this transformative technology serves humanity's best interests.

The Metaverse and Virtual Reality: Immersive Digital Experiences

The breathtaking advancements in the IoT naturally lead us to consider another frontier in computing: the "metaverse" and virtual reality (VR). While the IoT expands the reach of computing into the physical world, the metaverse and VR immerse us deeper into the digital realm, creating entirely new ways to interact with information and each other. It's a shift from simply connecting devices to constructing immersive, simulated environments where the lines between the physical and digital blur. The promise is captivating: a universe of endless possibilities, limited only by our imaginations and technological capabilities. However, as with any transformative technology, the path to realizing this vision is paved with challenges as well as opportunities.

The metaverse, in its broadest definition, is a persistent, shared, 3D virtual world. This isn't just about playing video games; it encompasses a range of applications, from virtual offices and classrooms to social gatherings and entertainment experiences. Imagine attending a concert from your living room, feeling as though you're in the crowd; collaborating on a design project with colleagues across the globe as if you're in the same room; or even exploring historical sites or fictional worlds with unparalleled realism. This interconnected, immersive digital space has the potential to reshape how we work, learn, socialize, and even experience the world around us.

Virtual reality is a key component of the metaverse, providing the immersive experience that makes these virtual worlds feel real. Through VR headsets and other devices, users are transported to simulated environments, able to interact with objects and other users in a way that feels natural and intuitive. This technology is already making inroads in various sectors. In healthcare, VR is used for training medical professionals, simulating surgical procedures, and even treating phobias and anxiety disorders. In education, VR offers immersive learning experiences, allowing students to explore historical events, dissect virtual organs, or even visit distant planets. In manufacturing, VR is utilized for design visualization, virtual prototyping, and employee training, reducing costs and improving efficiency.

Pixabay

The potential economic impact of the metaverse is substantial. New industries are emerging, creating opportunities for developers, designers, content creators, and entrepreneurs. The creation and sale of virtual goods, digital assets, and experiences represent a burgeoning market, with significant investment pouring into the sector. However, this potential is intertwined with significant challenges.

One of the most pressing issues is the development of interoperable standards. Currently, the metaverse is a fragmented landscape, with various platforms operating in isolation. The lack of interoperability limits the potential for seamless interaction between different virtual worlds and hinders the development of a truly interconnected metaverse. The development of common standards for avatars, digital assets, and interactions is crucial for fostering growth and preventing the metaverse from becoming a collection of isolated islands.

Accessibility remains another hurdle. VR headsets and other necessary hardware can be expensive, excluding a significant portion of the population. The digital divide, already a significant barrier to accessing technology, becomes even more pronounced in the context of the metaverse. Efforts to develop more affordable and accessible VR technologies are crucial for ensuring that the benefits of the metaverse are widely shared.

Cybersecurity is another critical concern. As the metaverse grows in popularity, it becomes an increasingly attractive target for cyberattacks. The theft of virtual assets, identity theft, and harassment are real threats. Robust security measures, including advanced encryption and authentication systems, are essential for protecting users and their data. The development of secure, decentralized platforms is also crucial for mitigating risks.

Furthermore, ethical considerations are paramount. Questions of data privacy, algorithmic bias, and virtual harassment need careful consideration. The potential for manipulation and misinformation in the metaverse necessitates the development of ethical guidelines and regulations to protect users and ensure responsible innovation. Transparency in data collection practices, user control over their data, and robust mechanisms for reporting and addressing harassment are crucial.

The immersive nature of the metaverse also raises concerns about addiction and mental health. The potential for individuals to become overly reliant on virtual worlds and to neglect their real-world responsibilities warrants careful attention. Research into the psychological effects of prolonged exposure to immersive technologies is crucial for mitigating potential risks. The development of healthy usage guidelines and support systems is essential.

The legal framework for the metaverse is still evolving. Questions of ownership, intellectual property rights, and the legal status of virtual assets need to be addressed. The creation of clear legal frameworks that protect users' rights and facilitate innovation is crucial for the sustainable growth of the metaverse. How do you enforce contracts in a space where jurisdiction is a jigsaw puzzle of server locations and user agreements? The legal frameworks lag far behind the technological possibilities, and until they catch up, expect some very strange court cases.

The evolution of AI is intricately linked to the future of the metaverse. AI plays a crucial role in developing realistic avatars, creating immersive environments, and powering intelligent virtual agents. AI-powered virtual assistants could become essential tools for navigating the metaverse, providing support and guidance to users. However, the use of AI also raises ethical concerns, particularly regarding algorithmic bias and the potential for misuse.

The convergence of VR, AI, and other emerging technologies has the potential to create truly transformative experiences. Augmented reality (AR), which overlays digital information onto the real world, complements VR by providing a seamless blend of the physical and digital realms. The combination of VR and AR could lead to entirely new forms of entertainment, education, and communication. Imagine having a virtual museum tour superimposed onto your living room, or collaboratively designing a building using shared augmented reality overlays. Or, how about fixing your car while a floating diagram guides your hand, or cooking dinner with a holographic chef egging you on? The applications are limitless.

Pixabay

The metaverse and VR are not merely futuristic concepts; they are technologies already impacting various sectors, shaping the way we work, learn, and interact. The challenges are significant, but the potential rewards—enhanced creativity, more efficient collaborations, and new forms of human connection—make the journey worthwhile. Navigating the complexities of this digital frontier requires a collaborative effort between technologists, policymakers, and society as a whole.

The future of computing is not just about processing power and data storage; it's about creating immersive, interactive, and meaningful experiences that enrich our lives. The metaverse, with its potential for both incredible advancement and potential pitfalls, represents a pivotal moment in the ongoing evolution of computing, a chapter still being written, but one with profound implications for humanity. The journey will be complex, fraught with unexpected twists and turns, but the destination—a richer, more interconnected, and potentially more immersive digital world—holds the promise of a future we can only begin to imagine. The story, however, is far from finished, and its final chapters will be shaped by the choices we make today.

Anecdotes, Musings, and Recollections

Hackers once exploited an IoT-connected fish tank to penetrate a casino's network. In mid-2017, cybercriminals targeted a smart aquarium thermometer in an unnamed North American casino lobby. By hijacking its connection, they gained a foothold, discovered the high-roller database, and siphoned off around 10 GB of sensitive data to a server in Finland.

CHAPTER 15

Reflections on the Past, Present, and Future of Computing and Technology

Key Themes and Lessons from the History of Computing

The history of computing's evolution isn't a straightforward march of progress. Looking back, several key themes emerge, offering invaluable lessons for future technological endeavors. One recurring motif is the unpredictable nature of technological adoption. We've seen time and again how superior technology doesn't automatically translate into market dominance. This underscores the critical interplay between technological advancement and effective market strategies. A product, no matter how innovative, needs a compelling narrative and a route to market to reach its potential audience.

This leads us to the vital role of user experience. The history of technology is littered with examples of technically advanced devices that failed because they were simply too difficult to use. The early personal computers, with their cryptic command lines and steep learning curves, are a case in point. The success of Apple, particularly with the Macintosh and later the iPhone, hinges on its unwavering commitment to intuitive design. They prioritized simplicity and ease of use, making technology accessible to a wider audience and driving adoption. This underscores the crucial lesson that technological innovation must be coupled with a profound understanding of the end-user's needs and capabilities. The lesson here: innovation that forgets the user ends up in the clearance bin.

Collaboration and the open-source movement have also played a significant role in shaping the landscape of computing. While proprietary software dominated the early days, the rise of open-source initiatives has fostered a culture of shared knowledge and collective innovation. Linux, a testament to collaborative development, stands as a powerful counterpoint to the closed ecosystems of proprietary operating systems. Its resilience and adaptability demonstrate the benefits of community-driven development, where diverse perspectives and expertise contribute to a constantly evolving product. Open source has democratized technology development, enabling individuals and organizations worldwide to contribute to the creation of innovative software. This collaborative approach has been particularly influential in specific sectors, such as web development, where open-source tools and frameworks have become the foundation for much of the internet's infrastructure. Shared knowledge, it seems, scales remarkably well.

The history of computing also showcases the ever-present tension between innovation and standardization. While innovation drives progress, standardization is crucial for widespread adoption and interoperability. The early days of personal computing were characterized by a bewildering array of incompatible hardware and software, creating a fragmented marketplace. The eventual emergence of industry standards, though sometimes slow and contentious, ultimately fostered a more unified and user-friendly computing experience. This highlights the inherent challenge of balancing the drive for technological advancement with the need for consistent and interoperable systems. Finding this balance is key to avoiding market fragmentation and maximizing the potential benefits of new technologies.

Ethical considerations have become increasingly prominent in the narrative of computing. From concerns about data privacy and security to the environmental impact of manufacturing and e-waste, the ethical implications of technology are no longer an afterthought but a central focus. The rise of AI and its potential societal impact has further intensified this conversation, highlighting the need for responsible innovation. The history of computing demonstrates the importance of embedding ethical considerations into the design and development process, rather than addressing them as an afterthought. Proactive ethical frameworks are essential to mitigate potential risks and ensure that technological advancements serve humanity's best interests.

The rapid pace of technological change is another recurring theme. Moore's Law, the observation that computing power doubles roughly every two years, has driven an exponential increase in processing power, storage capacity, and other key metrics. This unrelenting pace of innovation has transformed various aspects of our lives, but it also presents challenges related to obsolescence, sustainability, and the ability of individuals and societies to adapt to rapid change. This constant evolution underscores the need for continuous learning and adaptability in both the technological realm and in the wider society. The speed of change necessitates lifelong learning and the ability to embrace new technologies while critically evaluating their impact.

The history of computing is also a testament to the power of perseverance and resilience. Numerous individuals and companies have faced setbacks, failures, and near-extinctions, yet the field has continued to advance. The iterative nature of technological innovation, characterized by trial and error, constant refinement, and a willingness to learn from past mistakes, has enabled continuous growth and development. This resilience illustrates the importance of persistence, adaptability, and a long-term vision in the face of challenges and setbacks. The history of computing shows that even the most ambitious goals require ongoing dedication, continuous improvement, and a willingness to learn from failures.

Furthermore, the narrative of computing reveals a fascinating interplay between technological determinism and social constructivism. While technology undoubtedly shapes our world, it is also shaped by social, cultural, and economic forces. The adoption of technology isn't solely a function of its technical merits; it's deeply influenced by societal values, cultural norms, and economic structures. This understanding is crucial for comprehending the complex interplay between technology and society, and for predicting the future impact of technological advancements. Understanding these societal impacts is critical for ensuring that technological innovation benefits society as a whole and avoids exacerbating existing inequalities or creating new ones.

Finally, the history of computing underscores the importance of anticipating unforeseen consequences. Many technological innovations have had unintended side effects, both positive and negative. The internet, for example, has revolutionized communication and information sharing, but it has also facilitated the spread of misinformation, cybercrime, and online harassment. This highlights the critical need for foresight and careful consideration of potential unintended consequences when developing and deploying new technologies. Proactive risk assessment and responsible innovation are essential for mitigating potential harms and harnessing the benefits of new technologies while minimizing their risks. The constant evolution of technology necessitates a similarly evolving ethical and societal framework to navigate the complexities of its impacts. We must continually reflect upon the consequences of our innovations and adapt our approaches accordingly. The history of computing serves as a cautionary tale, reminding us that progress, unchecked, can be a double-edged sword. The future of computing hinges not just on technological advancement, but on our ability to harness its power responsibly and ethically.

The history of technology and computing reflects both remarkable progress and unforeseen complications. Breakthroughs such as transistors, the internet, and artificial intelligence have transformed society, but these innovations have also carried unintended consequences. From reshaping human interaction to redefining economies, tech's side effects often emerge slowly before becoming central challenges. Examining these outcomes alongside the triumphs is essential for understanding how technology influences our lives.

Social media is a good example. What started as a way to connect with friends and share news became a noisy arena full of misinformation, political polarization, amplification of extreme views, and online bullying. Algorithms originally meant to serve us content we'd "like" ended up pushing inflammatory posts that divide people even further. Similarly, e-commerce has revolutionized convenience and consumer access. Who doesn't love ordering paper towels at midnight? But it's also hollowed out small businesses and left a lot of once-busy main streets eerily empty.

Technology also takes a toll in other ways we don't always think about. Every gadget we buy depends on mining, production, and disposal that create serious environmental strain. Add to that the rise of automation, which often eliminates jobs just as fast as it creates new ones, leaving many workers scrambling to retrain. And let's not forget data surveillance: between phones, apps, and smart speakers, we've willingly surrounded ourselves with devices that constantly monitor our behavior, raising uncomfortable questions about whether we're trading too much privacy for convenience.

Still, it's not all negative. Some unintended consequences have been wonderful, like the rise of open-source software or the way the internet has allowed global communities to collaborate and share ideas instantly. This demonstrates that technology can also generate unforeseen benefits. We can't foresee every consequence, but we can cultivate the habit of looking around corners. The challenge is to approach new technologies with a bit more foresight: asking what could go wrong, who might be left behind, and how to design responsibly before problems spiral. If we can manage that, future innovations might bring more breakthroughs than headaches—helping technology serve us, rather than the other way around.

Glossary

This glossary defines key terms used throughout the book. It's been carefully crafted to avoid unnecessary jargon (as much as possible!).

2D: Short for two-dimensional materials—are like the ultra-thin pancakes of the material world: they're only one atom thick, but pack a punch in performance. These materials extend in just two dimensions (length and width), with negligible height, giving them some truly exotic properties.

Agile: Agile is an iterative approach to project management that emphasizes collaboration, flexibility, and customer satisfaction.

Algorithm: A set of instructions that a computer follows. Think of it as a recipe for solving a problem, but instead of cake, you get data.

BAL: Basic Assembly Language. Assembly language is closely correlated to machine language and is translated directly into binary by the computer.

BCE: Before Common Era

Binary Code: The foundation of all computing, representing data using only **0s and 1s**. It is a base-2 numeral system, meaning each digit (bit) can be either **0** or **1**, corresponding to electrical signals in a computer—**off(0)** and **on(1).**

Bit: The smallest unit of data, representing either a **0** or a **1**. (Yes, it's that simple—or that complicated, depending on your perspective.)

Blockchain technology: A distributed database that records transactions in blocks.

Each block is linked to the previous one, forming a chain. Once data is added, it's immutable—you can't change it without altering every subsequent block, which is nearly impossible without consensus.

Bug: A flaw in a computer program. Blame the cockroaches. I'm just kidding (mostly).

Cloud: A range of computing resources delivered over the internet. Instead of relying on local servers or personal devices for storage and processing power, users can access these resources remotely from anywhere at any time.

Compiler: A compiler turns a plain text file containing code (like COBOL) into a program that can be run on the computer.

Computing: Originally, the word computing was synonymous with counting and calculating, and the science and technology of mathematical calculations. Today, "computing" means using computers and other computing machines. It includes their operation and usage, the electrical processes carried out within the computing hardware itself, and the theoretical concepts governing them.

CPU: Central Processing Unit. The "brain" of the computer. It is a piece of hardware in a computer whose responsibility is to carry out arithmetical and logical operations from a set of instructions from a program.

Debugging: An essential part of the software development process. It helps in identifying and fixing errors, ensuring that the code runs smoothly and efficiently.

Decimal: Base-10 number system which uses digits 0 through 9.

Democratize: To make technology, data, or tools accessible to a broader audience so that more people can participate, create, and benefit—not just experts or elites.

Dump: A snapshot of a computer's memory at a specific moment, useful for diagnosing software issues.

Dynamic Memory Allocation: A process in which memory is allocated at runtime, rather than at compile time. Useful when the required memory size is unknown beforehand.

Flat File: Data is stored in a single table without relationships, making it simpler but less efficient for complex data management.

Floating Point Arithmetic: A method of representing and performing calculations on real numbers in computers. The format consists of: a sign (positive or negative), a significand (which holds the main digits of the number), and an exponent (which determines the scale or magnitude).

Functions: In programming, functions are reusable blocks of code that perform specific tasks.

Git: A distributed version control system that tracks changes in source code during software development. It allows multiple developers to work on a project simultaneously without stepping on each other's toes.

FOMO: Fear Of Missing Out on the latest tech innovations, updates, or digital trends.

Gallium: A soft, silvery metal with a melting point so low that it can literally melt in your hand. It is used in high-speed electronics and solar cells.

Germanium: Though it looks like a metal, it's actually a metalloid, meaning it straddles the line between metallic and non-metallic behavior. Used in the first transistors and still plays a role in high-speed electronics and fiber optics.

GPU: Graphics Processing Unit. A specialized electronic circuit designed to accelerate image rendering and graphical computations. Originally developed for gaming and visual applications, GPUs have evolved into powerful processors used in AI, ML, scientific simulations, and cryptocurrency mining. AGPU is optimized for parallel processing.

Gradient Descent: In ML, gradient descent works by helping an algorithm **learn** by adjusting its settings (parameters) step by step, moving in the direction that minimizes errors.

Graphene: One of the most extraordinary materials ever discovered—essentially a single layer of carbon atoms arranged in a honeycomb lattice. Despite being just one atom thick, it's 200 times stronger than steel and more conductive than copper.

GUI: Graphical User Interface. It's a visual way for users to interact with computers and software using graphical elements like windows, icons, buttons, and menus instead of text-based commands.

Hexadecimal (Hex): A base-16 numeral system that uses sixteen symbols: 0-9 & A to F representing values ten to fifteen. It provides a more compact and readable way to express binary values. E.g., Decimal 255 is 11111111 in binary and FF in hexadecimal.

HTML: HyperText markup language. It's the foundational language used to create and structure content on the web. It defines the structure of the web page.

HTTP: HyperText Transfer Protocol is the backbone of how information travels across the web. It is a communication protocol that governs how data is exchanged between your browser and a web server.

Immutability: In programming, immutable objects or data structures cannot be modified after they are initialized. Any changes result in the creation of a new object.

Integrated Circuit: Also known as a microchip or simply chip, is a compact assembly of electronic circuits formed from various electronic components— such as transistors, resistors, and capacitors— and their interconnections.

Internet: A vast, global network of interconnected computers and devices that communicate using standardized protocols—primarily TCP/IP (Transmission Control Protocol/Internet Protocol).

Interpreter: A type of program that executes code line by line, rather than compiling it all at once before running.

IoT: The Internet of Things. Refers to a network of physical devices—such as smart home appliances, industrial sensors, and wearable technology—that connect to the internet and exchange data.

Iterative: Repetitive, cyclical, progressive.

Loops: Control structures that allow a set of instructions to be executed repeatedly.

Low-level Language: A programming language that deals with a computer's hardware components and constraints. Low-level languages directly operate and handle a computer's entire hardware and instruction set architecture. They are often described as machine-oriented languages or as being close to the hardware. Programs and applications written in low-level languages require no interpretation, and they are directly executed on the computing hardware.

Machine Language: Machine language is binary code input directly into the machine and is the earliest form of programming language.

Memory: Hardware components that store data and instructions for processing.

Moore's Law: The observation that the number of transistors on a microchip doubles approximately every two years. It's been slowing down lately, but don't tell anyone.

MOSFET: The metal–oxide–semiconductor field-effect transistor (MOSFET, MOS-FET, MOS FET, or MOS transistor) is a type of field-effect transistor (FET), most commonly fabricated by the controlled oxidation of silicon. It has an insulated gate, the voltage of which determines the conductivity of the device. This ability to change conductivity with the amount of applied voltage can be used for amplifying or switching electronic signals.

Nanometer: One-billionth of a meter. In semiconductors, smaller nanometer sizes mean faster, more efficient chips.

Neuromorphic Computing: A bold reimagining of how machines think—by mimicking the brain itself.

Neuron: A specialized cell that processes and transmits information through electrical and chemical signals. It's the fundamental unit of the brain and spinal cord, and it's built for communication.

Octal: A base-8 numeral system that uses digits 0-7. Each octal digit represents three binary bits. For example: Decimal 54 1000000 in binary but 100 in octal.

Paradigm: At its heart, a paradigm is about comparison and demonstration, a way to show how things fit together. A paradigm shift, for example, is a fundamental change in the underlying assumptions of a field. So, that's my 20 cents worth.

Petabytes: A unit of digital storage that equals 1,000 terabytes (TB) or 1 quadrillion bytes. Yup! That's 15 zeros at the end.

Photolithography: The high-precision blueprinting technique behind nearly every microchip and nanodevice in existence. It's how we etch intricate patterns onto silicon wafers to build transistors, circuits, and memory cells—layer by layer, with light as the sculptor.

Polymorphic malware: Changes its code to evade detection.

Program: A set of instructions used to command the computer to perform various functions.

Push Notification: Alerts sent from Apps to your phone or computer, even when the Apps are not open. They serve to inform you about updates, reminders, or events, such as when someone likes your photo on social media or when you have a calendar event coming up.

QuBit: A quantum bit is the fundamental unit of information in quantum computing. A qubit (quantum bit) is the quantum version of a classical bit. While a classical bit is either a 0 or a 1, a qubit can be in a superposition of both states at once. Think of it like a spinning coin—until you measure it, it's both heads and tails. Still confused? Me too.

QR Code: Quick Response code is a type of two-dimensional barcode that stores information in a grid of black squares on a white background.

Quantum Computing: The next big thing (possibly). It involves... well, it's complicated. Let's just say it involves tiny particles doing very strange things.

QWERTY: Gets its name from the first six letters on the top row of the keyboard.

Race condition: This occurs when two or more threads (or processes) access and manipulate shared data concurrently, and the program's outcome depends on the unpredictable timing or order in which these accesses occur.

Ram: Random Access Memory. Referred to as "temporary memory" because data is stored on a temporary basis (while being accessed or edited) on the integrated circuit (chip) located on the computer. When the computer is shut down, the data is lost.

Rare Earth Material: A group of 17 metallic elements that are essential to modern technology. Despite the name, they're not actually rare in Earth's crust—but they're rarely found in concentrated, mineable deposits, which makes extraction tricky and geopolitically sensitive.

Refactoring: Code restructuring, optimization, revision

Register: An accumulator that stores values and increments of intermediate arithmetic and logic calculations that are being carried out by the CPU.

Relational File: Typically, part of a relational database where data is stored in structured tables with rows and columns. These tables are connected through relationships, often using primary keys and foreign keys.

Server: A computer or software system that provides services, data, or resources to other computers—called clients—over a network.

Silicon: Yay! Silicon is the unsung hero of the digital age! It is the backbone of modern electronics, the sparkle in quartz, and a silent workhorse behind solar panels and semiconductors. Silicon's ability to conduct electricity under certain conditions makes it ideal for transistors, microchips, and integrated circuits.

Silicon Carbide: It's a compound of silicon and carbon, known for its extreme hardness, thermal stability, and electrical versatility. It is ideal for high-voltage, high-temperature electronics--far outperforming traditional silicon in power applications.

Slack: Used for communication—it keeps teams connected, projects on track, and chaos at bay.

Subroutine: A mini-program living inside a larger program—it's a reusable set of instructions designed to perform a specific task. You "call" a subroutine from your main code, and it executes whatever instructions it's been given. Once it's done, it hands control back to the main program.

Stored Program: Program instructions that are stored in the computer's memory—right alongside the data they manipulate.

SQL: Standard SQL is designed to work with any compliant RDBMS, offering a wide range of features suitable for different use cases, from small-scale to enterprise-level systems.

SQL Server Express: SQL Server Express is targeted towards smaller-scale applications and development projects, with limitations on database size, memory usage, and CPU utilization.

Swiss Army Knife: A metaphor used to describe a tool, program, or device that's versatile, multifunctional, and compact—just like the iconic pocket knife it's named after.

Symbolic AI: Also known as classical AI or logic-based AI, is the term for the collection of all methods in AI research that are based on high-level symbolic (human-readable) representations of problems, logic, and search.

Synapses: They're the communication hubs of the nervous system, allowing electrical or chemical messages to leap from one cell to the next.

TCP/IP: A set of rules that governs how data is packaged, transmitted, and received across networks. It ensures that information can travel from one device to another reliably and efficiently.

Technical debt: Development backlog, accumulated inefficiencies

Transistor: A transistor is a semiconductor device used to amplify or switch electrical signals and power. It is one of the basic building blocks of modern electronics. It is composed of semiconductor material, usually with at least three terminals for connection to an electronic circuit. A voltage or current applied to one pair of the transistor's terminals controls the current through another pair of terminals.

URL: Uniform Resource Locator. The address you type into your browser to visit a specific resource on the internet, like a website, image, or video.

WWW: World Wide Web. A vast system of interlinked digital content that you access through the internet. Think of it as the "visible" part of the internet that you interact with using a browser. Invented in 1989 by Tim Berners-Lee at CERN.

Zero-day exploits: Attacks that exploit vulnerabilities unknown to software developers.

Index

2D, 177, 235

2G, 134, 135, 138

3D stacking, 187, 188

5G, 129, 130, 138, 143, 147

abacus, 8, 9, 10, 11, 22

ABC. See Atanasoff-Berry Computer

abstraction, 45, 46, 48, 49, 52, 53, 54, 55, 92, 104, 156, 165

access divide, 209

accountants, 8, 48

advanced persistent threats, 197

Advanced Research Projects Agency Network, 115, 116, 117, 119, 131, 190

AGI. See Artificial General Intelligence

Agile, 55, 235

AI. See artificial intelligence

Aiken, Howard, 27

airline reservation systems, 72

AirPods, 140

Alexa, 166, 169

ALGOL, 49

algorithm, 9, 11, 13, 14, 18, 43, 44, 45, 47, 71, 80, 83, 84, 85, 86, 87, 88, 89, 90, 91, 92, 94, 95, 122, 126, 130, 149, 157, 159, 160, 161, 162, 163, 164, 165, 166, 167, 169, 170, 171, 195, 197, 201, 211, 212, 213, 216, 217, 219, 226, 235, 236

algorithmic thinking, 83, 84, 86

AlphaGo, 95

Altair 8800, 99, 103, 113, 114

AM. See amplitude modulation

Amazon, 74, 77, 78, 122, 169

Amazon EBS, 78

Amazon Web Services, 74, 78

Amdahl Corporation, 34, 38, 39, 40

Amdahl, Gene, 3, 34, 39, 40, 41

amplitude modulation, 134

Analytical Engine, 11, 12, 13, 14, 15

analytics, 56, 75, 76, 78, 79, 89, 90, 126, 129, 196, 197

Android, 57, 137, 140, 141, 142, 143, 144, 154

ANNs. See artificial neural networks

Antikythera, 10, 11

AOL, 119, 125, 131

Apple, 57, 98, 100, 105, 108, 109, 113, 114, 137, 140, 141, 142, 143, 144, 145, 154, 231

Apple I, 100, 114

Apple II, 98, 114

APTs. See advanced persistent threats

Arab Spring, 126

ARPANET. See Advanced Research Projects Agency Network

Artificial General Intelligence, 218, 219, 220, 221

artificial intelligence, 21, 53, 56, 58, 76, 78, 79, 81, 82, 90, 94, 95, 124, 126, 130, 131, 143, 147, 156, 157, 158, 159, 160, 162, 163, 164, 167, 168, 169, 170, 171, 180, 194, 197, 198, 199, 200, 201, 212, 213, 215, 218, 219, 221, 223, 225, 226, 229, 232, 236, 240

artificial neural networks, 159

assembly, 43, 44, 45, 46, 47, 48, 49, 54, 58, 186, 199, 237

Atanasoff-Berry Computer, 26, 27, 28, 29, 35

AWS. See Amazon Web Services

Azure Blob Storage, 78

Azure Disk Storage, 78

Babbage, Charles, 5, 11

Backus, John, 47

BAL. See Basic Assembly Language

Bardeen, John, 174

base-60 system, 8

Basic Assembly Language, 235

BBSs. See bulletin board systems

Bell Labs, 173, 174

Berners-Lee, Tim, 119, 240

binary, 26, 27, 29, 30, 31, 43, 44, 65, 87, 91, 215, 235, 237, 238

biocomputing, 221, 222, 223, 224

biology, 221, 223

bit, 235

BlackBerry, 136, 140, 142, 154

BlackBerry 957, 136

blockchain, 130, 235

Blu-Ray, 69
Brattain, Walter, 174
bug, 37, 235
bulletin board systems, 192
Burroughs, 32, 40
C, 49, 51, 54, 56, 57, 114, 221
C++, 49, 51, 54, 56, 57
calculations, 8, 9, 10, 11, 13, 18, 19, 20, 22, 25, 29, 32,
    34, 35, 43, 47, 81, 105, 177, 187, 222, 235, 236, 239
California Consumer Privacy Act, 79
CAPEX. See capital expenditure
capital expenditure, 77
CASBs. See Cloud Access Security Brokers
CCPA. See California Consumer Privacy Act
CD, 69
CDC, 32, 33, 40
CD-ROM, 69
central processing unit, 12, 114, 236, 239, 240
Chinese, 8, 9, 40
Clojure, 52
cloud, 33, 34, 55, 69, 70, 74, 75, 76, 77, 78, 79, 81, 89,
    118, 119, 126, 142, 147, 162, 166, 183, 194, 196,
    197, 224, 225, 226
Cloud Access Security Brokers, 196
CNNs. See convolutional neural networks
COBOL, 48, 49, 50, 54, 58, 60, 235
Codd, Edgar F., 72
column-family, 73
Commodore, 100, 102
compiler, 48, 52, 58, 235
computations, 10, 12, 13, 19, 20, 47, 236
concurrency, 53, 56, 57, 73
confidentiality, 195
Control Program for Microcomputers, 102, 103, 104, 105,
    106
convolutional neural networks, 162, 165
Corporate Information Factory, 75
Coursera, 206
COVID-19, 210
CP/M. See Control Program for Microcomputers
CPU. See central processing unit
Cray, 26, 33, 35
cryptography, 216
cybercrime, 111, 152, 192, 193, 194, 233
cybersecurity, 57, 118, 131, 152, 189, 191, 192, 194,
    195, 196, 197, 198

Dartmouth Workshop of 1956, 157
data architecture, 3, 89, 90
data compression, 71, 81, 82
data lake, 76
data quality, 76, 90, 95
data storage, 10, 66, 68, 69, 71, 72, 76, 77, 78, 79, 80,
    81, 83, 130, 221, 222, 230
data variety, 75
Data Vault, 75
data velocity, 75
data veracity, 76
data volume, 75
data warehouse, 74
data warehousing, 74, 75, 76
database management system, 71, 72, 73
DBMS. See database management system
DDoS. See distributed denial-of-service
debugging, 45, 236
decimal, 29, 236, 237, 238
decomposition, 84
decryption, 195
deep learning, 159, 162, 163, 164, 165, 166, 167, 168,
    169, 170, 219
democratize, 236
design patterns, 52, 92
DevOps, 57
digital literacy, 112, 124, 128, 131, 153, 200, 207, 209,
    210, 211
Digital Research, Inc., 103
digital revolution, 11, 15, 18, 27, 97, 128, 133, 183
DiskOnKey, 70
distributed denial-of-service, 194
DNA, 80, 81, 221, 222
document, 73, 93, 193
documentation, 93
domain experts, 95
DVD, 69
dynamic memory allocation, 236
DynaTAC 8000x, 134
Eckert, J. Presper, 28, 29, 31
EDVAC. See Electronic Discrete Variable Automatic
    Computer
edX, 206
Egyptians, 8
Electronic Discrete Variable Automatic Computer, 30, 35

Electronic Numerical Integrator and Computer, 28, 29, 30, 35, 36, 43, 44

email, 83, 94, 111, 112, 123, 125, 135, 136, 148, 170, 193, 196

encryption, 118, 124, 193, 195, 197, 198, 216, 225, 228

ENIAC. See Electronic Numerical Integrator and Computer

ethical, 95, 129, 130, 131, 147, 151, 153, 163, 164, 167, 170, 171, 188, 201, 205, 208, 211, 212, 213, 214, 218, 220, 221, 223, 224, 225, 226, 227, 229, 232, 233

ethics, 111, 171, 213, 215, 223, 226

Excel, 8, 193

Expedia, 123

Explainable AI, 167

Facebook, 126, 145, 204

facial recognition, 159, 165

Fairchild Semiconductor, 178

fingerprint, 141, 197

Fischer, Todd, 113

flash drive, 70

flat file, 236

flexibility, 51, 73, 74, 75, 76, 77, 89, 92, 110, 123, 141, 196, 201, 205, 206, 219, 235

floating point arithmetic, 236

floppy disk, 66, 67, 68

floppy drive, 67

FM. See frequency modulation

FORTRAN, 47, 48, 49, 50, 54

FP. See functional programming

French, Gordon, 113

frequency modulation, 134

functional programming, 52, 53

gallium, 236

gallium nitride, 187

GaN. See gallium nitride

Gated Recurrent Units, 166

Gauss, Carl Friedrich, 22

GCP. See Google Cloud Platform

GDPR. See General Data Protection Regulation

General Data Protection Regulation, 79, 225

germanium, 236

gigabytes, 24, 69, 70

Git, 93, 236

Glenn, John, 22

Google, 16, 74, 77, 78, 121, 137, 140, 141, 142, 143, 144, 145, 149, 169, 208

Google Cloud Platform, 74, 78

Gore, Al, 131

gradient descent, 236

graph, 73, 88, 181

graphene, 237

graphical user interface, 53, 104, 105, 108, 114, 120, 138, 237

GRUs. See Gated Recurrent Units

GUI. See graphical user interface, See graphical user interface

Hadoop, 57

hard disk drive, 67

hard drive, 67, 68, 70, 71

Harvard, 27, 37

Harvard Mark I, 27

Haskell, 52, 55

HDD. See hard disk drive

Hewlett-Packard, 107, 108

hexadecimal, 237

hieroglyphic, 8, 93

Hindu-Arabic, 11

Hollerith, Herman, 16

Homebrew Computer Club, 113

Honeywell, 32, 33, 40

Hopper, Grace, 3, 37, 58, 59, 60

HP. See Hewlett-Packard

HTML, 120, 237

HTTP, 120, 237

human computers, 18, 19, 20, 21, 25, 35, 36

Hypatia, 22

IBM, 17, 27, 32, 33, 35, 39, 40, 47, 49, 63, 66, 73, 75, 89, 105, 107, 108, 109, 157, 192

IBM 1401, 31

IBM 650, 30, 35

IBM PC, 105, 107, 192

ICs. See integrated circuits

IDS. See intrusion detection systems

image analysis, 165, 170

iMaps, 145

immutable, 181, 235, 237

IMSAI, 100, 113

Inmon, Bill, 75

Instagram, 126, 165, 204

integrated circuits, 175, 176, 178, 179, 180, 182, 186, 239

Intel, 99, 101, 102, 114, 137, 181

internet, 5, 16, 56, 69, 77, 80, 112, 115, 116, 117, 118,
   119, 120, 121, 122, 123, 124, 125, 126, 127, 128,
   129, 130, 131, 135, 148, 162, 166, 192, 193, 194,
   196, 204, 206, 207, 209, 210, 211, 232, 233, 235,
   237, 240
Internet of Things, 56, 73, 79, 81, 128, 129, 130, 224,
   225, 226, 227, 230, 237
Internet Service Provider, 118, 119
interpreter, 237
intrusion detection systems, 195
intrusion prevention systems, 195
iOS, 57, 137, 140, 141, 142, 143, 144
IoT. See Internet of Things
iPad, 140
iPhone, 140, 141, 154, 231
IPS. See intrusion prevention systems
ISP. See Internet Service Provider
iteration, 85
Jacquard loom, 13, 15, 16
Jacquard, Joseph Marie, 15
Japanese, 8, 9
Java, 49, 51, 54, 56, 57, 58
Jobs, Steve, 105, 113, 114
Johnson, Katherine, 19, 22
JSON, 73
Kaypro, 102
key-value, 73
Kilby, Jack, 178
Kildall, Gary, 103
kilobytes, 24
Kimball, Ralph, 75
Kotlin, 57
Lebombo bone, 8
LEDs, 176
linked list, 87
Linstedt, Dan, 75
Linux, 93, 232
Lisp, 52
Long Short-Term Memory, 166
Lovelace, Ada, 5, 14
LSTM. See Long Short-Term Memory
machine learning, 56, 76, 78, 79, 81, 89, 94, 95, 124,
   143, 147, 157, 158, 160, 161, 162, 163, 164, 169,
   170, 188, 194, 197, 198, 199, 226, 236
Macintosh, 105, 108, 109, 114, 231
magnetic tape, 31, 66, 68, 70, 71

mainframe, 25, 26, 31, 33, 34, 39, 40, 49, 66, 73, 101,
   190
maintainability, 51, 57, 85, 92, 93
massive open online courses, 206
mathematicians, 7, 35, 43, 95, 156
mathematics, 8, 9, 10, 11, 200
Mauchly, John, 29
McCarthy, John, 157
megabytes, 24, 67, 68
memory management, 47, 88, 92, 102
merchants, 8, 22
Mesopotamia, 8
Mesopotamians, 8
Metal-Oxide-Semiconductor Field-Effect Transistor, 176
metaverse, 143, 227, 228, 229, 230
MFA. See multi-factor authentication
Microsoft, 74, 77, 78, 105, 121, 125, 131, 193
Microsoft Azure, 74, 78
minicomputer, 34
Minsky, Marvin, 157
MIT, 157, 206
ML. See machine learning
mobile, 57, 121, 124, 129, 133, 134, 135, 136, 137, 138,
   139, 140, 141, 142, 143, 145, 146, 147, 149, 152,
   205, 209, 222
mobile commerce, 124
Mobira Senator, 134
Model-View-Controller, 92
modularity, 50, 51, 53, 57, 92
MongoDB, 73
MOOCs. See massive open online courses
Moore, Fred, 113
Moore, Gordon, 137, 179, 181
Moore's Law, 137, 179, 180, 181, 182, 183, 185, 188,
   232, 238
Morrow, George, 113
MOSFET. See Metal-Oxide-Semiconductor Field-Effect
   Transistor
Motorola, 134
MSN Messenger, 125
M-Systems, 70
multi-factor authentication, 196
MVC. See Model-View-Controller
nanometer, 238
nanotechnology, 221, 223, 224
NASA, 19, 22, 24

natural language processing, 53, 158, 166, 169

Navajo, 24

NCR, 32, 40

neural networks, 157, 162, 164, 166, 188, 212, 219

neuromorphic computing, 238

neuron, 238

NLP. See natural language processing

node, 87, 88, 115

Nokia, 134, 139

NoSQL, 73, 74

Noyce, Robert, 178

object-oriented programming, 50, 51, 52, 53

octal, 238

OOP. See object-oriented programming

operational expenditure, 78

OPEX. See operational expenditure

Osborne, Adam, 113

Pandas, 56

papyrus, 8

paradigm, 46, 50, 52, 53, 54, 55, 72, 76, 94, 128, 136, 160, 175, 187, 214, 215, 227, 238

password, 196

personal computer, 97, 99, 101, 103, 104, 105, 106, 107, 109, 111, 112, 114, 115, 134, 181, 191

petabytes, 24, 79, 80

photolithography, 238

PL/I, 49

PNY, 70

pointer manipulation, 88

polymorphic malware, 238

programmers, 21, 35, 43, 44, 45, 46, 47, 48, 52, 53, 54, 58, 60, 61, 72, 74, 86, 92, 100, 101, 104, 106, 200

programming, 3, 5, 14, 15, 29, 32, 43, 44, 45, 46, 47, 48, 49, 50, 51, 52, 53, 54, 55, 56, 57, 58, 59, 60, 61, 62, 83, 84, 88, 92, 94, 99, 104, 113, 158, 160, 161, 212, 236, 237

Prolog, 53

punch cards, 6, 25, 27, 30, 31, 36, 74, 79

punched cards, 12, 13, 15, 16, 17, 65, 66, 68, 70, 71, 72

Pythagoras, 22

Python, 44, 49, 52, 54, 55, 56, 58

quantum computing, 58, 80, 81, 130, 180, 184, 187, 215, 216, 217, 218, 219, 221, 226, 238

qubits, 187, 188, 215, 217, 238

QWERTY, 136, 239

Radio Shack, 98

RAND Corporation, 117

recurrent neural networks, 162, 166

recursion, 84, 85

refactoring, 93

reinforcement learning, 95, 160, 161

relational database model, 72

RNNs. See recurrent neural networks

robotics, 95, 157, 160, 161, 199

Rochester, Nathaniel, 157

Roman, 8, 9, 11

Rust, 56, 57

SanDisk, 70

Scala, 52, 56

Scheme, 52

scholars, 7, 8

Scikit-learn, 56

Secure Sockets Layer, 195

Security Information and Event Management, 196

self-driving cars, 159, 162, 165, 167, 212, 214

semiconductor, 174, 175, 176, 177, 178, 181, 183, 184, 185, 186, 187, 188, 189, 238, 239, 240

servers, 56, 73, 77, 115, 120, 193, 235

service level agreement, 77

Shannon, Claude, 157

Shockley, William, 174, 175

Short Messaging Service, 135

SiC. See silicon carbide

SIEM. See Security Information and Event Management

silicon carbide, 187

Silicon Valley, 3, 4, 24, 40, 59

Singleton pattern, 92

Siri, 143, 166, 169

skills divide, 209

SLA. See service level agreement

SLAC. See Stanford Linear Accelerator Center

smartphones, 5, 124, 128, 136, 137, 138, 139, 140, 142, 144, 146, 148, 149, 151, 152, 153, 154, 175, 209

SMS. See Short Messaging Service

social networking, 123, 135

software engineering, 3, 51, 54, 91, 92, 93

soroban, 9

spam, 94, 170

Spark, 57, 98

speech recognition, 162, 166, 169

Sperry Rand, 32

spreadsheet, 8, 104, 162

SQL. See Structured Query Language
SSL. See Secure Sockets Layer
Stanford Linear Accelerator Center, 113
statisticians, 95
Stone Age, 8
storage arrays, 77
Structured Query Language, 72, 240
suanpan, 9
Sumerians, 8
supervised learning, 94, 161
Swift, 57
Symbian, 140, 142
System/360, 34
Tandy Corporation, 98
TCP/IP, 116, 237, 240
telecommuting, 110
terabytes, 24, 70, 80, 166, 238
Terrell, Paul, 113
Through-Silicon Vias, 187
TLS. See Transport Layer Security
transistor, 173, 174, 175, 176, 177, 178, 180, 181, 182,
    185, 187, 221, 238, 240
Transport Layer Security, 195
Travelocity, 123
TRS-80, 98
TSVs. See Through-Silicon Vias

Turing, Alan, 156
Twitter, 126, 145, 204
Univac, 32, 40
unsupervised learning, 95, 161
URL, 120
usage divide, 209
vacuum tubes, 27, 28, 29, 35, 173, 174, 175
version control, 93, 236
Viber, 125
Wayne, Ronald, 114
WhatsApp, 125
Windows, 106, 140, 142
World War II, 20, 27, 28, 98, 157
World Wide Web, 118, 119, 120, 121, 122, 193, 204, 240
Wozniak, Steve, 113, 114
WWW. See World Wide Web
WYSIWYG, 106
XAI. See Explainable AI
Xerox PARC, 104, 105
Yahoo! Messenger, 125
Yourdon, Ed, 3, 62, 63, 96
Zachman Framework, 89, 96
Zachman, John, 3, 89, 96
zero-day exploits, 240
Zilog Z80, 99, 102
Zoom, 207